A historical sensibility

Sir Michael Howard
and The International Institute for
Strategic Studies, 1958–2019

'Sir Michael Howard, one of the founders of the IISS was also, for six decades, its presiding spirit. Such was his reputation, both in academia and in the councils of the world, that his very presence was a guarantee of the Institute's intellectual independence, rigour and reputation.

A brilliant military historian and strategist, he was among the first in the immediate post-war world to realise that the thermonuclear age demanded not only a radically new strategic mindset but a new set of rules if the bombs were to remain unused in their bunkers. Today, when leaders seem increasingly unconstrained by rules, his thinking, on this issue alone, remains as relevant and urgent as ever.

This eclectic collection of his reminiscences, letters, articles, chapters and reviews, published in the Institute's journals over a period of 60 years, is, however, not only a memorial to one of the great historians and strategists of our time, but a reflection of how his thoughts – across as wide a range of issues as the years and crises that provoked them – remain acutely and enduringly perceptive and relevant. That the clarity of his thinking was matched by the equal clarity of its expression and a subtle, sometimes subversive wit, makes this anthology not only required reading for any student of our turbulent times, but a journey, as delightful as it is instructive, through a wise and elegant mind.

Sir Michael was famously dismissive of the cliché that we must learn from history if we are not to repeat it. Perhaps; but we will always have much to learn from outstanding historians like him.'

– *Fleur de Villiers CMG*

'In an era of instant analysis and social media polemics, Sir Michael Howard's depth of understanding, erudition and beautifully crafted prose serve as a welcome reminder that there exists another, better, way of gauging the forces of history and strategy. These are the writings of a man with rapier-sharp wit who speaks of war as someone with first-hand experience.'

– *Professor François Heisbourg*

A historical sensibility

Sir Michael Howard
and The International Institute for
Strategic Studies, 1958–2019

IISS The International Institute for Strategic Studies

The International Institute for Strategic Studies

Arundel House | 6 Temple Place | London | WC2R 2PG | UK

First published January 2020 by **Routledge**
4 Park Square, Milton Park, Abingdon, Oxon, OX14 4RN

for **The International Institute for Strategic Studies**
Arundel House, 6 Temple Place, London, WC2R 2PG, UK
www.iiss.org

Simultaneously published in the USA and Canada by **Routledge**
52 Vanderbilt Avenue, New York, NY 10017

Routledge is an imprint of Taylor & Francis, an Informa Business

The International Institute for Strategic Studies is an independent centre for research, information and debate on the problems of conflict, however caused, that have, or potentially have, an important military content. The Council and Staff of the Institute are international and its membership is drawn from almost 100 countries. The Institute is independent and it alone decides what activities to conduct. It owes no allegiance to any government, any group of governments or any political or other organisation. The IISS stresses rigorous research with a forward-looking policy orientation and places particular emphasis on bringing new perspectives to the strategic debate.

The Institute's publications are designed to meet the needs of a wider audience than its own membership and are available on subscription, by mail order and in good bookshops. Further details at www.iiss.org.

British Library Cataloguing in Publication Data
A catalogue record for this book is available from the British Library

Library of Congress Cataloging in Publication Data

ADELPHI series
ISSN 1944-5571

ADELPHI 472–474
ISBN 978-0-367-49562-6

Contents

EDITOR'S INTRODUCTION

Professor Sir Michael Howard's death in November 2019 left The International Institute for Strategic Studies (IISS) bereft of not only its president emeritus but the last of its founders and intellectual parents. Yet he bequeathed to us a magnificent legacy of scholarship and commentary. In tribute to Sir Michael and in celebration of his life and work, this volume collects a selection of his remarks and writings for IISS publications over six decades.

Combat in the Second World War had already equipped Sir Michael with a first-hand appreciation of conflict's realities by the time of the conferences and conversations that led to the Institute's foundation in 1958. His academic specialism, however, lay not in area studies, political science or the emerging field of strategic studies. Rather, it lay in history; initially, in fact, the history of England in the early seventeenth century. While he would go on to re-establish the Department of War Studies at nearby King's College London, he had believed that early modern England would be the focus of the assistant lectureship that first brought him there in the 1940s. Moreover, at the outset of his career, he was 'not in the least' interested in current events, as he said in a 2017 interview published for the first time here. He was – and remained – wary of facile 'lessons' derived from the past, remarking in a 1966 book review in *Survival* that 'if "history" teaches us anything, it is that men fall into quite as many errors in trying to learn from the past as they do trying to ignore it'.[1] Requesting that historians divine the future, he suggested at an IISS conference some years later, was just as futile: 'to ask a historian to look into and prescribe for the future is to invite a presentation consisting of as much past history as the author thinks he can get away with and as little prophecy and prescription as he thinks his audience will accept. Historians have seen too many confident prophets fall flat on their faces to lay themselves open to more humiliation than they can help.'[2]

Yet Sir Michael argued – and demonstrated – that while history 'provides few answers, it may shape our attitudes, engendering a scepticism, a humility, and an appreciation of the role of the contingent and the unforeseen in human affairs of a kind not always developed by a more positivist approach'.[3] His deep and broad historical learning brought with it a historical sensibility: the ability to see the present through the eyes of a historian; to be aware both of history's contingencies and its recurrent patterns; to be suspicious of immutable 'laws' of international relations; to be alive to the power of ideas in human events; and to locate contemporary developments within the *longue durée* for, as he put it, 'there is little point in considering where we should be going if we do not first decide where we are starting from'.[4] This sensibility entails an awareness of the subjective nature of an individual or nation's historical narrative and its determinative effect on their contemporary actions for, as he observed elsewhere, 'all we believe about the present depends on what we believe about the past'.[5]

This historical sensibility informed all of Sir Michael's work. Indeed, he embodied and epitomised it. He will forever remain a titan and exemplar not only for historians, but for all those who acknowledge the indispensability of history and the historical sensibility for any true understanding of present events. His learned, humane and *historical* approach to the study of strategy and conflict inspires the members and researchers of the Institute who hope to perpetuate his legacy.

The works selected for this volume are intended to serve several purposes. Firstly, it is hoped that they will reach a new generation of readers and be made more accessible to those fortunate enough to have read them already. The book also contains previously unprinted material: a tribute by John Chipman, the Institute's director-general; and the 2017 interview with Sir Michael.

Secondly, along with the tribute and interview, these articles, chapters, reviews and letters serve to illustrate Sir Michael's role in our creation and his abiding presence in the Institute's evolving intellectual life over 60 years. After beginning with a more recent recollection by Sir Michael, the publications are presented in chronological order. They serve as a historical document, tracing the development of strategic thought and preoccupations from the 1950s to the recent past. Yet Sir Michael's conclusions – whether on the paradoxes of European defence, the Arab-Israeli conflict or the relationship between modernisation and unrest, to name but a few – retain their immediacy and power. Beyond their historical value, these publications are of direct interest to any analyst of contemporary events.

Thirdly, this selection contains a number of obituaries and reminiscences Sir Michael wrote across the years to commemorate the lost colleagues who had played crucial roles in the Institute's establishment, growth and success. Their character and contributions are preserved in the articles, obituaries and recollections that he has left us. He, and they, serve as inspiration for the IISS to continue our work – not necessarily, as Sir Michael himself remarked in an article reprinted in this volume,[6] always focused on questions identical to those that occupied our founders, but with the same dedication and seriousness that marked a generation of thinkers who had experienced the horrors of total war at first hand and who understood the consequences of unclear thinking or self-deception.

Finally, these works are intended to demonstrate Sir Michael's style: lucid, direct and free of obfuscation or opacity. He was often witty; his book reviews show that he could sometimes be biting, especially when it came to those whose own writing or thinking was indirect or vague. To read him is to be in the presence of an erudite and powerful mind. His thinking enriches not only our understanding of the world, but our experience of the world itself.[7]

Notes

[1] Michael Howard et al., 'Book Reviews', *Survival*, vol. 8, no. 10, October 1966, p. 334.

[2] Michael Howard, 'Deterrence, Consensus and Reassurance in the Defence of Europe', in *Defence and Consensus: The Domestic Aspects of Western Security: Part III Papers from the IISS 24th Annual Conference*, Adelphi Paper, vol. 23, no. 184, 1983, p. 17.

[3] Howard et al., 'Book Reviews', vol. 8, no. 10, October 1966, p. 334.

[4] Howard, 'Deterrence, Consensus and Reassurance in the Defence of Europe', p. 17.

[5] Michael Howard, *The Lessons of History* (Oxford: Clarendon Press, 1991), p. 13.

[6] Michael Howard, 'The Remaking of Europe', *Survival*, vol. 32, no. 2, March–April 1990, p. 106.

[7] I am grateful for the advice and suggestions which I solicited from my colleagues during the preparation of this book. In particular, I would like to thank Dana Allin, John Chipman and James Hackett.

Professor Sir Michael Eliot Howard
OM CH CBE MC FBA FRHistS

Professor Sir Michael Howard died on 30 November 2019, a day after his 97th birthday.

He served in the Coldstream Guards and fought with special bravery in the first battle of Monte Cassino in the Italian Campaign of World War Two. He was famously Chichele Professor of the History of War at Oxford, Regius Professor of Modern History at Oxford, Robert A Lovett Professor of Military and Naval History at Yale University and founder of the Department of War Studies at King's College London. He produced truly extraordinary books and delivered always special lectures.

He fought, he taught, he wrote, he spoke, and he was always there to listen.

For all of us in the large IISS family, he was simply an icon.

He was one of the first founders of our Institute, and now the last to leave this world. He served on our Council, Executive Committee and Trustees, became President and then President Emeritus. On assuming this last role, at an advanced age, he quipped to me that this meant that he was too old to be President and 'deserved to be'.

He spoke with great fluency yet was never florid. He wrote with style, but shunned affectation. He adored the big stage and the important occasion, rising to both with a spring in his step and a glint in his eye. He was always impeccably dressed, though with just enough rumple to remind the onlooker that he had finer things to consider.

He knew that beautifully crafted sentences could inspire a sense of drama, and force even the most wayward to pay studied attention to his every word. This made him a supremely effective teacher. His intellectual followers were a happy flock. True to his profession, he always wanted to hear from the young. His bearing and reputation were such that no one dared to offer an opinion or advance an argument without due care. This rightly deterred the unprepared, but equally spurred on those with talent to do their best.

In 'committee', he listened judiciously, but with a dagger at his side lest anyone reason sloppily. When he summed up a discussion, his conclusions were crisp and dispositive of the case. There was usually nothing more to be said.

Like all excellent strategists, he had a cool head and a warm heart. He was among the first in the nuclear age to fuse history, ethics, politics, military strategy and policy judgement into one coherent and always elegant whole.

Sir Michael virtually invented a way of thinking that inspired generations intelligently to consider the many factors that needed to be weighed in questions of war and peace.

At the IISS we have always worked infused by his high standards, and now will do so in memory of his true greatness.

To the fortunate who knew him well, he will forever be, Dear Michael.

Dr John Chipman CMG,
Director-General and Chief Executive IISS, 1 December 2019

CHAPTER ONE

An interview with Sir Michael Howard

This interview was conducted by Dr Dana Allin, IISS Senior Fellow for US Foreign Policy and Transatlantic Affairs and Editor of Survival, *at Sir Michael's home in December 2017. It was organised by Hilary Morris, then the IISS Librarian and archivist. It has been edited for clarity and length.*

Dana Allin: The [Institute] came out of the Brighton Conference [of 1957]. [What role did you play in organising it?]

Michael Howard: I was not an immediate organiser [of the conference] but I belonged to one of the groups which organised it. There were three groups who were vaguely conscious of one another's existence and to some extent overlapped.

There was the group at Chatham House, which consisted primarily of Denis Healey, Richard Goold-Adams, Admiral Sir Anthony Buzzard – they were the major figures, and they had a study group of their own, looking into the problems of nuclear weapons. The leading figure there, in terms of thinking, was Denis Healey.

It overlapped with the second group, which was organised by the Council of Churches on International Affairs (CCIA), of whom the leading figure was the Bishop of Chichester [George] Bell, who was the leading church-man concerned about nuclear weapons, as he had been concerned about bombing during the [Second World War]. The actual bureaucrat connected with that was someone called Sir Kenneth Grubb, who was the chairman of the British end of the CCIA, and Alan Booth was the secretary. They were the people, I think, who got the Brighton Conference together.

There was the third group, which is where I came in to some extent, which was called 'the Military Commentators Circle', which was a dining club, got together by Basil Liddell Hart, consisting largely of the military correspondents in London at the time and a number of senior retired officers who were interested in the future of war in general. I was brought into that by Liddell Hart, who had got interested in what I had been writing, which was mainly book reviews about the whole question. The people who did the main organisation [for the conference] were Alan Booth for the CCIA, and Anthony Buzzard from Chatham House.

When we got together [at Brighton] – and this I have described very fully in my own memoirs [Michael Howard, *Captain Professor* (2006)] – we were divided into groups. I was in the junior group, which was not looking at any of the big subjects but was looking at the interesting questions of 'Where do we go from here? What do we do?' I found myself elected to the chair of that group. Modesty forbids as to why I should have been the chair, but the chair's a very good place to be if you have to be in anything! We did have, in our group, the idea that whatever we decide here about the way the world should be governed, we must have some kind of organisation which will carry things on, and that was then accepted by the conference as a whole.

The conference set up something called, at that time, I think, the Brighton Conference Association, whose main job was to continue to keep this question afloat and circulating and being discussed: a sort of mini-Chatham House, was the way we looked at it.

But the main thing was to get some money! The main person who had their fingers on the money was Denis Healey. Denis Healey was vitally important in getting things moving, because he got together with the Ford Foundation Secretary Shep Stone. [Healey asked for] a couple of thousand dollars just to sort of keep things going, and Shep Stone said 'well I'm sorry, we can't do that – we don't do anything less than twenty thousand dollars, but you'll have twenty thousand dollars left'. We agreed that we should use the money to get the thing established as a proper organisation, and then see.

First thing then, was to find a director, and the obvious man was Alastair Buchan, who was not only the leading defence correspondent for *The Observer*, but had also spent the last year in Washington and he knew what was going on there, and he knew all the people who were interested [in these questions] in the States, and they were the people who it was important to get over.

So, phase one was to have a conference which would bring over all the American pundits to tell us what they were doing and why they were doing it, and really to start interesting people in England about it. [The Institute] was, at that time, a truly English affair, and we had the money to run it as an English affair for three years. If at the end of that we hadn't achieved anything, then no more money. If we had achieved anything, then the Ford Foundation said they'd be interested in giving more money and it would become international after that.

DA: So, it was the Ford Foundation who sort of gave the impulse to the internationalisation [of the Institute]?

MH: That's right. So, we did two things: we organised conferences, and we set up this little journal called *Survival*,
which was simply getting together all the articles on the
whole question of nuclear weapons and publishing them
separately, and that was why it was called *Survival* and
continues to be.

Well, we had a couple of conferences. The first one was
at Oxford, where all the pundits about nuclear affairs
introduced themselves to one another. And a number of
those were from the United States who had previously
been not on speaking terms with one another – which
we discovered was a normal situation with American
pundits – but they came over and met one another, and
talked to one another, and talked to us, and got ideas
floating. That was fascinating, and that produced our first
book [Alastair Buchan, *NATO in the 1960s* (1960)], which
Alastair Buchan edited, about basically, extended deterrence: how effectively could American nuclear weapons
defend Western Europe, and should Western Europeans
have their own nuclear weapons?

The second conference which was about arms control
and disarmament, and that led to Hedley Bull's book [*The
control of the arms race: Disarmament and arms control in the
missile age* (1961)], and that had a terrific effect – not so
much on statesmen but on academics, because it really
changed the whole thinking of academics gradually about
international relations and international affairs, and what
could and could not be done by normal states. It was an
attack on total and complete disarmament.

DA: [And it instead proposed the] idea of arms control.

MH: Yes.

DA: Until that moment – in fact, even going back to the famous 1946 Acheson–Lilienthal Report – there was a lot of immediate utopian reaction to the atomic weapon …

MH: Yes. In his book, Hedley Bull said: forget about disarmament. Disarmament is irrelevant and counterproductive. Think about arms control. [That book was] the most important, long-term influence which we had during our first few years, because it extended so far beyond the whole rather narrow question of nuclear weapons.

It was three years of pretty hard work. [We had] set up Alastair as the director, and found an excellent secretary, and a couple of wonderful girls, who ran the whole thing between them – there's always wonderful girls around who run things!

We then said, okay, we need more money and so, okay, we will go international. We knew we were going to have to go international anyhow, so we did, and we set up an international council. Initially we had a [British] President, it then being a purely British institute: Clement Atlee, who represented, as it were, the sane branch of the left as he always had. That was where the interest lay, [not with] the conservatives who disapproved of the whole thing, and the left who thought total abolition [of nuclear weapons] was the only thing. [Atlee] actually was a good, sane and solid figure.

When we went international, we then had to look for an international president, and the obvious person was the Prime Minister of Canada, [Lester B.] 'Mike' Pearson. He was the obvious person, because Alastair Buchan was himself the son of John Buchan, who had been the [Governor-General] in Canada, and brought up Alastair as being half-Canadian anyway. This was in the immediate aftermath of the Suez [Crisis of 1956], where Mike Pearson was the person who, more than anybody else, somehow rescued the whole mess of the Suez affair, and was therefore, the flavour of the month. So he was a good international president.

When he died, we then get onto the Europeans. We wanted to have a European President, and so one of the – in fact the most distinguished European we got interested – had been Raymond Aron, and Raymond Aron was dragged kicking and screaming and made President [of the IISS] on the condition that he had absolutely no responsibility for doing anything at all…

DA: It's interesting that you said the obvious initial president was Clement Atlee. Was this, in a sense, an organisation of the centre-left? Were you serious when you said the conservatives were against the whole idea?

MH: Well, I exaggerate a bit. There were a number (as there always are) of very intelligent conservatives, who were interested in the thing, but the driving force did tend to come from the centre-left. But the major figures were not politicians; they were civil servants and military. Civil servants are, as you know, the people who really run the country, or did until recently. We were able to enlist some Foreign Office people, who were particularly prepared to see these ideas floating about – particularly Michael Palliser. One of the things which I take credit for is getting Michael Palliser in – an old army and schoolfriend, and a rising star in the diplomatic service.

DA: Was he with you in Italy [during the Second World War]?

MH: No, he was in North-West France, but I knew him before. I was with him at school, with him at Oxford, and our paths ran parallel for a long time. He was working in the Foreign Office on our behalf, as it were, making sure that the good young diplomats knew about us and came along to our discussions and were able to introduce the whole question of what is practical and what is not practical, who we should talk to in America, who we should talk to in Germany. They were most significant.

And then among the military, a major figure was Air Chief Marshal Jack Slessor – now an almost forgotten figure, but at the time [he] was our top airman. Although he didn't invent the concept of deterrence, he was writing about it before anybody in America.

Where do the British stand on the question of nuclear weapons? Up until then, and up until the beginning of the foundation of IISS, the whole question was basically an American one. They were the only people who had these things, and they were the only people who were going to be able to use them. In the 1940s, from 1944 until 1950 or so, the whole matter was a purely American one, because the Americans were the only ones who had the bomb, and so for the British – in so far as we thought about it at all, and not very many people did – it was simply a question of our relationship with the United States.

In the beginning of the 1950s two things happened. One was that we acquired our own nuclear weapons, and the other was the transition from nuclear to thermonuclear weapons. That transition was something of vital significance. With purely [fission] weapons, it was possible to regard a nuclear weapon as just a larger kind of bomb. We had destroyed Hiroshima with just one bomb, but we had inflicted far greater damage on Tokyo, with conventional weapons. So to go from one thing to another was not really a change of category at all. With [the first test of a thermonuclear weapon on] Enewetak Atoll, then you are in a different, nightmarish world. And it is then that people started thinking, in this country and elsewhere, about nuclear weapons as a question affecting us. It is then that we start getting CND [the Campaign for Nuclear Disarmament]. This was something in the air that was affecting all of us. 1957, which was when the Brighton Conference began, was at the time when the Americans had, I think, declared [their policy of] massive retaliation. And then what do the British do about that with their little bomb? The simultaneous foundation of CND and IISS, not in conscious competition with one another, but two different social groups reacting to what was seen as the innate global problem.

I think it was then that another question arose about the split between, or the relationship between, CCIA and IISS. I think that Alistair [Buchan] and all the rest of us wanted to keep in touch with the Christians for as long as we could. Not only because one of the key figures there actually continued to run the IISS – Alan Booth, who was a wonderful, efficient, charming bureaucrat who did an enormous amount of hard work on our side. There was a very strong Christian element – not particularly strong *inside*, as it were, with Alastair and me and others – but we were brought up in the churches, we wanted to retain our links with the churches. But people like the Bishop of Chichester apart from anybody else, and all the active Christians thinking about it, wanted to go on concentrating on the ethics. The people who were putting up the money and the people who were providing the ideas wanted to talk about actualities all the time. And so I think in a perfectly friendly way, it was felt [best to] gently separate, and do our own thing in our own way, without any sense of hostility or rivalry, but with partnership continuing.

DA: I think you've confirmed that there was sort of this utopian CND movement, that your circle was much more practical or at least anti-utopian. Was there a current of Strangelovian sort of disregard – that these were just bombs and we needed to use them, the sort of things that Donald Trump says about atomic bombs today [during his presidential campaign]? You mentioned massive retaliation. Did the Eisenhower administration see massive retaliation as a war-fighting doctrine or as a utopian, ultimate deterrence doctrine? It was probably a mix.

MH: Certainly, in the 1950s, in the days of General [Curtis] LeMay and [Allen] Dulles and all the rest of it, it was a war-fighting doctrine, without the slightest doubt about it. Where Trump is now is where they all were then, including Eisenhower as far as one can see: that in the event of the Russians doing anything stupid, we will do what we think is appropriate at a time or place of our own choosing, and we will use nuclear weapons on whatever scale we consider necessary. I think that within the US Air Force [the attitude was]: 'we've got it, we're going to use it.' Well, how many people are you prepared to kill? 'As many as it takes.' How many are you prepared to have killed on your own side? 'Well, we reckon that, so long as it's no more than ten million, we can survive.' And that is the way in which the thinking went at that time.

DA: The original IISS crew, including you and Alastair Buchan – what was their attitude towards that kind of thing?

MH: I was sent over [to the US] by Alastair in the first year of the foundation of IISS, to sniff around and find out what the Americans were thinking about it. And of course, as with all Americans, they were thinking about it from A to Z! But in Washington, one met highly intelligent State Department officials and very concerned professors and others, who said if we have to use [nuclear weapons], we have to be very careful about it. And there were Dr Strangelove figures, and there were General LeMay figures, who said 'we've got the bomb, why not use it?' And one went over to RAND corporation in Los Angeles, and I was really scared there that they were living in a different universe. The whole thing for them was simply abstract, but then one went back to the Charles River [in Cambridge, Massachusetts], and they were on track with us. And so, one of the things we did succeed in doing at the IISS, was to get these Americans to talk to one another. Dr Strangelove was a very, very real figure at that time.

With the Cuban Missile Crisis, the whole thing becomes real. That is when, in 1962, IISS has been going for five years or so, and there was, I think, then a complete change of mode. Dr Strangelove more or less disappeared. The internal politics of the US Air Force at that time would be interesting to know about – whether the more realistic people did find themselves getting promoted into the top jobs. After that, when I started journeying over to the States on a regular basis, which I did about once a year for the rest of my life, I didn't meet any Dr Strangeloves in the Air Force. I still met quite a lot down at RAND Corporation. Albert Wohlstetter I always regarded as a very, very sinister figure, although I liked him very much and respected him. And he was, of course, a very formidable figure in the education of people like Donald

Rumsfeld, and the extreme right. He was simply one in a not-very-typical group of academics, who were not, at that stage, in the least dominant.

DA: You write about this in your memoirs: that there was a big difference in worldview between Santa Monica and Cambridge, Massachusetts. From the beginning, on the Charles River, people who thought about nuclear weapons were immediately thinking about restraint. This included [Henry] Kissinger?

MH: Everything includes Kissinger! ... Henry was very helpful and very supportive at that time, and has been throughout his life actually, and one of the major works at that early time was Kissinger's own book [*Nuclear Weapons and Foreign Policy* (1957)]. He was acting as a rapporteur of a study group, so he could almost say this was not his idea. But he believed in tactical nuclear weapons and thought that this would be the answer – that one would be able to keep the [nuclear conflict] at a level that one could manage. I doubt whether he held that view for very long.

Henry approached things, basically, as a historian of international affairs, and war as being an instrument of policy and, if we start from there, then where do nuclear weapons fit into war as an instrument of policy. He had a very subtle, very European and a very Jewish kind of mind, with wonderfully clear, analytical thinking, based on a thorough knowledge of the past. Everything that he has written about has been intelligent, important – but not necessarily cohesive or coherent – trying to find the practical answer to the problems of the moment. He was always a benign figure in the background, and he was always very close to Alastair [Buchan], but the moment of course that he gets into power [in 1969], he has to think in terms of power. Once he's out of power, he thinks in terms of possibilities, desirabilities – all those things.

DA: The enormity of the problems that the IISS was established to study – was there already that sense of enormity after World War Two because of the total nature of that war? In other words, was there a continuum between strategic bombing as practiced by the United States and the UK, and the idea of nuclear weapons?

MH: Yes, and that is where P.M.S. Blackett becomes important. He was a figure, politically, [who was] pretty far left, but he had also been an officer in the Royal Navy in the First World War. He had been enormously important in developing operational analysis. He realised that [nuclear weapons] could not be abolished, he believed that the British could not afford them, and the Americans were going ahead with them, and therefore it was a British problem for us to think about. Blackett, Slessor – the airman who also had been involved in bombing – introduced an expertise which we lacked on the whole, and therefore they were both very much in favour of being closely allied with the United States but – as we have felt, if I may say so, constantly ever since then about the United States – 'they're wonderful people but we've got to control them'.

DA: You weren't that interested in current events. That seems to be what you are saying.

MH: Yes. I wasn't, not in the least.

DA: You were an historian.

MH: I was an historian. My speciality was English history of the early seventeenth century, and I was employed, by King's College London, as an assistant lecturer, in early modern English history.

DA: Then you were asked to start the War Studies Programme.

MH: Even before I was employed by King's, my regiment had got hold of me to help with their official history. So I did have a lingering interest in military affairs, but one which I had no intention of pursuing for very long. Then the decision to offer me the job at King's was simply the fact that (a) I was already there, and had established good contacts and everything, and (b) I had got form in writing a little military history.

DA: Even though you were a military historian, you were still an historian. How did you become engaged with the central strategic question of contemporary politics and warfare?

MH: Through my contact with Liddell Hart, who had read various reviews that I had written in the New Statesman and elsewhere and was interested in the things that I had said. I had made various references to him I think, in the review, which he agreed or disagreed with, or wanted to get in touch with me about. Anyhow we got together, and we clicked, and I think he saw me as being a possible disciple of his.

I had also got involved with Chatham House. I had acted as a rapporteur of a study group at Chatham House on [US] disengagement from Europe. The study group was set up, and I was appointed rapporteur of that, and so there was a book published about [US] disengagement [Michael Howard, *Disengagement in Europe* (1958)]. I was the rapporteur but nonetheless, I was the author of it. And that got me involved, as it were, as a specialist on contemporary European problems.

DA: I recall from *Captain Professor* that Chatham House wouldn't publish that book.

MH: Yes, that's right. Interestingly enough, the person who damned it was Jack Slessor. My God, he had a good mind! He went through it, just tearing it to pieces and he said no, it shouldn't be published. Alastair Buchan however, who was a major figure in the writing of it, said: we're not going to allow this ignorant airman to trample over us. He got onto the publishers at Penguin and got them to publish it instead.

DA: Where did it fit between the Kennan and Acheson arguments about disengagement?

MH: I said it wouldn't work.

DA: You were closer to Acheson.

MH: That was the general sense of the study group, but I put an awful lot of punch into what, I must admit, seemed like a crazy idea.

Kennan came as a guest of honour to a dinner given by the Military Commentators Circle. He then defended the idea of disengagement in Europe, and I attacked it, in terms which were rather brutal, I'm afraid, at the time. I will never forget that George Kennan, whom I admired and loved, and was one of the great good men of our time, that as I got more and more cutting about the idea, his face sort of crumpled. I was causing him personal anguish, I could see that. And I thought 'Oh God, what have I done, what am I doing?' because I'd made him really, really unhappy. He didn't see this, obviously, as something to come back at me with, which I'd rather assumed, and what I then realised was that he felt deeply and personally about everything, which made him both a very sympathetic but a rather vulnerable person.

DA: After Alastair Buchan was appointed Director, was your involvement in the Institute purely intellectual, or were you involved also in decisions about publications and operational decisions as well?

MH: They were concerned with general overall policies, I would say. Alastair managed a very tight ship, and managed it with great efficiency, but he would consult me about such questions such as what the subject matter of the next conference should be.

DA: What would you consider the milestones or the major achievements of the Institute?

MH: John Chipman's appointment. John virtually re-founded the Institute. Before John, it was more of a cottage industry, it was run more or less on a shoestring, and it was John's idea not to become simply international, but global.

Earlier, when we had Bob O'Neill as Director, he broadened our scope out to the Far East. Being Australian, he did have a different view of the world and that was interesting and important. But the decision actually, to broaden us, and to think in terms of millions rather than tens of thousands of pounds; if you're talking of steps: internationalisation from ISS to IISS; globalisation with Bob O'Neill, and then universalisation, or whatever you like to call it, with John [Chipman].

DA: Maybe it was just geographical that [the Institute] became such a central place for transatlantic debate. Was it because of sheer geography that it was important?

MH: Well, it did help. When it was founded, I wouldn't say 'the special relationship' worked, but London was the focus of the West, in a way which nowhere else was. I think that that was why the Ford Foundation were interested in us. There was nobody on the mainland of Europe in the immediate post-war world who could be anything of the kind. And the United States was too far away from Europe and Britain, and the American specialists were so busy fighting one another, that [establishing the Institute in the US] would have been just [produced] another American think tank, without any particular influence anywhere particular. So, I think London was the obvious place so far as the Ford Foundation was concerned.

DA: In some place you wrote that the Institute was criticised for not engaging with the question of Vietnam.

MH: We discussed often as to whether we should not be doing more about the question of Vietnam. But it was Alastair's view throughout that this was too painful for the Americans. Almost anything that we wrote or published about Vietnam would cause pain to our friends and allies. Politically it was understandable, for sure, and I don't think actually that our reputation suffered.

DA: What was your sense of what the Ford Foundation was doing at that time [in the context of the Cold War]?

MH: The Ford Foundation was definitely an American weapon in the Cold War, and the Ford Foundation poured money into Western Europe, to keep it sweet. And they saw IISS very much as one of their tools, keeping the Western Europeans onside. Had I been told that the Ford Foundation were doing this to keep us onside, I would think 'fine, OK, me too!', in the same way as people say of the magazine *Encounter* – 'you should not have subscribed to that – that was a Cold War instrument', I would say 'OK, but I'm on that side in the Cold War!' The same would be applied to most people, I think, who were associated with *Encounter* or CIA or anything else back then.

When the Cold War went cool [in military terms] after the Cuban Missile Crisis, it didn't get frozen so far as politics were concerned and, in some ways, it became even more ferocious underground than it did when it had been over-ground. There was a sense in Washington that it was clear that we couldn't use nuclear weapons to deter [the Soviets], so we have got to use everything else which is available.

After the end of the Cold War, [the Russians] could not escape this shadow of the KGB. They could not believe that there was not somebody there watching and reporting on them. To be quite open and frank was not in their genes, and it was going to take a generation to thaw them out. Dealing with them was a matter of very, very long-term sensitivity.

One of the people who can deal with them is Trump. Trump understands ruthlessness, he understands power. He has the same kind of cruel sense of humour. They're adversaries now, they'll be friends tomorrow, they will stab one another in the back if that suits them, they know that that's going to be the case, so they have a great deal more in common with one another than they do with ordinary honest people.

DA: I can't remember reading you on the subject of NATO enlargement – what was your view?

MH: At the time, I don't think I had a view quite honestly, because I wasn't particularly conscious of what was going on. I think all that happened when I was at Yale and felt rather out of things. If asked about it I would have said go easy, keep it cool for the moment. If consulted, I think I would have had the wit to say that at the time, but I wasn't consulted about it and I didn't really think about it all that much.

DA: Well, thank you so much for having us.

MH: You've made me think about things that I haven't thought about for a very long time. It's been most enjoyable. And I hope that in the answers that I gave, I wasn't deliberately misleading about anything.

I have a request to make. It's a posthumous request. It is that, when I die, a really good party should be given … An excellent party with very, very good champagne. I see no point in dying if people aren't going to enjoy it.

CHAPTER TWO

Present at the creation

Survival 50-1, 2008

The International Institute for Strategic Studies was originally established as The Institute for Strategic Studies in November 1958, and the first issue of its journal, *Survival*, appeared in March–April 1959. It was then a purely British institution, and its priorities were determined by the British circumstances of the 1950s.

Some three years earlier, on 1 March 1955, Winston Churchill had revealed to the House of Commons the full implications for the British people of the 'hydrogen bomb' – the thermo-nuclear weapon that the United States had successfully tested at Eniwetok in 1952, to be followed by the Soviet Union a few months later. Half a dozen such bombs, Churchill told his audience, would make the British Isles uninhabitable, and no defence could possibly be guaranteed. Their use, he admitted, could only be 'deterred'; so Britain was building its own 'deterrent' to threaten comparable damage against any attacker. But in the event of nuclear war Britain would be wiped off the face of the map, whatever happened to its allies or its enemies. 'It may well be', Churchill concluded hopefully, 'that we shall, by a process of sublime irony, have reached a stage where safety will be the sturdy shield of terror, and survival the twin brother of annihilation.' But such a happy outcome could by no means be guaranteed.

It took some time for the implications of Churchill's revelations to soak in. Too much else was occupying the foreground of public events. A year later, in 1956, the British government and its Conservative supporters would be thrown into confusion by the humiliation of the Suez campaign. Simultaneously the Labour opposition, especially the fellow-travelling left wing, was equally disoriented by the Soviet invasion of Hungary. The first event showed that the United States could not always be relied on to protect British vital interests; the second, that the disappearance of Stalin did not mean that the antagonism between the Soviet Union and the Western world was in any way abated. Meanwhile the British Armed Services were engaged in bitter in-fighting, between an Army concerned with the defence of the European mainland, a Navy defending sea communications to British overseas commitments, an Air Force charged with maintaining 'the deterrent', and a Treasury reluctant to provide money for any of them. Debates in the House of Commons were monopolised by Conservative members demanding more money for the Services and Labour demanding less; while among the general public there was a massive lack of interest.

Public opinion became seriously concerned by the nuclear threat only when in the spring of 1957 a tough defence minister, Duncan Sandys, tried to solve his problems by making massive reductions in 'conventional' forces – including the abolition of National Service – and making it explicit that the defence – indeed the survival – of the United Kingdom would henceforth depend entirely on the credibility of its own nuclear deterrent. But already there had been private stirrings. On the left, the prospect of nuclear annihilation had revived traditional demands for disarmament, if need be unilateral, that were to crystallise a few years later in the vastly popular Campaign for Nuclear Disarmament. But others, not least many within the Armed Services themselves, were equally concerned over a policy that seemed to raise more questions than it answered. Given the enormous power of the American nuclear arsenal, was a British 'deterrent' necessary at all? Was it affordable? Was it credible? If used, should its strike be pre-emptive, or retaliatory? If the first, was it justifiable? If the second, was it feasible? How were nuclear weapons to be factored in to the defence of Europe? And given the horrific consequences of a nuclear strike, was it justifiable ever to use one, even in retaliation?

These, it was felt, were not questions to be dealt with in profound secrecy by a small group of specialists in the Ministry of Defence. They were not just military but, in the profoundest sense, political. More, they were moral. And more even than that, they were existential. At stake was not just the 'security' of the United Kingdom but the survival, possibly, of mankind. At very least such matters demanded widespread debate of the kind they were already receiving in the United States. But Britain had no specialist bodies to promote such debate on the model of the RAND Corporation, or centres for concerned scientists such as MIT. Few people were aware of the work being done in the States by such thinkers as Bernard Brodie, Albert Wohlstetter, Thomas Schelling and Herman Kahn. But among those who were so aware were Denis Healey, one of the very few members of the Labour Party who took an informed interest in defence questions; a small number of well-informed journalists, notably Richard Goold-Adams of *The Economist* and Alastair Buchan of *The Observer*; and the Nobel-winning scientist P.M.S. Blackett, whose work *The Military and Political Consequences of Nuclear Energy* was one of the very few British contributions to the nuclear debate.

British scientists did not on the whole agonise so publicly about the development of nuclear weapons as did their American colleagues who published *The Bulletin of Atomic Scientists*, with its clock ticking inexorably towards midnight. But the moral dilemma posed by nuclear war was being urgently considered by a group of British clergy under the leadership of Bishop Bell of Chichester, one of the few clerics who had publicly objected to the 'area bombardment' of German cities during the Second World War. The British Council of Churches was thus a major focus of debate. Another was 'the Military Commentators Circle', an informal club of journalists, politicians and retired military figures presided over by the doyen of military experts, B.H. Liddell Hart. A third was the Royal Institute for International Affairs at Chatham House, a sibling of the New York Council on Foreign Relations that had sponsored the young Henry Kissinger's *Nuclear Weapons and Foreign Policy*, a work that created considerable interest in Britain. It was at Chatham House that Blackett, Healey and Goold-Adams came together, joined by a retired senior naval officer Sir Anthony Buzzard, to discuss and publish a pamphlet that examined the possibility of limiting the use of nuclear weapons. Buzzard, a dedicated Christian, then enlisted the help of the British Council of Churches to organise a conference in Brighton in January 1957 at which politicians, journalists, churchmen and senior retired military officers were invited to discuss the whole problem of nuclear war.

I was invited to that conference: since I was then in the process of creating what was to become the Department of War Studies at King's College London, I was one of the tiny number of British academics who showed any interest in the subject. Somewhat to my disappointment I was allotted, not to one of the groups discussing the substance of the subject, but to that whose task was to recommend what should be done about it.

That group agreed that we neither could nor should form any kind of pressure group, or propose any specific course of action. The best thing we could do would be to create an informed body of public opinion, so that decisions could at least be taken, and judged, against a background of informed discussion. To this end we recommended that we should set up a body whose primary, if not main, purpose should be the collection and dissemination of information about nuclear weapons and their implications for international relations. It was a proposal that the conference, perhaps sobered by discussions that revealed how little they knew about the subject, endorsed with some enthusiasm. And so the Institute was born.

In the half century since its foundation the Institute has expanded both its interests and its membership far beyond those modest beginnings, and gladly recruits members of all views and interests from all over the world. But at its core there remains the existential question: in a world of sovereign states with differing ideologies and interests, how can conflicts, even if they cannot be peacefully resolved, at least be kept within bounds that prevent them from escalating to mass holocaust, if not indeed to the 'annihilation' against which Churchill had warned? The founders of the Institute had been concerned, not so much with the ineffable goal of 'peace' – a term that attracts so much goodwill but begs so many questions – but rather with the condition that necessarily precedes peace of any kind: survival. Hence the title of our journal.

CHAPTER THREE

Book Reviews: Sociology and the military establishment

Sociology and the military establishment, by Morris Janowitz (New York: Russell Sage Foundation, 1959)

Survival 1-4, 1959

Sociologists have never taken the military establishment as seriously as it deserves. So at least argues Dr. Janowitz, echoing those economists, historians and academic lawyers who constantly complain that their colleagues regard military affairs as something peripheral and exceptional, and barely worth the attention even of specialists. This short book attempts only to indicate where sociology has been of practical value to the armed services, and to outline some of the peculiarities of the military establishment particularly interesting to the sociologist. The impatient layman may feel that many of the points somewhat ponderously made by Dr. Janowitz are obvious to the common sense of the intelligent observer and could be much more pithily expressed. Such sentences as, "The contradictory interplay of practices designed to stimulate group initiative and those practices required for organizational co-ordination are again widespread bureaucratic processes" or "While generalizations in this area are most hazardous, it does seem that weapons systems which maintain close physical proximity of team members and enhance the process of communication contribute most to primary group cohesion" seem to obscure rather than illuminate truth. But for those with the patience to thread their way through the tortuous thickets of his style Dr. Janowitz says many wise things in a very short space. He analyses the change which new weapons-systems and new forms of warfare are effecting in the traditional format of the armed services, and the tensions which thereby result. He dwells on the different functions, of command and co-ordination, which confront the officer, and the difficulty of devising a training system to develop both forms of skill. He speaks of the increasing part which persuasion, rather than command, plays in the complex military bureaucracies of our time; and, perhaps most important of all, he emphasizes the contribution to morale in combat of what the layman would call 'comradeship' and the sociologist labels 'group cohesion'.

It is certainly a cause for wonder that sociologists should not have shown greater alacrity in availing themselves of the excellent material for field-work which they would find in the military social organisms on their doorsteps; and Dr. Janowitz shows the sort of contribution which applied sociology has made and can make to solving problems of military organization. But so long as he and his fellows express their conclusions in such esoteric terms they are likely to be regarded with continuing suspicion by those military organizers who have the greatest need of their help.

CHAPTER FOUR

Book Review: Deterrent or defence

Deterrent or defence: a fresh look at the West's military policy, by B.H. Liddell Hart (London: Stevens & Sons, 1960)

Survival 2-5, 1960

The sub-title of Captain Liddell Hart's book is a little misleading. This volume is, as the author makes clear in his preface, a collection of studies written over the last two or three years – two indeed date back to the first half of the decade – some of which have already appeared in print. In spite of skilful blending and extensive re-writing the chapters still give an impression of having been written separately, without reference to any overall scheme of work, and in response to different historical stimuli; and the publishers would add to the interest of the book, without in the least detracting from its value, if they gave some indication as to which of the contents had already been printed, in what form, where, and when. It would at least provide scholars with a useful key to the evolution of the thought of the most penetrating military critic of our time.

Captain Liddell Hart brings to the study of military affairs two qualities, neither unusual in itself, but in combination virtually unique. The first is a grasp of grand strategy, based on a wide study of history which has led him to develop a philosophy of war comparable to that of Clausewitz in its insistence upon the necessary primacy of political considerations in all military operations. The second is an expertise in the *minutiae* of tactics, weapons and organization for land warfare which is kept meticulously abreast of the unfolding technology of war. This expertise to some extent determines his approach, especially in this latest book. The sailor will find curiously little about global strategy and sea power. The airman will complain, possibly with more justification, that the author ignores those subtle and unending speculations over massive deterrence, finite deterrence, minimal deterrence, and first and second strike forces, of which military theory is coming increasingly to consist. For Liddell Hart the battle is the pay-off, and ground forces exist, not to trigger off any global process of mutual extermination, but to fight battles – and fight them economically, efficiently, and decisively.

This belief has made him a constant critic of the posture and philosophy of NATO; and it has made his the most powerful voice raised in protest against the increasing dependence of the West on 'tactical' nuclear weapons whose use, it is almost universally agreed, could not be confined to the battlefield. But his criticism is always constructive. Instead of reliance on weapons whose use would, for Western Europe at least, involve national suicide, he re-emphasizes the viability of conventional weapons in the defence, even against overwhelmingly superior odds. Here his mastery of tactical detail is invaluable. He shows how the number of men required to hold a given length of front has, as weapons have developed, steadily shrunk. Twenty thousand men were needed to the mile in Napoleon's day; 2,000 was usual in the Second World War; while in the Normandy campaign – to quote no examples from the Russian front – the Allied troops, fresh, superbly equipped and with complete dominance of the air, seldom succeeded in breaking the German lines with a superiority of less than five to one. On this analogy, the West could with little difficulty raise and equip enough conventionally armed divisions to defend NATO's central front against the strongest forces that the Russians are likely to deploy against it. Nuclear weapons should be held only by special units and used only as 'a last but one resort'. For the vulnerable Northern and Central Fronts it would be wise to provide, as reinforcements, forces of those highly mobile amphibious troops whose value, both military and political, is analysed in one of the most instructive articles in this book. And finally, the fighting effectiveness of all these front-line forces should be maximized by new tactics of 'controlled dispersion'; by the extensive use of night action; by light, hard hitting, air-transportable tanks; by helicopters, and zero ground-pressure vehicles; and if necessary by the use of a weapon far more humane than nuclear armaments – gas.

There remains one gap to be filled in the chain of Captain Liddell Hart's argument. The forces which he has in mind are designed primarily to deal with emergencies and provide 'a non-nuclear fireguard and fire-extinguisher'. He attacks the 'soldiers (who) still think in terms of a lengthy war and of winning it, (who) tend to put the requirements – in men, equipment, and money – much higher than the statesmen feel they can meet'. Yet if a purely conventional defensive system did prove effective in repelling a conventional attack, and nuclear war was not unleashed, a lengthy war of the Korean type might easily ensue; and there would enter into the battle not only the elements, which he discusses so shrewdly, of Force and Space, but a third to which he devotes little attention: Duration. Military organizers are not misled in being worried by this aspect of conventional war, and it raises problems which mobile elite troops are not well equipped to solve. Captain Liddell Hart is not blind to this question. He touches interestingly on the idea of militia-type forces, 'a superior type of Home Guard, (which) would provide a deep network of defence, yet need much less transport than the present NATO type, be much less of a target, be less liable to interception, and become effective with far greater training'. But he does not seem to have devoted to this problem quite the amount of sustained thinking which is evident elsewhere in the work. Perhaps that will soon be forthcoming. Fire-extinguishers can deal with accidents; but we would be rash if we assumed that accidents were the only emergencies for which the West had to prepare.

CHAPTER FIVE

Book Review: Verteidigung oder Vergeltung

Verteidigung oder Vergeltung, by Helmut Schmidt
(Stuttgart: Seewald Verlag, 1961)

Survival 3-4, 1961

German voices have been notably absent from the debates on strategy, deterrence and arms control which have occupied the Anglo-Saxon world during the past decade. With one or two exceptions – Professor von Weizsacker and Adelbert Weinstein come to mind – German military thinkers have occupied themselves with the technical and tactical problems of their growing *Bundeswehr*, about which they have already created a formidable literature; and they have relied on the Americans for directives about higher strategy. (The new directives which they must now be getting, incidentally, are likely to come as a shock to Herr Strauss and his officials.) Germany's recent history makes this not altogether surprising, but it is still a pity. Germany has produced not only many of the world's greatest soldiers but a tradition of military thought, through Clausewitz and Delbruck, which, with its insistence on the interpenetration of policy and strategy, we can ill afford to see die out; and if Germany's leaders have twice in a generation ignored the advice of her wisest teachers, that is no reason for us to reject those teachers as well.

A renaissance of German strategic studies is overdue, and Helmut Schmidt's book is all the more welcome because of this. He does not, it is true, belong to any distinctively German tradition of thinking. His mentors are the Americans – Kissinger, Wohlstetter, Gavin, King – and the British – Buchan, Buzzard, Blackett. He writes largely, he admits, to bring the conclusions of these Anglo-Saxon thinkers to the attention of a German public quite uninstructed in defence matters. But in doing this he himself makes an outstanding contribution to the literature of the subject. In the first place, he has written a summary of contemporary strategic issues, not in NATO alone but throughout the world, which is so complete, so balanced and so clear that it deserves to be translated as a guide to the public of this country and that of the United States as well as of his own Germany. Nothing published here during the last few years can rival it. He surveys the general development of weapons and the doctrines and controversies to which they have given rise during the past decade: first and second strike forces, hard and soft-based weapons, counter-force and counter-city blows. He discusses the implications of tactical nuclear weapons, and the degree to which they can replace conventional forces. He outlines the various proposals for disarmament and arms control; and he makes a specific study of the problems of NATO defence. His conclusions are those which one is tempted to define as the defence doctrine of all sensible men. Multiply mobile and hard-based strike forces so as to secure as stable a balance of deterrence as may be possible. Increase conventional forces so as to raise the nuclear threshold. Put tactical nuclear weapons under a distinct command, and adopt any measures of conventional rearmament that may be needed to free NATO from the necessity for initiating their use. Study arms control measures as a matter of urgency; and understand that the vital victories in the world today must be won in fields other than military. In all this Herr Schmidt speaks, not simply as a German, but as a perceptive member of Western civilization.

In addition to this, however, Herr Schmidt has provided a specifically German view of these problems, which Germany's allies will find of the greatest interest and importance. Germany's position is peculiar in three ways. First, she would be the greatest sufferer from any 'limited' nuclear war waged in Europe. Secondly, her rearmament is regarded with foreboding by many of her Western allies and is followed beyond the Iron Curtain with quite intelligible alarm. And thirdly she is a divided country whose leaders are immovably dedicated to the intention of restoring her unity. If Herr Schmidt makes the second of these points with a frankness which is unlikely to be welcome to his own countrymen, his affirmation of the third is passionate: *Einigkeit und Recht und Freiheit fur das deutsche Vaterland!* And for this unity, West German integration into a Western European Community can never provide a substitute.

All these considerations lead Herr Schmidt to put forward by far the most interesting proposal for a reshaping of NATO and for a controlled 'non-nuclear' zone in central Europe that this reviewer has yet seen. His scheme, like M. Rapacki's, embraces both Germanies, Poland and Czechoslovakia. The armed forces of these states would be subject to international inspection, kept to certain limits and possess no nuclear weapons. The forces of Russia and of Germany's Western allies would be reduced to symbolic frontier detachments with the same function as the Berlin garrison: to act as guarantees of the continuing interest of these powers in the preservation of the military balance within this area. Outside the area, the great powers could make whatever disposition of bases and of nuclear weapons that they pleased. On the frontiers of the area radar-warning systems would be set up, the Western on the Russian frontier, the Eastern on the Rhine. Such provisions, claims Herr Schmidt, would reduce the danger of accidental war without diminishing the security of the West. It would provide a useful testing-ground for an inspectorate. It would make German reunification considerably easier; and it would allay the fears raised on both sides of the Iron Curtain by the spectre of Western Germany's armament with nuclear weapons.

This is not the place to discuss Herr Schmidt's proposal. It must be studied in his own words, together with his rebuttal of all the obvious objections; and here is another reason to have this most important book translated as quickly as possible. It is enough to say that his arguments are of a piece with the rest of his work: cool, practical and realistic. We hope to hear a great deal more of them in the near future – and a great deal more of Herr Schmidt himself.

CHAPTER SIX

Letter to the editor

Survival 4-1, 1962

Dear Sir:

In his letter in your issue of November 1961, Professor Strausz-Hupé three times uses the word 'blackmail' to describe Soviet foreign policy. Strictly speaking he is quite correct. 'Blackmail' in its original sense certainly meant the attempt to impose one's will on another party by the threat of force, and in civil society this is rightly considered a heinous offence; involving as it does a contempt for the due process of law and striking at the foundations of the State.

In international affairs however the situation is hardly comparable. We have not yet created a World State. In relations between sovereign states force is still, regrettably, the *ultima ratio*, and every Power with the capacity to do so uses the ultimate threat of force as an indispensable element in its policy. Blackmail is still, as it has always been, an intrinsic part of power politics. In a world of nuclear weapons this attitude may be archaic and eventually fatal to mankind; but it is certainly not peculiar to the Soviet Union. Mr Khrushchev was not the first and has not been the last national leader who has assured the world and his own people, at moments of crisis, of the overwhelming might of his national armoury. Such assurances are usually meant to cow one's adversaries and reassure one's friends. It is seldom that they do either.

No great Power is at present in a position to accuse another of 'blackmail'. The question at issue is whether or not one approves of the policy in furtherance of which the use of force is ultimately threatened. If one accepts the *status quo* one will condemn any threat to use force in changing it. But even here moral judgments are not easy to make. A policy which attempts to disrupt the *status quo* is not *ipso facto* wrong. If one party considers the existing situation intolerable and has failed to persuade its colleagues to change it, it is not unusual for it to have recourse to arms; and the knowledge that it may do so is a vital element in the negotiations. Professor Strausz-Hupé himself does not hold the *status quo* sacrosanct; his latest book indeed is an eloquent plea that it is not. He may conceivably be right in urging the United States to use more ruthlessly both the traditional and the new techniques of power politics. But in doing so he disqualifies himself from condemning the Soviet Union when it attempts to do the same. The only people in any position to condemn 'Soviet blackmail', or blackmail in general as an instrument of policy, are those who are working to create a world order in which even the mightiest States will be subject to the rule of law. It is far from clear, on the evidence of his recent writings, that Professor Strausz-Hupé and his associates are to be numbered among them.

Yours faithfully,

Michael Howard
London

CHAPTER SEVEN

Book Reviews: Introduction à la stratégie; Le grand débat

Introduction à la stratégie, by André Beaufre (Paris: Armand Colin, 1963); **Le grand débat: initiation à la stratègie atomique**, by Raymond Aron (Paris: Calmann-Lévy, 1963)

Survival 6-3, 1964

The simultaneous appearance of these two strategic studies, the first by one of France's most literate and distinguished soldiers, the second by one of her foremost political thinkers, is not only a happy coincidence but an event of major importance in the history of strategic thought. It is a sign that, after an almost totally negative decade during which this continent could only gape in wonder at the ideas being produced in the United States, Europe is at last coming of age and beginning to make her own contribution to what Professor Aron rightly calls The Great Debate. Hitherto European writers have tended either to ignore and dismiss the more sophisticated American thinking, or uncritically to swallow it. These two writers examine it with respect, but do not entirely accept it; and give very valid reasons why they cannot.

Each approaches the problem of strategy in the nuclear age from his own professional standpoint, and much may be learned by comparing the two books. General Beaufre, the professional soldier, searches for a theory, if not a formula, which will provide a guide to action. Strategy he defines as 'une méthode de pensée permettant de classer et de hiérarchiser les événements, puis de choisir les procédés les plus efficaces'. He attempts, in his own words, to construct 'an algebra of war'. As Clausewitz tried to create an intellectual system which would be valid both for the limited wars of the eighteenth century and the total war of the Napoleonic period, so Beaufre tries to create a system which will bring together 'classical military strategy', in which all operations were directed towards the Battle, nuclear strategy, and 'indirect strategy', in which he includes not only guerrilla and political warfare but almost all the maneouvres of the cold war. Professor Aron, the philosopher, is concerned rather with explaining the predicament which afflicts all of mankind in the face of nuclear weapons, and with devising techniques for mastering it which will have universal applicability, for the Russians as well as ourselves. He has little to say about the cold war, but a great deal about arms control. For him the enemy is not, as it is for General Beaufre, an orthodox – or unorthodox – adversary; it is nuclear annihilation in a world where 'le risque de violence est inséparable de la pluralité des Etas souverains, probablement même de la condition sociale de l'homme'.

General Beaufre writes with that beautiful clarity and logic characteristic of his nation, imposing order on his chaotic subject-matter in masterly fashion. Sometimes he is almost too masterly. For example, he traces the connection between 'military' strategy and the 'deterrent' strategy of the arms race, suggesting that to secure a nuclear superiority is the 'deterrent' equivalent of a military attack, that the revelation of the Soviet lead in missile technology was the equivalent of a military surprise, the deceptive Soviet bomber programme of 1955 the equivalent of a feint; and so on. This is surely to read into the contigent and accidental world of politics a degree of military precision that it seldom possesses? Indeed in stating, quite correctly, that strategy today embraces political as well

as military elements, General Beaufre sometimes comes peril-
ously close to regarding international politics as a military
weapon. That he realizes the fallacy of so doing he makes clear:
'Politique au dessus, stratégie totale (i.e., cold-war strategy) au
dessus' he firmly states. But even this over-simplifies the situation. The current of politics (and the plural form in English
gives a far better indication of their inevitable complexity and
self-contradiction than does the singular French) often turns in
directions completely opposed to that of 'national strategy', as
both the Americans and the Russians have several times found
out. The maintenance of objective and overall plan which is
mandatory in 'classical' war is not always a realistic ambition
in the pluralistic word of peace. It is natural for soldiers to
wish to fashion their political masters in their own image, but
seldom possible; even when that political master is a General.

Professor Aron is descriptive rather than analytic: he has no
time for beautiful systems, as he makes clear in dismissing the
writings of another French soldier, Pierre Gallois: 'ce systéme
intellectuelle a de quoi séduire certains esprits, plus épris de
simplification que soucieux de reconnâitre les complexités
du réel et les equivoques d'un univers inconnu.' The search
for an 'algebra' can be pushed to extremes. His book, which
contains in succinct form many of the ideas of his great *Paix
et Guerre entre les Nations*, is written in an attempt to explain
the American doctrine of 'flexible response' to his countrymen,
and the European objections to it to the Americans. 'Flexible
response', he points out, is simply arms-control during a
period of crisis; for arms-control itself is 'à la fois la politique
d'armament avant la crise, et la conduite de la diplomatie-stra-
tégie durant la crise.' He ably rehearses the arguments for such
a policy as against those for maximising deterrence by massive
response, and points out also the weaknesses in counter-force
doctrine admitted by the Americans themselves. 'Ceux qui

imaginent refuter le secrétaire d'Etat en insistant sur les limites de la stratégie contre-force' he sums up crisply, 's'abusent eux-mêmes ou abusent leurs lecteurs.'

But he recognises that Europeans cannot be expected to endorse Mr McNamara's doctrine with any degree of enthusiasm. 'Que cette stratégie soit ou non la meilleure, elle paraît trop pleinement conforme à l'intérêt national des Etats Unis pour ne pas inspirer des soupçons aux Européens'. A strategy which, ideal for the whole, is not ideal for the individual members; and 'ce que craignent les Européens raisonnables, c'est moins l'abandon de l'Europe par les Etats Unis qu'une stratégie américaine qui, a force d'annoncer l'assouplissement de la réplique, finirait par élargir exagérément la zone d'opérations située au dessous de seuil atomique'. The answer for him does not lie in any national *Force de frappe*, whose credibility would in fact be far less than that of the American. Nor does it lie in the MLF. It might eventually lie in the development of a European deterrent, for in spite of all their differences, 'les Etats Européens ont des problèmes de défense communs, à certain égards différents de ceux de Etats Unis'. The main argument in favour of the French *force de frappe* he considers to lie precisely in this, that it might one day constitute the nucleus of such a European force. But he admits also that it has forced the United States 'd'entretenir, sur le sujet de stratégie, un dialogue avec l'Europe'; and that it constitutes 'un début d'assurance contre l'imprévisibilité de l'avenir diplomatique'.

British specialists will read what Professor Aron has to say about the *force de frappe* with particular interest, if only because, in his discussion of it, he virtually ignores the existence of the British independent deterrent. This is, from so eminent and moderate an expert, both chastening and significant. It is an indication, if one were needed, that the discussions between British and French specialists, which are going on under the auspices of the Institute for Strategic Studies, are long overdue. Let us hope that one day soon such discussions may open on a more official level.

MICHAEL HOWARD

Book Review: Deterrence before Hiroshima: the airpower background of modern strategy

Deterrence before Hiroshima: the airpower background of modern strategy, by George H. Quester (New York and London: Wiley, 1966)

Survival 8-10, 1966

Historians, if they have any sense, hesitate for a long time before suggesting that we can learn any precise 'lessons' from a past of which our knowledge is inevitably incomplete and filtered through doubtfully reliable channels. There has been something refreshing about the attempts made since 1945 to think through the problems of nuclear war by the light of pure reason, on the assumption that the quantitative development in the power and range of weapons invalidates all theories derived from earlier wars. If 'history' teaches us anything, it is that men fall into quite as many errors in trying to learn from the past as they do in ignoring it. But although it provides few answers, it may shape our attitudes, engendering a scepticism, a humility, and an appreciation of the role of the contingent and the unforeseen in human affairs of a kind not always developed by a more positivist approach.

Dr Quester's valuable study of theories of deterrence in the pre-nuclear age was not written, and should not be read, as a critique or amplification of the theories which have been developed since 1945; but it does equip us with a perspective and a certain amount of data by which these theories can be evaluated. The idea of using strategic air power to bring direct influence to bear on the adversary's will is, as he shows, as old as the century. Douhet is only the best known, although by no means the first, the most influential or the most profound, of these early thinkers about air war. At the beginning of the First World War such British writers as Lanchester and Spaight were discussing the respective merits of counter-force and counter-value strategies. The former had written, 'The power of reprisal and the knowledge that the means of reprisal exists will ever be a far greater deterrent than any pseudo-legal document'. The latter was already advocating the separation of military from civilian targets, the strengthening of aerial defences and the subterranean siting of strategic objectives. The connection between the hardening of the base and the credibility of the deterrent was stated very explicitly by Winston Churchill in 1935. The problem of the instability of a balance of first-strike forces was widely discussed in the 1930s, when Jonathan Griffin wrote, 'It would be a balance of terrors – for that is what the balance of power, loaded with bombs, should truly be called. In the end one group must strike'. Finally Dr Quester shows how escalation, as a threat, as a policy, and as a largely inevitable process, was as familiar in 1914-18 as it became in 1939-45.

This study makes many interesting points, some of them strikingly original. It properly emphasizes the remarkable absence of serious analysis lying behind the assumption that civilian populations subjected to aerial bombardment would demand an end to the war. The reaction of the Londoners, on whose panic in 1917 all subsequent calculations were based, was to call for intensification of reprisals against Germany; and none of the British advocates of area-bombing in 1940-45 was able to adduce any evidence that German civilians would feel any differently. Dr Quester is on slightly shakier ground when he argues that in August 1940 Churchill *deliberately* escalated the British attack from counter-force to counter-city by the first raid on Berlin, to divert the Luftwaffe from its assault on RAF airfields to the less decisive target of London. On the basis of available evidence, it is difficult to make such a charge stick. He also overemphasizes the restraint and rationality with which Hitler conducted his air war, but here his basic point is a good one: that Hitler was not the hopelessly irrational adversary that Allied leaders assumed. It was not, he suggests the impossibility of negotiating restraints with Hitler that led to the Allied policy of unrestricted bombing; it was Hitler's inability to hit effectively back. But here also the verdict must be non-proven. Would an earlier development of V-weapons really have led to a tacit agreement and mutual limitation on bombing attacks? It is very difficult to visualize.

With the advent of thermonuclear weapons, the objective of strategic air power shifted decisively from the enemy's *will* to carry on the war to his actual *capacity* to carry on either war or anything else. It can therefore be reasonably argued that Dr Quester's study is of little direct relevance to the problems of nuclear war today, once a nuclear exchange has taken place. But it is certainly relevant to such operations as the British bombing of Egypt in 1956, the American bombing of Vietnam in 1965-66, or any other attempts to use air power to intimidate or deter. These events suggest that a great deal of hard study still needs to be done on the use of air power as an instrument of policy; and to this study the experience of the recent past would certainly be highly relevant.

CHAPTER NINE

Book Review: Neither liberty nor safety: a hard look at US military policy and strategy

Neither liberty nor safety: a hard look at US military policy and strategy, by
General Nathan F. Twining (New York: Holt, Rinehart & Winston, 1966)

Survival 9-4, 1967

This is not an easy book to review, for either you share General
Twining's assumptions about the world in which we live or
you do not. If you do, then his criticisms of American defence
and foreign policy will probably seem cogent and his proposals
for improving them reasonable. If, like this reviewer, you do
not, the former will appear naive and the latter both stupid
and dangerous. What is beyond dispute is that the views of
the Chairman of the American Joint Chiefs of Staff from 1957
to 1960 cannot be dismissed as insignificant, and that General
Twining is probably not the only senior officer in the United
States Armed Forces to hold them.

It is for General Twining a fact 'which cannot be disputed
by rational men' that the Free World confronts a monolithic
Communist conspiracy 'which for over forty years has been
dedicated to an unswerving objective to destroy free institutions, the free way of life and free republican governments'.
To deal with this, he considers, the US policy of 'containment'
was unsatisfactory, since it offered 'no real plan for the ultimate resolution of our conflict with the Sino-Soviet bloc' (the
schism within which the General 'cannot take too seriously').

He would have preferred 'containment plus initiative'. This, he assures us, 'would not *necessarily* have required a calculated and deliberate first nuclear blow against Communist powers' (my italics); but 'the United States could have said "the United States does not intend to initiate military conflict, but it will have to begin it if the USSR and Communist China persist in their attempts to enslave more of the free world"'.

If General Twining has little patience with 'containment', he has still less with the sophisticated doctrines of limited war, stable balance and damage limitation which now rule in the Pentagon, or for the 'transient non-professionals' who devise and implement them. 'In the old days' he recalls nostalgically, 'war was war and peace peace. . . . When the nation was at war, Americans were at war, and Americans did what was necessary to win'. To that situation he wishes the United States to return. It should maintain a position of unchallengeably superior military technology and devote itself to 'eliminating' or 'neutralizing' the system which threatens it, withholding all aid from allies and neutrals who do not toe the line. If, on the other hand, the United States were to decide that the Communist objectives were no longer 'as stated by that conspiracy', it should, concludes the General rather surprisingly, 'disarm at once'.

Those who do not believe that General Twining gives an accurate description of the existing condition of world affairs or a correct diagnosis of the causes of international tensions are likely to put this book down with mixed feelings: thankfulness that we survived the years when the chief military appointment in the United States was held by a man of General Twining's outlook; respect for a political system which could use his outstanding military abilities but yet hold him in check; and perhaps a certain reluctant sympathy for Lord Russell's Peace Foundation. Even those who share the General's views may regret certain things about his book. There is, for example, his rather cavalier attitude to historical facts. ('In September 1938 Prime Minister Chamberlain had travelled to Munich to shake his umbrella in Hitler's face and to issue an ultimatum that Hitler halt his aggressive moves in Europe. In face of the appalling German war machine made clear to him at Munich, Chamberlain miserably switched to a policy of appeasement'.) Then there is the manner in which he treats those with whose views he disagrees – 'members of the scientific fraternity who had wriggled their way in as advisers on national policy'; 'anti-nuclear intellectuals'; 'armchair strategists, do-gooders, appeasers'; 'young political and military sophists, steeped in text-book analysis'; 'scientists with a bad conscience'. People such as these, argues the General, in a passage which will not increase the number of his admirers, 'like the sound of the term limited war. . . . "Little people", civilian soldiers by the millions, if necessary, can do the fighting and dying by bayonet and bullet in limited war, but the intelligentsia will have the traditional safety of a bomb-proof job'.

General Twining's principal targets are of course the men, headed by Mr Robert McNamara, who were brought in by President Kennedy to advise him in 1960, and who have shaped the policy which the General so much dislikes. But abuse of this sort is no substitute for the kind of hard argument which General Maxwell Taylor used in his book *The Uncertain Trumpet* when, under very similar circumstances, he presented to the public the case he had failed to carry within the Administration. General Twining dodges argument. He confesses indeed that 'it is difficult to find specific fault' with the objectives of the Kennedy Administration. He complains only that 'the sum total adds up to a defence of mediocrity and passiveness'; which does not get us much further.

Most of all General Twining's sympathizers may regret that he has adulterated, with views on international affairs which carry no more weight than the next man's, judgements on the matters about which he can speak with unchallenged authority: military organization, administration, and the procurement of weapons systems. On Mr McNamara's handling of these questions he could probably have presented a formidable indictment if he had set himself to it. As it is, he can have done his cause little good by publishing this book. The views it expresses and the manner in which they are presented are likely to convince waverers that the 'civilianization' of the Department of Defense did not come a moment too soon. The qualities which enable a man to rise to the top of the military profession are not necessarily those best suited to the formulation of defence policy in the nuclear age.

MICHAEL HOWARD
Stanford, California

CHAPTER TEN

Israel and the Arab world: the crisis of 1967

Adelphi Paper 41, 1967
By Michael Howard and Robert Hunter

Preface

We do not attempt in this paper to give a detailed account of the Third Arab–Israeli War of June 1967. We try simply to set the conflict in its historical and political perspective, to examine its immediate origins, to account for the remarkable course which it took, and to discuss its significance for a world which shows fewer signs than ever of abandoning the use of violence as an instrument of policy. For many years to come the war and its antecedents will provide valuable data for analysts both of military and of political affairs. It is for them that this study is primarily intended, rather than for a general public for whom a number of vivid accounts have already been provided by skilled journalists and for whom more detailed histories will no doubt be produced in course of time.

The audience to whom this study is addressed will immediately observe its shortcomings. Apart from anything else, it is not documented; it draws more heavily upon Israeli than upon Arab sources; and it does not attempt the kind of impartiality which can be achieved only by refraining from any interpretation of the events it describes. The lack of documentation is due to the fact that much of the information used has been obtained from participants or observers under seal of confidence. The lack of balance in sources is due less to any lack of co-operation from Arab governments than to the extraordinary helpfulness shown by Israeli officials, soldiers, and politicians at all levels. If as a result our presentation is in any way incomplete or unfair, the responsibility is ours alone.

We make no apology, however, for attempting an interpretive history rather than – if such a thing is ever possible – a dispassionate chronicle. We are aware that our interpretation will be acceptable neither to those who believe that the war was the result of a Soviet attempt to embarrass the United States and gain a bargaining counter for use in the conflict over Vietnam; nor to those – perhaps, unfortunately, still a majority in the Arab world – who see it as the outcome of a plot by the imperialist powers, using Zionism as their cat's-paw, to frustrate the aims of the Arab revolution and reassert their hegemony over the Middle East. We realize also that much information was not available to us, in the time at our disposal, which might have made us reconsider our conclusions. We hope, however, that within its limits this paper will be found of some value to students of international relations, and even to those who are unfortunate enough to have to conduct them.

We wish to thank those many officials, scholars, soldiers, and observers in London, Washington, New York, and the Middle East who have given us such generous assistance. Any errors of fact or judgment, however, are our responsibility alone. But most of all our thanks are due to the Director and Staff of the Institute for Strategic Studies, who accepted with every appearance of cheerful resignation this heavy additional burden on their time.

> M.H.
> R.H.
> *September 1967*

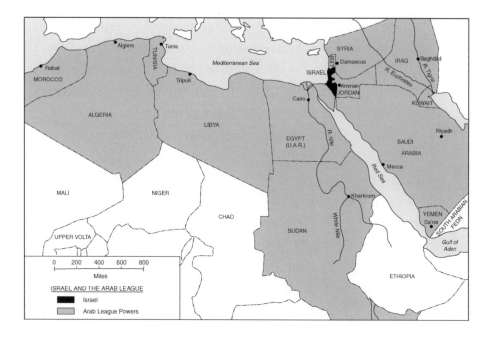

I. The conflict

Historians who like to trace the origins of political regimes to such written documents as the Declaration of Independence, Magna Carta, or the Oath of the Tennis Court must accord a similar respect to the 'Balfour Declaration'; that remarkable assurance which the British Government gave to the Zionist Organization in November 1917.

This document, the product as much of political calculation as of generous idealism, ran as follows:

> His Majesty's Government view with favour the establishment in Palestine of a National Home for the Jewish People and will use their best endeavours to facilitate the achievement of this object, it being clearly understood that nothing shall be done which may prejudice the civil and religious rights of existing non-Jewish communities in Palestine or the rights and political status enjoyed by Jews in any other country.

Significant as this promise was to the eventual establishment of a Jewish State, it did not create the Jewish nation. The very existence of a Zionist Organization with ambitions to 'return' to Palestine and sufficient influence to gain the support of one of the greatest powers in the world showed how strong and effective Jewish nationalism had already become in a world where nationalism was rapidly replacing religion as the chief ideological driving force of mankind. The wording of the second part of the Declaration, however, showed that the British Government fully realized that the Palestine which it proposed to 'liberate' from the Ottoman Empire was not a blank space to be freely settled with politically congenial immigrants. It was not only the loosely worded promises which Sir Henry MacMahon, British High Commissioner in Egypt, had made to Hussein, Sharif of Mecca, to 'recognize and support the independence of the Arabs' which had to be reconciled with the Balfour Declaration. Nor were the complications introduced by the Sykes-Picot agreement, dividing the Middle East into European spheres of influence, to create the greatest ultimate difficulties. Little regarded at the time, but eventually to constitute the greatest problem of all, was the reaction in such cities as Cairo, Damascus, and Beirut of men educated according to a European pattern, in nationalism of a European style, who objected strongly to the introduction of an alien element into their community by an equally alien power; and one which had bid for their own sympathies with very similar promises of national self-fulfilment.

This conflict between Jews – a nation without a State – and Arabs – a nation divided into too many States – was evident to some experts from the beginning. But it was slow to acquire international significance.[1] Arab nationalism became more vocal and influential as the economic and political development of the Middle East dissolved its traditional social structure; yet so long as the number of Jews in Palestine did not increase significantly – the total was 80,000 when the British assumed their Mandate from the League of Nations in 1922 – the conflict might have remained latent and Arab objections academic. But the number did increase. In 1924 the imposition by the American Government of quotas on immigration to the United States cut off the Jews of Europe – particularly Eastern Europe – from the haven where most of them would have preferred to find refuge. Even then there was little about the arid lands of Palestine to attract Jews from the European communities where they had lived, precariously but not uncomfortably, for so many centuries; until in 1933 the advent to power in Germany of the Nazi regime, and the development of similar regimes elsewhere in Europe, made their life in those communities grimly intolerable.

Until then, the British authorities in Palestine had little difficulty in restricting immigration, as their policy demanded, to the economic capacity of the country to absorb new arrivals. Now humanitarian considerations led them to increase the immigration quota yearly, until by 1939 the Jewish population stood at 450,000: nearly one-third of the total population of Palestine.[2]

The Arab population reacted naturally and violently to this influx. Rational reflection might have persuaded them – as it might, under not dissimilar circumstances, have persuaded the indigenous inhabitants of North America – that the advent of all these skilled and hard-working immigrants would increase the productivity of the country and provide a better life for all its inhabitants. But they preferred to fight to preserve their land as they knew it. The first serious clashes came in 1929. Thereafter there was a continuing pattern of conflict between Jews and Arabs. In 1936 the Arabs precipitated what the British termed a 'rebellion' but what the Arabs themselves regarded as a war to repel invaders from their native soil. Within three years the conflict was to cost 4,000 lives. The British gave the immigrants what protection they could, but it was not enough. The Jews had to organize the military defence of their own settlements. This was nothing new to many of them: in the ghettos of Eastern Europe they had lived surrounded by populations quite as hostile and often as violent as the Arabs, and had developed techniques of communal defence which were now revived and adapted by their semi-official defence organization, the Haganah. The Jews in Israel in fact had to assume the burden of defending themselves against their enemies ten years before the British abandoned the Mandate and left them on their own.

It was not only the Arabs whom the Haganah learned to fight. By now the British had realized the full difficulty of the task they had taken on. Unless there was to be continual warfare in Palestine the Arabs had somehow to be reconciled to the new arrivals. In 1937 the Peel Commission proposed a straightforward partition of the country – as the United Nations were to do ten years later. Neither party would accept this solution. To impose it by force would have involved a military effort which the British, belatedly arming to meet an even greater menace, had neither the will nor the capacity to make. Instead, in 1939 the British Government adopted a policy set out in a White Paper, which for a whole generation was to be *the* White Paper, in an attempt to meet the Arab objections.[3] This set, as the limit to Jewish immigration, the proportion of one-third of the population of Palestine, which meant in practice that a further 75,000 Jews might immigrate over the next five years. After that, no further immigration would be allowed without Arab consent. The White Paper also declared unequivocally that the British Government did not intend that 'Palestine should become a Jewish State'. Instead it visualized a Palestinian State in which

Jews and Arabs would 'share authority in such a way that the essential interests of each are secured'.

The White Paper did little to pacify the Arabs, and it infuriated the Jews. Not only had the Zionist craving for an independent State, as opposed to a 'National Home', increased as the Jewish population of Palestine swelled, but also the prospective check on immigration, at a time when their race was suffering a persecution unparalleled even in their own terrible annals, appeared to them – and not only to them – as a policy of intolerable heartlessness. For five years, however, the question rested in suspense, while British and Jews fought an adversary who threatened the survival of both. But as the war ebbed from the Middle East the conflict re-emerged, and the Jewish extremists, with improved weaponry and military expertise, began to direct their energies against British as well as Arab targets.

As for the Arabs, the war had done nothing to appease their anger, and much to exacerbate it. Their political and social system had been violently disrupted. British occupation forces had been ubiquitous, exigent, and not always tactful. In the Middle East, as elsewhere in the world, the Second World War had shattered the image of placid invincibility which had enabled the British to maintain so vast a suzerainty in the area with so small an expenditure of force. Now Arab nationalism was ready to explode not only against the humiliating foreign domination, but also against the native monarchs and oligarchies who were prepared to sustain it. The British were wise enough not to attempt to impose direct rule, but tried to preserve their influence, in an area which they still regarded as vital to their strategic and economic interests, by collaborating with the native rulers: a policy whose total failure in Egypt was partially balanced by its success in the Hashemite monarchies of Transjordan and Iraq. But friendship with these or any other Arab states could be preserved only by maintaining the White Paper policy on Palestine; and this meant turning back the boatloads of homeless Jews who were flocking from the ruins of post-war Europe, and infuriating their influential sympathizers in the United States.

Britain's first post-war Foreign Secretary, Mr Ernest Bevin, rashly staked his reputation on solving the Palestine problem. He failed. Eighty thousand British troops were pinned down in peace-keeping operations between two peoples whose dislike for themselves they grew heartily to reciprocate, for purposes which not only imposed a financial burden that the over-stretched British resources could simply not afford but were of doubtful relevance to British interests. It is not surprising that in 1947, thirty years after the ill-fated Balfour Declaration had been issued, the British abandoned responsibility for Palestine to the United Nations and announced their intention of relinquishing the Mandate in May of the following year. Britain, declared her Government, 'was not prepared to undertake the task of imposing a policy on Palestine by force of arms'.

The United Nations Special Committee on Palestine recommended, as the Peel Commission had done ten years earlier, that Palestine should be partitioned into a Jewish and an Arab State, with economic union and an international regime for the city of Jerusalem. The frontiers they proposed looked curious on the map, each State being allotted three separate areas which only touched at two single points. The Jewish State was allotted the north-east, a coastal strip embracing Tel Aviv and Haifa, and a wedge containing Beersheba and the Negev Desert with an outlet on the Gulf of Aqaba. But the frontiers followed the lines of settlement with reasonable accuracy, and the Jews, who were concerned at this stage rather to establish their sovereignty than to extend their lands, declared themselves ready to accept them.[4] The Arabs remained implacable. There now existed, in the Arab League (which had been formed largely under British auspices in 1945), a political mechanism making possible the joint action of all Arab States. In October 1947 the League set up a Military Committee and agreed in principle to establish a joint command.

In principle the Arabs were unanimously hostile to the establishment of a Jewish State. In practice, then as now, their hostility varied in intensity. At one extreme stood Syria, for long the focus of extreme Arab nationalism, and Iraq. The United Nations partition proposals touched off violent riots in Damascus and Aleppo. In Syria, compulsory service was introduced, military appropriations were voted totalling $2 million, and army officers resigned their commissions to serve in an Arab Liberation Army, units of which began to raid Jewish settlements over the border early in 1948.[5] At the other extreme stood Saudi Arabia, less directly interested, more responsive to Western influence, its rulers less subject to pressure from university students and city mobs. Pressure of this kind could be, and was, brought to bear on the Egyptian Government in Cairo; but a military involvement was the last thing its Army Command wanted. Egyptian participation, however, was virtually forced by the serpentine policy of King Abdullah of Transjordan. Abdullah viewed the United Nations proposals with equanimity, for he proposed, with British acquiescence, to annex the Arab territories of Palestine on the West Bank of the Jordan, including Jerusalem itself. The prospect of such gains made it easy for him to accept the creation of a Jewish State in the coastal valley; but the prospect of so great an extension of Jordanian territory and influence was so unwelcome to the Egyptians that they accepted common action in Palestine as the best way to balance it.

When, on the eve of the formal ending of the British Mandate on 15 May 1948, David Ben-Gurion proclaimed in Tel Aviv 'the

U.N. partition recommendations
November 1947

Arab   Zionist

Neutral

establishment of the Jewish State in Palestine, to be called Israel', fighting had already been in progress, and increasing in intensity, for about four months, as the two sides jockeyed for advantage. Now both rushed in to fill the vacuum left by the withdrawing British troops. As at the outset of all civil wars, local success or failure was determined by local circumstances, and often by a hair's breadth. The Haganah, with its spearhead of shock-troops the Palmach, was ready to fight the Palestine Arabs, but it was not prepared either in armament or in organization to deal with the regular forces of Syria, Iraq, Jordan, and Egypt when these began to close in on them from

Armistice lines and Israeli
border from Spring 1949
to present

Kissoue

Tyre

LEBANON

SYRIA

GALILEE

Acre

Safad

Sea of
Galilee

Nazareth

Dara

Irbid

SAMARIA

Qal at el
Mafraq

Mediterranean
Sea

R. Jordan

Tel AVIV

Jaffa

Lydda

Jerusalem

Amman

Qal et ed
Daba

Bethlehem

Gaza

Dead Sea

Hebron

Rafah

El Qatrana

ISRAEL

El Karak

El Auja

JORDAN

NEGEV

Quseima

El
Ghanu

Qal at
Anelza

U.A.R.
(EGYPT)

Petra

El Kuntilla

Maan

Ras an Naqb

SINAI
PENINSULA

Elath

Aqaba

0   10   20   30   40   50

Miles

north, east, and south. Courage, ingenuity, and the clumsiness
of their opponents enabled the heavily outnumbered Israelis
to check the Syrian and Egyptian advance, but they could not
prevent the Jordanians from overrunning the West Bank of the
Jordan, capturing the Old City and the heights dominating
Jerusalem, and severing the road to the coast. The four-week
cease-fire imposed by the United Nations on 11 June was
accepted with relief by both sides as a necessary breathing
space, but no more.

When the truce ended on 9 July the Israelis were in considerably better shape. The old Haganah protective forces were

rapidly developing into an army organized for regular warfare, and heavy weapons – mainly paid for by American contributions – were being flown in from Europe, principally from Czechoslovakia. When the Mandate ended in May, the Israeli Army had numbered only 35,000 men and women, with four guns, no heavy mortars, and 1,500 machine guns between them. By October they were 80,000 strong, with 250 guns, 45 heavy mortars, and 7,550 machine guns.[6] But more important still was the growth in their skill, self-confidence, and ruthlessness. In July they conquered the Arab areas of central and northern Galilee, linking up their settlements in the Upper Jordan Valley with the coastal area round Tel Aviv; and by driving the Arabs from Lydda and Ramle they gained a broad corridor to the beleaguered city of Jerusalem. These were areas of unquestionably Arab settlement. Their inhabitants, uprooted from homes they had occupied for centuries, fled east towards Syria and Jordan or south to the protection of the Egyptians at Gaza. In the week from 9 to 18 July, when the United Nations were able to negotiate another cease-fire, Israel transformed itself from a collection of settlements scattered among an alien community into a compact and formidable State.

Still neither side was prepared to accept the new situation as definitive. The Arabs expressed their fury and resentment by repeated breaches of the truce. The Israelis also had unfinished business. In the south of the country round Beersheba, isolated Jewish settlements were still surrounded by Egyptian forces. These were relieved by attacks in October, and in December the whole area of the Upper Negev was cleared.[7] This opened up the Lower Negev, an area of the greatest potential importance to the new State. Its mineral wealth was considerable; it gave access to the Indian Ocean, by-passing the Suez Canal; and it separated Israel's two most dangerous adversaries, Egypt and Jordan. On 10 March 1949 the Israelis established themselves in

Eilat, and a month later the Armistice Agreement with Jordan confirmed their frontier to the east.

The frontiers finally established by the Armistice Agreements were far from ideal. In the north the Syrians still held their old frontiers on the heights dominating the Upper Jordan Valley. In the centre the Jordanian positions reached to within twelve miles of the coast, and the salient at Latrun cut the direct road from Jerusalem to Tel Aviv. In the south the Egyptians occupied the coastal strip from Gaza to El Arish, which flanked the southern Israeli settlements and was to become a festering plague-spot of miserable refugees.[8] But in comparison with the position at the beginning of the year the Israelis had much to be thankful for. It is not surprising that their statesmen were quite ready to convert the Armistice Agreements into a definitive peace.

These agreements were reached during the course of 1949, separately negotiated by Israel with each of the principal belligerents: Egypt, Lebanon, Jordan, and Syria.[9] In all of them it was emphasized that they did not constitute a political settlement and that their provisions were 'dictated exclusively by military considerations and [were] valid only for the period of the Armistice'. It was further recognized, in the words of the Egyptian agreement, 'that rights, claims, or interests of a non-military character in the area of Palestine covered by this Agreement [might] be asserted by either Party, and that these, by mutual agreement being excluded from the Armistice negotiations, shall be, at the discretion of the Parties, the subject of later settlement'. In particular it was laid down that the Armistice Demarcation Lines established between the belligerent forces were not to be regarded as political or territorial boundaries – only as lines beyond which the armed forces of the contracting parties were not allowed to move. But the belligerents did agree in equally emphatic terms to keep the peace. They affirmed that they would not resort to military force in settlement of the

Palestine question; that there would be no aggressive action 'undertaken, planned, or threatened' by their armed forces against one another; and that each side would respect the right of the other to its security and freedom from attack. Arrangements were made for the peaceful enforcement of the armistice agreements, which we will consider further below.

With the exception of Abdullah of Jordan, whose acquisition of the Old City of Jerusalem and the West Bank of the Jordan left him no less satisfied than the Israelis, the Arabs regarded the armistice as a humiliating defeat imposed on them by *force majeure*; the force, not of Israel alone, but of the Great Powers, who, acting in rare unanimity, had brought the United Nations to recognize the State of Israel and permit her to retain the *de facto* borders established by her military power. For the swelling forces of Arab nationalism, the loss of Palestine to an alien invader was a blow as bitter as the loss of Alsace-Lorraine had been to France: a reverse never to be forgotten and certainly never to be accepted as permanent. The Syrians immediately overturned the government which had led them to defeat; in Egypt a similar movement, primarily among the younger officers, was to operate more slowly but no less drastically to bring about the revolution of 1952, which eventually brought President Nasser to power. As for Jordan, the assassination of the over-subtle Abdullah in July 1951 provided a grim warning to his incompetent son Talal and his formidably competent grandson Hussein when they succeeded him. If the war had brought the Hashemite house territory and prestige, it had also brought some half a million Palestinian refugees who, settled on the West Bank of the Jordan with full rights of citizenship, saw to it that Jordan did not lag behind its neighbours in its imprecations against the common foe.

The existence of these refugees would have ensured, if such insurance had been necessary, that time would do nothing to appease Arab feelings. During the war whole communities had fled from Palestine, encouraged by their leaders and certainly not discouraged by the Jews. Such actions of Jewish extremists as the abominable Deir Yassin massacre were exceptional, but they lost nothing in the telling. In December 1948, after the fighting had died down, the General Assembly of the United Nations resolved that all refugees who so wished be allowed to return to their homes and that those not wishing to do so should be compensated by the Israeli Government. On this and later resolutions Israel constantly prevaricated. How could 700,000 Jews allow the return of nearly a million Arabs to their lands without risking the destruction of the Jewish State? Yet how could they refuse it without inflicting on innocent people an injustice reminiscent of so many which the Jews had themselves suffered throughout their own melancholy history? And why should the Arab governments compound this injustice by persuading the Palestinians to forget their past and find a home in new lands? By 1966 the number of these refugees registered with the United Nations Relief and Works Agency was 1.3 million: 700,000 in Jordan, 300,000 in the Gaza Strip, and 300,000 divided between the Lebanon and Syria. Their presence continued to demonstrate vividly why the State of Israel, however defensive and conciliatory its policy, constituted by its very existence a standing provocation to the whole of the Arab world.[10]

The States of the Arab League, therefore, though accepting the military armistice, refused recognition to Israel, and made war on her with all the economic weapons that lay to hand. A state of belligerency, they insisted, still obtained, and gave them full rights of blockade. Pressure was exerted against firms dealing with Israel, airlines were not allowed to include both Arab States and Israel in the same routes, and ships were not allowed to visit Arab States after touching at Israeli ports.

There were regional boycott offices, a Prize Court – in fact all the paraphernalia and regulations of nations at war. After the revolution of 1952 the Egyptian Government sharply increased its pressure until, in October 1955, it imposed a comprehensive prohibition of all commercial and financial dealings with 'the enemy'.

Egypt was in a better position than any other Arab State to do Israel economic harm. From the very beginning she had established a blockade on Israeli shipping through the Suez Canal. This was extended in 1953 to include all goods being shipped to Israel. Israel appealed to the United Nations in vain. In 1951 a United Nations condemnation was ignored by Egypt. In 1954, when the question was raised again, a Soviet veto prevented any effective action being taken on Israel's behalf. As Israel's economy expanded and her volume of international trade grew, these restrictions became increasingly irksome. They might in the long run have been intolerable, if she had not been able to develop an alternative outlet to the south and east from the Negev port of Eilat, at the head of the Gulf of Aqaba. But shipping from the Gulf of Aqaba could only reach the open sea by passing through Egyptian territorial waters at the Straits of Tiran; and that remote passage began to acquire an international importance rivalling that of the Dardanelles.

The legal position respecting these waters has long been a point of contention. The Straits of Tiran certainly lie within Egypt's territorial waters. But are there high seas within the Gulf of Aqaba itself? If so, then right of passage through the Straits cannot be abridged; but if not, then passage through the Straits becomes subject to Egyptian regulation, though not – for merchant vessels at least – prohibition.

On the other hand, if the littoral states could agree among themselves, the Gulf could be closed to all shipping. But is Israel a littoral State? The Arabs deny it every time they deny Israel's right to exist; Israel is strongly supported on this point by her Western friends. Even if Israel's right to exist were granted, the Arabs would still contend that she has no right to a stretch of coastline on the Gulf.[11] Beyond this, Egypt takes her stand on belligerent rights. The Security Council adopted a resolution in September 1951 which asserted in passing that 'the Armistice regime . . . is of a permanent character [and] neither party can reasonably assert that it is actively a belligerent or requires to exercise the right of visit, search, and seizure for any legitimate purpose of self-defence'. But Egypt ignored this resolution, and averred that she was under no obligation to convert the Armistice Agreement into a definitive peace. Here the issue rests, though it is conceivable that the international community would not choose to tolerate this claim of belligerency.

For the Israelis the free use of the port of Eilat appeared essential, if not to survival, then certainly to the development of their State; and it is never easy to distinguish between the two. The mineral resources of the Negev, especially its phosphates, its potash, and its methane gas, provided the basis for an industry to balance the agrarian settlements of the centre and north. For David Ben-Gurion and many of his old Zionist followers, the area satisfied a still deeper need, a hinterland where the pioneer spirit could be nourished to balance the thriving cosmopolitan conurbations of the coastal plain. Little could be done to develop Eilat during the first ten years of Israel's existence. In 1957 the port was handling only 41,000 tons of cargo a year. But by 1959 that figure had tripled; in 1965 it had reached 500,000 tons,[12] including 90 per cent of Israel's oil imports; and Israeli planners expected that by 1970 the tonnage would have topped the million mark. Any threat to Eilat was thus seen as a threat to the future of Israel itself – something of which the Arabs were very well aware – and to repel it the Israelis were prepared if necessary to fight.

The first time they found it necessary to do so was in 1956. In 1953 Egypt had begun to restrict Israeli commerce through the Straits, making all shipping subject to inspection by Egyptian coastguards. These measures increased in intensity until, in September 1955, Egypt broadened the blockade and included a ban on overflights by Israeli aircraft. This definitive closing of the Straits led the Israeli Government to order its Chief of Staff, General Moshe Dayan, to prepare contingency plans for capturing the Egyptian positions at Sharm-el-Sheikh, at Ras Nasrani, and on the islands of Tiran and Sinafir, from which the blockade was enforced. The Prime Minister, Mr Ben-Gurion, wanted to strike at once, but was restrained by his colleagues. A full year passed; a year during which raids on Israeli territory by Palestinian Arab *fedayeen* based on the Gaza Strip and the West Bank of the Jordan increased in frequency and provoked massive reprisals. Then the opportunity which Israel needed was provided by the decision of France and Great Britain to respond by force to President Nasser's nationalization of the Suez Canal.

In spite of the reluctance of successive British governments to reveal the full details of this curious episode, the essential facts are now clearly established. On 29 October 1956, with the approval and foreknowledge of both France and Britain, Israeli forces invaded the Sinai Peninsula, ostensibly in response to the *fedayeen* raids. The following day Britain and France sent Egypt and Israel an ultimatum, calling upon both countries to withdraw their forces ten miles from the Suez Canal, and further calling upon Egypt to permit a joint expeditionary force to occupy the Canal Zone. On 31 October, British and French aircraft began air attacks against military targets in Egypt, while Egypt sank ships to block the Canal. The destruction of the Egyptian Air Force, the rapid withdrawal of Egyptian forces, and the failure of Egypt's allies Jordan and Syria to come to

her aid must not be allowed to obscure the remarkable achievement of the Israeli Army in overrunning the greater part of the
Sinai Peninsula within six days and, on 5 November, hoisting
the Israeli flag over the Egyptian fort at Sharm-el-Sheikh.[13] The
same day French and British forces began to land near Port Said.

The United Nations General Assembly had called for a
cease-fire on 2 November. With British and French vetos
preventing any action by the Security Council, the General
Assembly seemed faced with the alternative of taking drastic
action under the famous 'Uniting for Peace' resolution (which
had been introduced by the Western powers in 1950 after the
Korean experience) or pursuing the anodyne course of requesting the Secretary-General to negotiate directly with the powers
concerned. In the event, a third course of action was adopted;
one which was to prove effective in bringing about the withdrawal of foreign troops on Egyptian soil, in fostering eleven
years of relative security for Israel, and in preventing a return
to a *status quo* that had entailed a long-term threat to Israel's
economic development and a pattern of constant border
disturbances. This was the establishment of the United Nations
Emergency Force. The concept was largely that of Mr Lester
Pearson, at the time Canadian Minister for External Affairs. Its
successful implementation, however, was due entirely to the
pertinacious diplomacy of Mr Dag Hammarskjöld, Secretary-
General of the United Nations.

The role of the Force, in Mr Hammarskjöld's words, was
simply 'to enter Egyptian territory with the consent of the
Egyptian Government, in order to help maintain quiet during
and after the withdrawal of non-Egyptian troops and to secure
compliance with the other terms established in the [cease-fire]
resolution of 2 November 1956'.

Its establishment was finally approved by the General
Assembly on 7 November; and on the same day, two days

after Israel, Britain and France accepted the cease-fire. On 15 November UNEF landed in Egypt, and the withdrawal of the invading forces began. By 22 January Israeli troops had evacuated all territory beyond the original Armistice Demarcation Lines, with the significant exceptions of the Gaza Strip and the east coast of the Sinai Peninsula down to the Straits of Tiran. There, in spite of constant pressure from the United Nations, they remained. When at length, in March 1957, the Government of Israel consented to withdraw them, it was only on receiving explicit assurances from the United States Government (with which France and Britain were to associate themselves) that no nation had the right to prevent free and innocent passage in the Gulf of Aqaba. 'The United States', declared President Eisenhower on 20 February, 'was prepared to exercise this right itself and to join with others to secure general recognition of this right'.[14]

In different ways, the outcome of the 1956 crisis was satisfactory both for Egypt and for Israel. For the Israelis it ended the *fedayeen* raids from Jordan and the Gaza Strip; and a United Nations presence, backed by guarantees from the principal Western powers, appeared to assure free use of the Gulf of Aqaba. For President Nasser it brought an immense increase in prestige in that he was able to claim victory in repelling the Anglo-French invasion from Egyptian soil. The longer-term effects of the crisis were still more satisfactory for the Arab world. Britain's inept intervention destroyed such influence as she had left in the Middle East. The position of her friends became untenable. Saudi Arabia imposed oil sanctions; Hussein of Jordan denounced the Anglo-Jordanian Treaty of 1946 and renounced his British subsidies in return for a promise of help from Egypt, Syria, and Saudi Arabia; even Nuri es-Said in Iraq, Britain's oldest client in the Middle East, tried to insure himself – in vain, as it turned out – by demanding Britain's expulsion from the Baghdad Pact. The United States, fearing that the Soviet Union would exploit the situation thus created, tried to take Britain's place. In January 1957 President Eisenhower pledged American help to any Middle East State against aggression by 'States controlled by International Communism'; a label, it would be charitable to assume, intended rather to placate a suspicious Congress than to indicate the State Department's true assessment of the Middle East situation. Thus empowered, he was able to send arms and aid to Jordan, the Lebanon, and Saudi Arabia. The left-wing regime in Syria was beyond wooing by such means and replied to the advent of the Americans by defiantly stressing their links with the Soviet Union. This flirtation with Moscow, alarming as it appeared to the West, was short-lived, and the following year Syria contracted instead her unhappy marriage with Egypt in the United Arab Republic.

But even outside the borders of Syria, American influence and protection was shown to be no more welcome than British. The Lebanese and Jordanian Governments accepted it at the cost of bloody internal strife, which spilt over into Iraq and precipitated, in July 1958, the overthrow of Nuri es-Said's pro-Western regime. For a moment it looked as though the Lebanese and Jordanian Governments might go the way of Nuri's, and American marines and British paratroops were rushed in to sustain them. But by the end of the year it was clear in both Washington and London that there could no longer be any security for Arab governments which rested on the support of Western bayonets. It was clear also, from the course of events both in Egypt and in Iraq, that the Arab world had its own bulwarks against the Soviet penetration whose prospect had caused the West such acute alarm. And it was clear that, if the Russians had little prospect of dominating the Middle East in the immediate future, the West had even less. The influence which any Great Power could henceforth expect to exercise in the area would depend on its use of the traditional techniques of diplomacy, trade, economic assistance, and cultural influence. The Great Powers might, acting in concert or by mutual consent, set limits to the activities of the Arab States and of Israel; but they could do little positively to direct or control them. This somewhat belated recognition on the part of the outside world marked a new stage in the history of Middle Eastern affairs.[15]

The slackening of the tension which had been created by the Western interventions between 1956 and 1958 meant that Arab politics now fell into natural disarray. During these years when the forces of Arab revolutionary nationalism from the Maghreb to Syria could plausibly contend that they were being subjected to a concerted counter-attack by a Holy Alliance of Western imperialism, President Nasser provided a focal point for the Arab world, if not precisely a leader behind whom all were prepared to rally. With the ebbing of the alleged imperialist threat – though few Arabs would allow that this ebbing was anything but temporary – old rivalries reappeared, complicated by new clashes of personality. Kessim's Iraq proved to be no more friendly to Egypt than that of Nuri es-Said, and Kessim's revolutionary credentials were quite as good as Nasser's. Within the United Arab Republic (UAR) the centralization of authority at Cairo proved as unwelcome to the forces of the Left in Syria as the sweeping measures of socialization which Nasser promulgated in July 1961 were disagreeable to those of the Right. In September 1961 a group of army officers seized power in Damascus, announced Syria's secession from the UAR, and installed a conservative government which annulled most of the socialist measures which Nasser had introduced. It was not long before this regime, and Kessim's, were replaced by others more friendly towards Egypt; but the success of the reactionaries led Nasser to press forward the more ruthlessly with his own revolution in Egypt; to renew his attacks on the monarchist regimes in Jordan and Saudi Arabia; and stridently to demand unity against imperialism, reaction, and Zionism, which 'despite apparent contradictions, have common aims and march in one procession directed by imperialism'.

Nasser in fact was quite happy to play the Mazzini of the Arab Revolution when he could not play the Cavour. Whichever role he played, whether the visionary promoter of the Arab social revolution or the sagacious architect of Arab unity, the theme remained the same: *fuori i stranieri!* The imperialists might have removed their physical presence, but they had left a bridge-head behind in Israel, sustained by Western capital and Western arms. The more nationalism took on the hue of social revolution the more Israel came to be seen as the spearhead of the Western imperialist conspiracy. In Syria, the home of the Ba'athist Party which formulated these ideas with the greatest violence and precision and where a succession of increasingly extremist regimes displaced that which had broken with Egypt, willingness to attack Israel became the acid test of revolutionary zeal. As a revolutionary, Nasser could not allow himself to be outdistanced by the Ba'athists, whose influence had spread far beyond Syria. And any aspiring architect of Arab unity knew well that the most effective cement for that precarious structure was the hatred of Israel which was felt throughout the Arab world and, even where it was not felt, still had to be professed by every figure in the public eye.

All this must be taken into account if we are to understand why, by the 1960s, hatred of Israel had acquired so self-generating a quality within the Arab world and had become so intrinsic and necessary a part of Arab politics. Even if the fact of Israel's existence might, after fifteen years, have been accepted, the *idea*, and all the implications Arab intellectuals read into it, remained utterly intolerable. But the inconvenience of the fact itself was brought uncompromisingly to the fore when, in late 1963, work neared completion on an Israeli project designed to pump fresh water out of Lake Tiberias to irrigate the Negev Desert.[16]

This question of the Jordan waters would be one of great technical complexity even if it were not confused by bitter political dispute. Briefly, the River Jordan above Lake Tiberias, before it becomes adulterated by the saline affluents farther downstream, was a major source of fresh water for the irrigation schemes both of Israel and of Jordan, and could also be put to valuable use by Syria and the Lebanon. In 1955 Mr Eric Johnston, of the United States, presented a plan which allotted to each State enough water to fulfil its estimated needs. Although his proposals were acceptable to the technical experts of all the countries concerned, the Arab governments continued, for political reasons, to withhold their consent.[17] So the Israelis went ahead on their own, and began to build at Eshed Kinrot on Lake Tiberias a pumping station to raise water from the lake 1,100 feet over the Galilean watershed to flow down through the coastal plain and irrigate the Negev Desert. The Jordanians complained that this action, besides being of doubtful legality, complicated their own irrigation problems, since the reduction of the fresh water content of Lake Tiberias increased the salinity of the southern outflow on which they themselves largely depended. This the Israelis denied. They also maintained that they were drawing off from the Jordan no more than the quota allotted to them under the Johnston scheme; to which the Arabs riposted that the capacity of the irrigation works under construction indicated an intention of exceeding this considerably. In any case the Eshed Kinrot pumping station was due to begin operations early in 1964, and the prospect caused sufficient concern for the Arab States temporarily to suspend their differences and meet to discuss what should be done.

The Israeli action created among the Arabs a degree of unity, however illusory and however impermanent, such as had not been seen since the Western interventions five years before. Nasser-Mazzini once again gave place to Nasser-Cavour. In December 1963, Heads of the Arab States were invited to attend a conference in Cairo the following month. The monarchs of Jordan and Saudi Arabia, those doubtful allies of the Arab social revolution, were treated with unwonted geniality. The Syrian extremists were given stern warnings by a unusually sober and statesmanlike Cairo Press. The shrill demands from Damascus for immediate war against Israel met with the reply, 'The UAR will not let itself be pushed into a battle with Israel before the attainment of unity among all Arab countries'. Nasser himself was even blunter. 'We cannot use force today', he said, 'because circumstances do not allow us'. What circumstances he would have considered auspicious it is difficult to judge. They would certainly have included the acquiescence of the Soviet Union, if not the United States, on whose aid the Egyptian economy was at that stage still very dependent.[18]

The only measures President Nasser was meanwhile prepared to adopt were long-term ones. At the Summit Conference in Cairo in January 1964, the Arab States agreed to reply to the Israeli water-diversion scheme by one of their own which would drastically reduce the amount of water available to Israel. Two of the streams which feed the Upper Jordan originate outside Israeli territory, the Hasbani in Lebanon, the Baniyas in Syria. The Hasbani was to be diverted westward into the Litani River, and irrigate the Lebanon. The Baniyas was to be diverted south-east by a canal through Syrian territory into the River Yarmuk in Jordan. Since the Baniyas rises within a few hundred yards of Israeli territory, and the configuration of the ground would keep the course of the canal close to the frontier for much of its length, the Baniyas scheme would be highly vulnerable to Israeli attack. In order to deter such an attack, military dispositions would have to be made, and an Arab Unified High Command was established under the Egyptian General Ali Ali Amer to plan them.

Finally, the Palestine refugees were enlisted in the struggle. It was after all on their behalf that all these efforts were being made; and the confrontation was likely to enlist more sympathy, especially among the developing countries, if it could be presented not as one between an alliance of Arab powers and the small State of Israel, but as the concern of the native people of Palestine fighting, as the people of Algeria had so successfully fought, to drive out a settlement of alien colonialists. A Palestine 'Entity' was therefore created, and the eloquent M. Ahmed Shukeiry, until recently Saudi Arabia's representative at the United Nations, was appointed its spokesman. Four months later this Entity was accorded a formal unveiling – if that is the *mot juste* – at a great conference in Jerusalem, opened by King Hussein himself.

The programme inaugurated at Cairo in January 1964 was further developed at Summit Conferences in Alexandria in September 1964 and Casablanca in 1965. The practical problems involved, combined with the presence of the conservative Jordanians and Saudi Arabians and the moderate Moroccans and Tunisians, gave these conferences a cautious and pragmatic tone. On the recommendation of the Algerians, it is true, the Palestine Entity was clothed with flesh as the Palestine Liberation Organization, authorized to establish a Liberation Army, and set up headquarters at Gaza on Egyptian-administered territory. But King Hussein, who considered with some reason that M. Shukeiry was as interested in subverting the Hashemite regime as that of the Israelis, refused to permit him to operate from Jordanian territory. No other Arab State was prepared to offer him much in the way of practical help; and his bellicose pronouncements aroused, outside Algeria and Syria, only chilly disapproval. Poor M. Shukeiry was so disillusioned that at the Casablanca Conference he offered his resignation; but his sponsors did not find it convenient to accept it.

Little progress was made in any other direction. The States not immediately concerned in the confrontation (Kuwait, Egypt, Saudi Arabia, Libya, Algeria, Morocco, and the Yemen) set up a fund to provide weapons for those which were (Syria, Lebanon, and Jordan).[19] But General Amer had to report, at Alexandria, that he saw no prospect of his command being ready for action until 1966; and his task was made more difficult by the blank refusal of any of the three States concerned to accept Egyptian forces on her territory. All had good reason to assess the military threat from Israel remote in comparison with the undesirable impact which the presence of such troops would make on the delicate balance of their own internal politics. In any case, the Casablanca Conference concluded hopefully, the problem was not an immediate one. War with Israel was inevitable; but it would not come for some five to ten years.

For two years, therefore, the Arab world was able to put up a remarkable show of unity and moderation; even checking the virulent mutual abuse which had become so familiar a feature of their radio programmes. For this President Nasser deserves much of the credit. His prolonged involvement in the Yemen civil war disinclined him to adventures anywhere else, and so long as the Israel question could be made the common concern of the whole Arab world, the Syrians could be effectively curbed. Cairo was in friendly relations with both Jordan and Iraq, in spite of the severity with which their governments treated President Nasser's more intemperate supporters within their own borders. Egypt and Saudi Arabia appeared to be working amicably together to find a solution to the Yemen civil war. President Nasser seemed to have abandoned the cause of the Arab social revolution in the interests of Arab unity, and the question of Israel was interred in a multiplicity of expert committees.

What happened to reverse this situation over the next eighteen months – and reverse it so totally that in May 1967 President Nasser stood at the head of an Arab world apparently united on a policy of immediate war? Perhaps the most significant factor was the rise in the Arabian firmament of a star rivalling even Nasser in brilliance: King Feisal of Saudi Arabia, who succeeded to the throne of his brother Saud in November 1964. With its feudal economic and social structure, its friendliness towards the West, and the rivalry it posed for control of South Arabia after the British withdrawal, Saudi Arabia was anyhow among the least likely of Arab States to become an obedient satellite to Egypt. Now it began to appear as a formidable rival. In December 1965 Feisal visited his brother monarch the Shah of Iran. The following month he visited Hussein of Jordan. He placed substantial armament orders with Western firms. In January 1966 he floated the idea of an 'Islamic Summit'. Although he blandly denied that this would in any way disrupt the fabric of Arab unity to which he professed unchanging devotion, and stressed that he was concerned only with emphasizing the spiritual ties which bound Islam together, the implications of this move were evident. Feisal had set himself up as a rallying point for all the forces in the Arab world which resented the speed and the direction of the Arab social revolution.

Syria – where a yet more radical regime came into power in February 1966 – at once denounced his manoeuvre and demanded a counter-summit of Egypt, Iraq, Syria, and Algeria to frustrate it. The search for Arab unity was at an end. Nasser did indeed delay taking sides for as long as he could. Not until March did he openly attack Feisal. Thereafter, however, his denunciations become more ferocious until, in July, he publicly abandoned the principle of Arab summits altogether since, as he put it, they were being perverted to reactionary purposes.[20] The refusal of the United States in May to open negotiations for an additional $150 million in economic aid may have done something to confirm him in this change of course. In November he signed a defence pact with Syria, and the following month went on record accusing Feisal, Hussein, and President Bourguiba of Tunisia – whose consistently moderate attitude he must have found both a trial and a menace – of aping the example of Nuri es-Said and selling out the Arab nation to the forces of imperialism.

In all this it is likely that he was receiving active encouragement from the Soviet Union. The reappearance of a pro-Western bloc in the Middle East, which threatened to embrace Iran, could not have been welcome to Moscow. Mr Kosygin visited Cairo in May 1966, and Soviet interest in Damascus had never entirely disappeared since the flirtation of 1957–58. The least that can be said on the basis of available evidence is that the Soviet Union no doubt viewed the re-establishment of unity between the revolutionary Arab States – Egypt, Syria, Algeria, and Iraq – with at least as much approval as the West had viewed King Feisal's efforts to combat them. How far either was due to the direct action and encouragement of outside powers it is not at present possible to assess. But the turn of events was one which brought war with Israel closer.

For the Syrians with whom Nasser had once more entered into close alliance were, if possible, even more violent in their attitude towards Israel than they had been two years earlier, when he had so successfully diluted the Syrian bitters with the cold water of Arab summitry. It has been suggested indeed that the defence pact of November 1966 was primarily a device to restrain them. The Syrians had not regarded M. Shukeiry's Palestine Liberation Organization, operating – or, rather, not operating – under strict Egyptian control, as any substitute for action on their own part. They had sponsored an organization of their own, *El Fatah* ('Conquest'), whose commando units began in 1965 to attack, usually infiltrating through Lebanese and Jordanian territory to raid northern Israel, much as, ten years earlier, the *fedayeen* of the Gaza Strip and the West Bank had harassed the south. The Israeli reaction was, as usual, one of massive retaliation.[21] In May 1965 their armed forces attacked the Jordanian frontier villages of Qalqiliya, Jenin, and Shuleh, which they suspected of harbouring *El Fatah* units. In October they struck at the Lebanese village of Houlé. Whatever their effect on the Lebanese and Jordanian Governments, these measures did not, apparently, dismay the Syrians. In May 1966 President Al Atassi demanded a war of liberation against the Israelis on the lines of that being fought against the United States in Vietnam. In Damascus a Higher Defence Committee was set up to 'make all arrangements for preparing all sectors of the public and mobilizing them in the battle in face of Israeli threats and aggressive intentions'. A spiral of raid and counter-raid seemed to be opening which was likely to lead, as it had in Gaza ten years before, to a climactic and formal recourse to force.

The situation in the north was the more complicated in that the Syrians had considerable *bona fide* grievances against Israel, arising out of the original armistice agreements of 1949. By these agreements a Demilitarized Zone was established on the Israeli-Syrian borders.[22] The agreement laid it down that these arrangements were 'not to be interpreted as having any relation whatsoever to ultimate territorial arrangements'; but Israel claimed the Demilitarized Zone as part of her national territory. Further, Israel installed fortifications and stationed border police there, to which the Syrians objected as a breach of the demilitarization agreement; and, finally, Israeli farmers had begun to cultivate some of the territory, which seemed to the Syrians to be a deliberate attempt to gain an advantage, in direct contradiction of the principle laid down in the agreement that 'no military or political advantage should be gained under the truce'.

To deal with problems arising out of interpretation and implementation of the Armistice Agreements the United Nations had set up a Truce Supervision Organization (UNTSO), which was assisted in its duties by Mixed Armistice Commissions of the appropriate belligerent powers.[23] The Israelis had attended no regular meetings of the Syrian Commission since 1951, and had shown considerable reluctance to permit UNTSO observers to investigate some of their activities within the Demilitarized Zone. By 1967, however, mutual complaints had reached a level which made both sides regard the Commission as a useful vehicle for their protests. Each had raids and counter-raids to complain of.[24] In addition, in July 1966, the Israelis had attacked, with artillery and aircraft, the works on the Baniyas water-diversion scheme just across their border; while the Syrians had repeatedly fired on Israelis attempting to cultivate land in the Demilitarized Zone. Predictably the Commission broke up, disagreeably and inconclusively, after only three emergency meetings. But meanwhile two incidents occurred which transcended the normal level of border dispute. The first was the Israeli attack on the Jordanian village of Es Samu on 13 November 1966. The second was the air battle on 7 April 1967, when Israeli aircraft, without loss to themselves, shot down six Syrian MiG fighter aircraft. The repercussions of these events were, as we shall see, to be very considerable indeed.

The Samu raid followed the failure of Israel to get any satisfaction after a complaint to the Security Council about mines laid on her territory by *El Fatah* units. The incident was repeated near the Jordanian frontier; so the Israelis took matters into their own hands with a daylight attack by armour, aircraft, and infantry which did considerable damage to the village and killed eighteen Jordanians.[25] Public opinion even in Israel objected to the violence of this blow against the mildest of their adversaries, and Israel was condemned by the Security Council. But in view of the failure of the Council to condemn the activities of the Syrians, she was naturally unimpressed. 'If Hussein has control of the West Bank and failed to prevent terrorism', asked Yigal Allon, her Minister of Labour, 'why is he entitled to our indulgence? And if he does not exercise control there, what interest have we in preserving his regime? . . . The action at Samu demonstrated to the Powers that Israel is not willing to submit its security to diplomatic bargaining'. In fact the Samu raid precipitated such angry demonstrations in Jordan that Hussein took stern measures to repress his dissident elements; which were seized on by supporters of the Israeli action as further proof of its effectiveness. It had, they suggested, given Hussein the excuse he needed to show himself master in his own house.

The second incident arose over one of the Israeli attempts to cultivate land in the Demilitarized Zone. Syrian small-arms fire against an Israeli tractor was answered by fire from Israeli forces who somehow happened to be in the neighbourhood. Artillery, tanks, and ultimately aircraft joined in, the Israeli aircraft silencing the Syrian gun positions, shooting down six aircraft of the intercepting fighter patrol sent up to meet them, and sweeping on over Damascus in jubilant demonstration of their victory. Even more than the Samu raid, this demonstrated Israel's ability and willingness to react, indeed to over-react, to provocations of the kind which the Syrians had no intention of discontinuing. And like the Samu raid it showed the disunity that still obtained among Israel's principal enemies. Hussein's purge of his activists infuriated the Syrians, who redoubled their attacks on his regime, both in the Press and over Damascus Radio. The Jordanians retaliated by jubilantly broadcasting details of the Syrian aircraft forced down over Jordanian territory; and both Syria and Jordan complained loudly of the Egyptian failure to do anything to help them, taunting Nasser – significantly in view of later developments – with sheltering behind the United Nations Emergency Force. Considering that Hussein refused to allow Egyptian units on his territory and that Syria refused Egypt's offer to establish an air base on her soil, they really had little cause for complaint. But Nasser could not stand by indefinitely and watch his allies suffer such humiliating reversals; and more important, neither could the Russians. M. Gromyko, Soviet Foreign Minister, visited Cairo in April. It is likely that this question had an important place on his agenda.

Were such humiliations likely to continue? The Israeli Government derived no satisfaction from inflicting them, and fully realized the dangers it incurred in doing so: dangers arising not simply from another war fought, like that of 1948, on three fronts against superior forces, but from antagonizing the Great Powers. The Prime Minister, Mr Levi Eshkol, like David Ben-Gurion before him, believed in the need to retain, almost at any cost, the sympathy of the United States. He was almost as anxious to avoid antagonizing the Soviet Union; and the Soviet Union, he knew, watched with paternal concern over the fortunes of the kaleidoscopic regimes in Damascus.

Yet opinion in Israel would not indefinitely put up with the kind of provocation offered by the *El Fatah* raids.[26] Mr Eshkol's reputation was one for sagacity rather than for decisiveness. He presided over an uneasy coalition delicately responsive to shifts in public opinion – a coalition itself under heavy criticism from the Rafi party founded by Ben-Gurion in 1965, through which such colourful figures as Moshe Dayan, Shimon Peres, and Teddy Kolleck demanded greater drive in government, a more positive foreign policy, and in general a more vigorous and forward-looking 'style'. These demands were attractive to the younger generation of Israelis – 'Sabras', born in Israel, justly proud of their achievements, impatient of the older generation of East European immigrants who still so largely dominated the government, less conscious than that generation of Israel's debt to diplomacy and good fortune as well as to her own energy and military force. The last thing Mr Eshkol and his colleagues wanted was a military adventure which would darken the already gloomy economic situation and complicate relations with the Great Powers. But if the Syrians went on with their raids, how was such an adventure to be avoided?

From September 1966 to May 1967 Mr Eshkol and his colleagues – including a little surprisingly, General Rabin, the Chief of Staff – went on record with a series of increasingly vehement statements threatening Syria with condign punishment if the offensive incidents continued. We have seen how little effect these had as a deterrent to the Syrian Government. They may have been more effective in quietening public opinion in Israel itself. What is beyond question is their contribution to the general sense of uneasiness in the Middle East. They came to a climax on 13 May, when Mr Eshkol declared, both in a press conference and in a live broadcast, that Israel would react in her own fashion to the harassing of her borders – 'at the place, the time, and in the manner we choose. . . . We shall not recognize the limitations they are trying to impose on our reprisals. If they try to disturb our border, then their border will be disturbed'. Furthermore, Israel would react to any attempt to divert the headwaters of the Jordan or to interfere with the freedom of her shipping to the Red Sea. Her armed forces were being overhauled and receiving new equipment, and would be able to fulfil any demands that might be made on them. At the same time General Rabin, speaking to a military audience, was reported as saying that so long as the government continued in power in Damascus the *El Fatah* raids were likely to continue; not an unreasonable appreciation, but one which was seized on by the Arab press and inflated into a threat to overthrow the Ba'athist regime by force.

Mr Eshkol's remarks were unusually strongly-worded, but it is doubtful whether Israeli public opinion would have been satisfied with anything less. It was perhaps his domestic audience that he had in mind when he made them: certainly he can hardly have anticipated their effect abroad. The whole Arab world exploded into wrathful activity and the Great Powers suddenly realized that they had on their hands a crisis of major proportions; an imminent conflict between client states to whose survival their own prestige and power were deeply committed.

II. The crisis

The celebration of the foundation of the State of Israel in the spring of each year always increased tension between Israel and her Arab neighbours.[27] For the Arabs, particularly the Palestinian exiles, it was an occasion for mourning. For the Israelis it was a day of rejoicing and of military parades, the main national celebration being held in each large Israeli town in turn. In 1967, for the first time since 1961, it was the turn of Jerusalem. This always caused trouble. Apart from the natural sensitivity of the Jordanians to any ceremonies in this disputed city, Jerusalem lay within the 'defensive area' as defined by the Armistice Agreement, in which the deployment of armed forces was rigorously limited. In 1961, in defiance of a ruling by the Security Council, Israel had ignored these limitations. This year she intended to be more cautious. The Government hoped to obtain the attendance of the diplomatic corps at an event which so signally marked the status of Jerusalem as an integral part of Israel, and as a bait they reduced the military parade to dimensions compatible with the Armistice Agreement. They did not succeed. Not even the Western powers sent official representatives. The Arabs lodged a protest with the United Nations just the same; and the absence of heavy units gave credibility to the rumours that they were being reserved for action somewhere else. Nonetheless Mr Eshkol came under heavy criticism in the Knesset and the press for making such concessions. Nationalist sentiment in Israel, already irritated at his failure to respond effectively to the *El Fatah* raids, saw this as further evidence of weakness. Should not Independence Day, it was asked, be a moment for national self-assertion rather than diplomatic finesse?

Foreign observers in Tel Aviv considered that pressures of this kind were very largely responsible for the crop of bellicose statements by Mr Eshkol, General Rabin, and their colleagues during the week leading up to Independence Day. Many believed that the Israeli Government was primarily anxious to prevent any further action by Syria which might intensify a demand for retaliation, and that it was to deter such action, as well as to disarm their own critics, that its members spoke as they did. But there is much about the situation that still remains obscure. Rumours of an impending blow against Syria were current in Tel Aviv. These may have been purely self-generating; they may have been deliberately kindled by the Israeli Government as part of their general programme of deterrence; or they may have been rooted in fact (indeed, it is possible that Israeli forces were conducting demonstrations near the frontier for the Syrians' benefit). Whatever the origins of these rumours, they appear to have reached Damascus and Cairo in the form of specific reports of Israeli troop movements indicating that a massive attack was being mounted on Syrian territory. President Nasser was later to be very precise about this. 'On 13 May', he said on 22 May, 'we received accurate information that Israel was concentrating on the Syrian border huge armed forces of about 11–13 brigades. These forces were divided into two fronts, one south of Lake Tiberias and one north of the Lake. The decision made by Israel at the time was to carry out an attack against Syria starting on 17 May. On 14 May we took action, discussed the matter, and contacted our Syrian brothers. The Syrians also had this information'.

They had indeed, and the indications are very strong that they received it from the same source – the Soviet Union. It was natural enough that the Soviet Union should have warned her friends of rumours of an impending attack. To report specific troop movements, however, was more serious. No such movements had been detected by UNTSO observers, according to the Secretary-General's Report of 18 May. A force of the size reported could hardly have been concentrated without extensive mobilization measures which would have been generally observed and discussed by the many foreign visitors to Israel. Besides, a large concentration of this kind was quite alien to the Israel military style. A punitive expedition capable of striking deep into Syrian territory could have been rapidly mounted from the area round Haifa by rapidly assembled forces within a few hours. The Soviet Ambassador was invited by Mr Eshkol to inspect the alleged concentration areas for himself. He refused. The evidence for a concentration of the kind described by President Nasser is at present so tenuous as to be entirely unconvincing. But in discounting it we cannot entirely exclude two hypotheses: first, that an attack of some sort was intended; and, second, that the Israeli Government, for the reasons discussed above, wished such an intention to be generally believed at home and abroad, and encouraged rumours accordingly.

The effectiveness of a threat does not depend only on the credibility of the threatening party. Important also is the vulnerability of the party threatened, and the Syrian Government, the product of the last of an apparently ceaseless succession of *coups d'état*, was very precarious indeed. Another Israeli blow like that of 7 April might easily have caused its overthrow, a further period of instability, and embarrassment both to its Soviet patrons and to its Egyptian friends. But how could such a blow be deterred? The Syrian Army, a political rather than a military force, was in no state to resist serious attack. Relations with Jordan were sulphurous: Jordanian 'reactionism' ranked with Zionism and Imperialism in the diabolical Trinity accused of plotting the downfall of the Arab revolution. And Egypt, with no bases on Syrian soil, could bring at best only indirect help. But President Nasser had already twice failed to assist Arab States against Israeli attack. He could not afford to stand by yet a third time without suffering a serious loss of prestige – and one which his rivals in Jordan and Saudi Arabia would be glad to exploit. All these factors, it may be conjectured, played some part in the Russian decision to issue such categoric warnings to Cairo and Damascus on the basis of such flimsy evidence. They may not have believed an Israeli attack to be quite so imminent as they alleged; but the possibility of one was self-evident, and it was better to be safe than sorry.

If the Russians had any doubts about the reality of the danger, they were not widely shared in Cairo or Damascus. On 13 May the Cairo newspaper *Al-Ahram* wrote that the statements by Mr Eshkol meant that an attack on Syria was imminent. 'If Israel now tries to set the region on fire, then it is definite that Israel herself will be completely destroyed in this fire, which will surround it on all sides, thus bringing about the end of this aggressive racist base'. In Damascus the Foreign Minister informed ambassadors of the States represented on the Security Council of the threatening Israeli aggression. The following day, Sunday 14 May, General Mohammed Fawzy, Chief of Staff of the Egyptian Armed Forces, flew to Damascus to examine the situation and co-ordinate plans with the Syrian Government. On the Monday the Egyptian Army began to move, in an obvious and spectacular fashion. Convoys converged on Cairo from camps farther south, passed through the city for hours, causing major traffic dislocation on their way, and headed out in the direction of Alexandria and Ismailia. Next day, 16 May, a state of emergency was proclaimed for the Egyptian armed forces. 'If Israel attempts to fulfil its foolish threats', quoted Cairo Radio from the newspaper *Al-Akhbar*, 'it will find forces ready to face it, forces specially maintained for this purpose. Measures laid down by the joint Syrian-UAR defence agreement are already being implemented'.

Spectacular as these troop movements were, their scale was not such as to cause the Israelis serious alarm. They were seen as a military demonstration to satisfy Arab public opinion rather than as a preparation for serious attack. General Gavish, Commander of the Sinai front, normally had only a single battalion to observe both the Egyptian and the Jordanian frontiers; the Israeli Army Command quietly increased his strength to two brigades, and awaited events. So far the situation was well under control. A potential threat had been checked by a counter-threat. If Israel had seriously contemplated an attack on Syria she would now know that this would precipitate hostilities with Egypt as well, and would no doubt have been effectively deterred. The Russians had shown themselves wise counsellors, and President Nasser a loyal ally. At this point the matter might have rested, save for two factors. The first was Arab public opinion. The second was the presence of the United Nations Emergency Force.

The Syrian cry for help and the Egyptian military demonstration set off throughout the Arab world a wave of emotion such as could hardly have been predicted and which was to have considerable influence on the course of events. There was hardly an Arab city from Casablanca to Baghdad where demonstrations of some kind did not occur. No Arab government, whatever its political complexion, could afford to be backward in pledging both moral and material support in the battle apparently provoked by aggressive Zionism. Iraq promised help on 15 May. On the 17th both Iraq and Jordan placed their forces in a state of alert. Lebanon called off a courtesy visit by the American Sixth Fleet.[28] On the 18th Kuwait placed its forces under the United Command already established by Egypt and Syria, and three days later Jordan offered to do the same. Libya and the Sudan pledged their support on 22 May. On the 23rd King Feisal of Saudi Arabia declared at the conclusion of his state visit to London that 'any Arab who falters in taking part in this battle, which may mark his destiny, is not worthy to have the name of Arab'. King Hassan of Morocco sent his personal adviser, M. Ahmed Balafrej, to Cairo with promises of support. Algeria declared a state of alert and called for volunteers from the old FLN. Even M. Bourguiba of Tunisia informed the Secretary-General of the Arab League on 25 May that his country was 'bound by obligations taken by it during the first and second Arab Summits . . . concerning the problem of Palestine and the possibility of Israeli aggression against any Arab State'. By 27 May all thirteen members of the Arab League had declared their solidarity in aiding any of their members who had to defend itself against Zionist aggression; and in their van was the Palestine Liberation Organization, whose radio stations in Cairo poured out against Israel an uninterrupted stream of threats and abuse. For the Palestinians this was *Der Tag*, the moment of revenge and return for which they had waited so impatiently. 'The menace and challenge of Israel have persisted for too long', cried the Palestine Service of Cairo

Radio on 16 May. 'The very existence of Israel in our usurped land has endured beyond all expectation. An end must be put to the challenge of Israel and to its very existence. . . . Welcome to aggression by Israel, for it will send us into action to destroy it! . . . Welcome to the battle for which we have long waited! The hour of battle is imminent. In fact, this is the hour of battle'.

The views of the unfortunate Palestinian Arabs and the violence of their spokesmen should not be regarded as typical of the whole Arab world. Nevertheless the feeling was clearly general that a crisis was at hand, that the whole question of Palestine was once more reopened, and that an opportunity had arisen to reverse the settlement of 1956, if not indeed that of 1949. It was a feeling that President Nasser himself evidently came quickly to share; but even if he had not, it was too strong to be ignored or suppressed. The Arab world, in appearance at least, was suddenly united and looking to him for action. It is doubtful whether under such circumstances any Arab states-man could have told the demonstrators to go home, politely refused all offers of military help, muzzled M. Shukeiry, and declared that his objectives were now achieved.

This swelling support, the confidence he derived from it, and the realization that if he did not exploit it others would, may do something to explain President Nasser's actions over the next two weeks. And the first which require some explana-tion are those respecting the United Nations Emergency Force and the Straits of Tiran.

The United Nations Emergency Force, behind whose shel-tering skirts the radio stations of Damascus and Amman had been repeatedly accusing Nasser of hiding, consisted by now of 3,378 men. A Yugoslav reconnaissance battalion patrolled most of the international frontier in the Sinai Desert, with a platoon at Sharm-el-Sheikh. The northern end of the frontier and the western part of the demarcation line in the Gaza Strip was the responsibility of a Brazilian infantry battalion, while Indian and Swedish infantry battalions patrolled the eastern part of the line. UNEF Headquarters were in Gaza itself. Its commander, Major-General Rikhye of the Indian Army, was in Gaza on the evening of 16 May when the liaison officer of the United Arab Republic arrived with a message from the Egyptian Chief of Staff, General Fawzy, demanding the withdrawal of all UN forces along Egypt's borders.[29] The officer added, according to General Rikhye's own account, that the posts at El Sabha on the Sinai border and at Sharm-el-Sheikh on the Straits of Tiran must be evacuated immediately, since Egyptian forces would occupy them that night. It is still not clear whether this additional demand, which was to have such major international repercussions, was made on the instructions of General Fawzy alone, or on those of President Nasser himself. In any case, General Rikhye pointed out that the whole procedure was grossly improper. Any such request must be made to the Secretary-General; whom he at once informed.

Next morning the Yugoslav contingent at El Sabha found its observation posts already occupied and their camp surrounded by Egyptian forces. The situation grew increasingly tense. At midday on the 17th General Rikhye received a further demand for the withdrawal of his forces in Sinai, which he again refused. On the morning of the 18th the Egyptians forced Yugoslav troops out of their positions at El Amr and El Kuntilla, and at noon the commander of the contingent at Sharm-el-Sheikh was given fifteen minutes to withdraw his forces – an ultimatum he rejected. That night, however, instructions reached General Rikhye from the Secretary-General to withdraw UNEF as requested. He at once complied. Israeli and Egyptian forces again confronted each other directly in the Sinai Desert and the Gaza Strip.

The legality of the Secretary-General's action in withdrawing UNEF has never been called into question. The force derived its right to be on Egyptian soil from the Egyptian Government, and once the consent of that government was withdrawn it had no legal basis for remaining. The refusal of the Israelis to accommodate the force – a refusal which their representative at the United Nations repeated on 18 May – well illustrated the rights of sovereign States in the whole question. U Thant's wisdom in complying so rapidly with the Egyptian request, and the propriety of his doing so without referring the matter either to the Security Council or to the General Assembly, was however questioned, immediately and publicly, both by the President of the United States and by the British Foreign Secretary. It has been suggested, not only that U Thant could legitimately have played for time and thus provided the opportunity for passions to ebb, but also that President Nasser expected him to do so, and was as surprised as anyone else by his immediate acquiescence. On this last point many informed observers speak with conviction, but evidence is hard to come by. Certainly the actions of the Egyptians forces on the ground, where they were already forcibly taking over the UN positions on the morning of 17 May, do nothing to bear out this interpretation.

The Secretary-General published on 26 June a comprehensive reply to his critics chronicling and justifying his actions, and in this the difficulties under which he operated are made very clear. The message from General Rikhye showed that rapid action was imperative. A little more than an hour after receiving it U Thant was in conference with M. El Kony, the Permanent Representative of the UAR at the United Nations, who denied all knowledge of his government's request. U Thant stated the position as he saw it. If Egypt made a formal request for the withdrawal of the force, he would be compelled to comply. But the temporary withdrawal of the force from all or part of the demarcation line and the international frontier would be unacceptable 'because the purpose of the United Nations Force in Gaza and Sinai is to prevent a recurrence of fighting, and it cannot be asked to stand aside in order to enable the two sides to resume fighting'. Next day U Thant consulted informally with the representatives of the countries providing contingents for UNEF. The Canadian representative pointed out forcefully, and, as it proved, accurately, what was likely to happen if the force was withdrawn, and advised delay. The Indians and the Yugoslavs insisted that Egypt was acting within her rights and that they must comply with her request. The forces of these two countries were those immediately involved and their political leaders had long enjoyed particularly friendly relations with President Nasser. Moreover, they were powers of medium size in the uncommitted world, and the importance of asserting the principle of national sovereignty was bound to bulk large in their minds.[30]

It was in the knowledge of this division among the nations directly involved that U Thant had to decide how to act when he received, on the afternoon of 18 May, the formal Egyptian request for UNEF's withdrawal; which was accompanied by the warning that any appeal to President Nasser to rescind it would be rebuffed. He referred the matter to the UNEF Advisory Committee, where the same views were expressed formally as had been informally aired the previous day.[31] The Indian and Yugoslav representatives made it clear that their contingents were likely to be withdrawn as soon as their governments were informed of the situation. Mr Ignatieff of Canada urged consultation with the Security Council powers, but the idea did not find favour. Nobody, apparently, proposed that the Committee should exercise its right of requesting a meeting of the General Assembly. It was accepted that the Secretary-General should comply with the Egyptian request and report his actions to the Security Council and the General Assembly. This he did in appropriately sombre terms.

> It is true [he concluded his report on 18 May] that UNEF has allowed us for ten years to ignore some of the hard realities of the underlying conflict. The Governments concerned, and the United Nations, are now confronted with a brutally realistic and dangerous situation. . . . I do not wish to be alarmist, but I cannot avoid the warning to the Council that in my view the current situation in the Near East is more disturbing, indeed I may say more menacing, than at any time since the fall of 1956.

Could U Thant have acted otherwise? It must be remembered that he was presented on the ground with a virtual *fait accompli*. United Nations forces were already being jostled out of their positions by Egyptian troops. They were dependent for maintenance and supply on Egyptian good will. There was at best only the slenderest legal grounds for delaying their withdrawal, and such delay would have aroused strong objections from a substantial number – perhaps indeed a majority – of member States of the United Nations, including two who were providing a considerable part of the force. Soviet action would certainly have paralyzed the Security Council; the General Assembly would certainly have ended its deliberations in deadlock; the position of the forces on the ground would rapidly have become impossible; but a day or so might have been gained for President Nasser to reflect on all the possible consequences of his actions. Dag Hammarskjöld might have played a lone and perhaps a successful hand.[32] But U Thant had been appointed to his post, and held it successfully for six years, precisely because he was not a Hammarskjöld. His actions were correct, if unimaginative. And it is significant that the criticisms levelled against them in North America and Great Britain have found few echoes in Communist countries or the Third World; to whom, in the United Nations, the Secretary-General owes a responsibility no less than that to the Western powers.

The withdrawal of UNEF brought the crisis into a new and very much graver stage. It was no longer possible to see the Egyptian movements in Sinai as a mere promenade. Israel ordered a limited mobilization of reserves, to which Egypt, on 21 May, replied in kind. But eyes were now fixed, not on Sinai, but on Sharm-el-Sheikh, which UNEF finally evacuated on 23 May.[33] Two days earlier Amman Radio had taunted Nasser, in very typical fashion, with the dilemma he now faced. 'This is the question all Arabs are asking: will Egypt restore its batteries and guns and close its territorial waters in the Tiran Strait to the enemy? Logic, wisdom, and nationalism make it incumbent on Egypt to do so. . . . If she fails to do so, what value would there be in military demonstrations?' The Israelis had given repeated warnings that they would regard such an act as a *casus belli*. They had done so in 1956: the growth of the port of Eilat made it still more probable that they would again in 1967. Such a step would transform the Egyptian actions from a massive deterrent demonstration – and one which had probably served its purpose – into a deliberate challenge to war against an adversary who had twice within the past twenty years defeated them in the field.

By what calculations and by what stages President Nasser decided to take this step is still obscure. Indeed it remains the central mystery of the whole crisis. There is no cause to suppose that the Soviet Union gave him any encouragement. She had at no time endorsed Egypt's case on the Gulf of Aqaba – one which would have disagreeable implications for herself in the

Baltic and the Black Sea. Her military advisers knew as much as anyone, and more than most, about the comparative state of armament, training, and morale of the Egyptian, Syrian, and Israeli armed forces. The protection of Syria and the humiliation of Israel was one thing; open war in the Middle East between the protégés of the Communist and Western worlds was quite another. It is generally believed that the Russians were now regarding with alarm the spread of the holocaust which they had so insouciantly touched off. But if the Soviet Ambassador was advising caution, the press of the Arab world was demanding just the opposite. Once Egyptian forces occupied Sharm-el-Sheikh, any action short of restoring the *status quo ante* 1956 would have been painted by Nasser's enemies and rivals as weakness and betrayal. The only way lay forward – a *fuite en avant*, even if necessary into war.

All this must at present remain in the realm of speculation. Whatever his reasoning, President Nasser announced his decision in the course of a visit to his forces in Sinai on the evening of Monday 22 May.

> The armed forces yesterday [he declared] occupied Sharm-el-Sheikh. What does this mean? It is affirmation of our rights and our sovereignty over the Gulf of Aqaba, which constitutes territorial waters. Under no circumstances will we allow the Israeli flag to pass through the Gulf of Aqaba. The Jews threaten war. We tell them you are welcome, we are ready for war, but under no circumstances will we abandon any of our rights. This water is ours.

The army, he said, was ready to defend the rights of the Arab people as a whole. 'They are all behind you, praying for you day and night and believing that you are the pride of their nation, of the Arab nation. This is the feeling of the Arab people in Egypt and outside Egypt. We are confident that you will honour the trust.'

But the Arab unity to which he referred had its limits. President Nasser was still the revolutionary, warning his people against the reactionaries, those running dogs in the imperialist-Zionist plot.

> Reaction casts doubt on everything and so does the Islamic alliance. We all know that the Islamic alliance is now represented by three States: the Kingdom of Saudi Arabia, the Kingdom of Jordan, and Iran. They are saying that the purpose of the Islamic alliance is to unite the Muslim against Israel. I would like the Islamic Alliance to solve the Palestine question in only one way – by preventing the supply of oil to Israel. . . . It is an imperialist alliance, and this means it sides with Zionism because Zionism is the main ally of imperialism. . . . They say they want to co-ordinate their plans with us. We cannot co-ordinate our plans with Islamic alliance members because it would mean giving our plans to the Jews and Israel.

It will be seen how large a part 'anti-imperialism' played in President Nasser's declarations, even before the Western powers had made their position in the dispute clear. Already Syrian and Egyptian newspapers were describing the imminent Israeli offensive in terms of an imperialist plot against the revolutionary Arab world. Such assumptions could only accentuate the division between the revolutionary Arab States and those which, however sincere their detestation of Israel, still tried to retain their links with the West. Jordanian offers of military co-operation were cold-shouldered in Cairo. In Damascus, press attacks on the Hashemite Kingdom reached a new peak of intensity. And on 23 May, in consequence of a terrorist bomb explosion in a frontier town in which 14 Jordanians were killed, Jordan broke off diplomatic relations with Syria. Whatever the aspirations of its statesmen and thinkers, Arab unity was still far from being an accomplished fact.

The blockade of the Straits of Tiran, however, was. On 24 May *Al-Ahram* reported that the Straits had been closed not only by guns and patrol-boats but also with mines: a report which Western official circles received with justifiable scepticism. Israeli vessels, it said, would be exposed to fire; others would be asked to stop for inspection of their cargoes. On 25 May the Egyptian Foreign Minister, M. Riad, gave further details. The United Arab Republic would, he declared, consider the entry of an Israeli ship into her territorial waters as an act of aggression which would 'oblige us to take all measures to ensure the integrity of our territory and territorial waters and the safety of our armed forces'. In addition 'any attempt by any nation to use our territorial waters to send strategic materials to Israel would be considered an unfriendly act constituting assistance to the Israeli war effort against the UAR and all Arab countries'. Finally he asserted that the claim of the 'imperialist States' to act as guardians over what they termed an international waterway was prejudicial to the sovereignty of the UAR.

For the imposition of the blockade had brought prompt reaction from Israel and the West. The crisis was now one of international proportions. Israel had withdrawn from the Straits in 1957 only after she had received from the Western powers the most explicit assurances that these powers would guarantee freedom of passage for her ships. Mr Eshkol, speaking in the Knesset on 23 May, now demanded publicly, as Israeli diplomats were doing privately, that those powers should live up to their obligations. 'This is indeed a test for a solemn and clear international commitment on the implementation of which depends the existence of a regime of international security and law. ... In view of this situation I again call on the Great Powers to act without delay to maintain the right of free access for shipping to our southern port'. And Mr Abba Eban, Israel's Foreign Minister, was despatched to Paris, London, and Washington to secure the necessary assurances.

Mr Eshkol's statement was described in the Israeli press as 'restrained'. Certainly there were those, especially in the senior ranks of the army, who found it inadequate and would have preferred to attack at once before the Egyptian forces in Sinai had time to consolidate. But it was agreed not only by the Cabinet but by opposition leaders – including Mr Begin, General Dayan, and Mr Ben-Gurion – that the intentions of the Western powers should be sounded before Israel risked action on her own.[34] Nevertheless there were, and still remain, strong rumours that an immediate attack was intended and was called off only on the urging of the United States. Here again, as with Israel's intention towards Syria ten days earlier, we can only speculate. The rumours may have been founded on fact – though it is improbable that such an attack could have been launched before 26 May. They may have been totally false. Or they may have received covert official blessing in order to force the hand of the Western powers.

The knowledge that Israel was likely to take action on her own unless something was done for her was certainly a major factor in the calculations of Washington and London. Those calculations were not simple ones. The United States was deeply involved in Vietnam. The Department of Defense could only regard the possibility of another conflict, which would make further demands on their resources, with undiluted dismay. Sympathetic as public opinion was to the cause of Israel, it was doubtful how far that sympathy would stretch in terms of an official commitment which might come to resemble, in its open-ended demands on American blood and treasure, that to the Republic of South Vietnam. In any case, as the Senate Foreign Affairs Committee made clear to the Secretary of State, there could be no question of the United States again assuming such a commitment without effective allies. This time America must not go it alone. For the British the problem was still graver. To support Israel meant antagonizing the entire Arab world, including her traditional allies and the oil-producing States. A withdrawal of Arab sterling balances and an interruption of oil supplies would be blows which her chronically sick economy would find it hard to bear. The disadvantages of such a course were depressingly obvious. The gains were less easy to assess.

Yet unless the Western powers took some action, the Israelis undoubtedly would, and no one could calculate the consequences. On 23 May, when the news of the blockade reached Washington, President Johnson issued a statement to the effect that 'the United States considers the Gulf to be an international waterway and feels that a blockade of Israeli shipping is illegal and potentially disastrous to the cause of peace. The right of free, innocent passage of the international waterway is a vital interest of the international community'. The following day, in the course of an address to a trade union meeting in Margate, Mr Harold Wilson recalled the British declaration of March 1957 that the Straits of Tiran constituted an international waterway, 'through which the vessels of all nations have a right of passage', and that Britain would 'assert this right on behalf of all British shipping and [was] prepared to join with others to secure general recognition of this right'. 'The declaration then made', went on Mr Wilson, 'remains the view and policy of Her Majesty's Government and we shall promote and support international action to uphold this right of free passage'. To this end, he said, the Minister of State at the Foreign Office, Mr George Thomson, was being sent to Washington, and to confer with the United Nations Delegation in New York.

While Mr Thomson flew to America, the Foreign Secretary himself, Mr George Brown, set off on a deferred visit to Moscow. There he held talks which he afterwards described as 'very full, very detailed, exceedingly friendly, and constructive'. 'What we are all concerned with', he told the press on 26 May, 'is seeing that a conflagration does not break out'. Privately he reported signs of dissension within the Soviet Government over the best course to pursue. Similar exchanges were in progress between Moscow and Washington through normal diplomatic contacts, and the West was satisfied that the Soviet Union was urging restraint on the Arabs. The Soviet Ambassador indeed roused President Nasser at 3.30 on the morning of 26 May to advise him to take no rash initiative.[35] Mr Kosygin also sent to Mr Eshkol a note urging him 'emphatically to take all measures to prevent a military conflict which would be fraught with very grave consequences to the cause of peace and international security'.[36] But whatever pressure the Soviet Union may have been applying behind the scenes, she did not vary her public posture of support for the Arab case; and she used it to frustrate all attempts by the Western powers to gain support for their position in the United Nations.

When President Nasser announced the closing of the Straits on the evening of 22 May, U Thant was already on his way to Cairo on a visit which, arranged some time earlier, had now been accelerated. In spite of his absence, Canada and Denmark, the two states who had at the meeting of the UNEF Advisory Committee most strongly opposed UNEF's withdrawal, called for an immediate meeting of the Security Council. When it met on 24 May, with the representatives of Israel and Egypt in attendance without votes, Canada and Denmark put forward a resolution which expressed full support for U Thant's efforts in Cairo to pacify the situation, requested all member States to refrain from steps likely to worsen it, and invited the Secretary-General to report back on his return. M. El Kony, for Egypt, strongly objected to this as an attempt to cut the ground from under U Thant's feet, and attacked Britain and the United States for 'an intensive and brutal policy beyond their boundaries and far away from their territories'. Dr Fedorenko for the Soviet Union took the same line. 'Is there not more of a concealed desire here to interfere in the affairs of someone else rather than a true concern for the peace and security of the Near East'? Even among less implacably hostile States it was difficult for the Western powers, who had already made their attitude to the closing of the Straits so clear, to gain support for a motion even so innocuously worded. They could not obtain the nine votes necessary to secure acceptance of the motion, or even persuade their colleagues to enter into private discussions about it. The representatives of India, Ethiopia, Nigeria, and Mali broadly supported the line taken by Dr Fedorenko. It was clear that the Western powers' claim to impartiality carried little conviction at the United Nations. The declarations already made by their leaders revealed them to be already strongly *parti-pris*.

They could not even speak with a united voice among themselves. General de Gaulle was *a priori* unlikely to toe a line which had been drawn in Washington and London. Israel had been a good customer for French armaments and a useful ally during the days when France, struggling to retain Algeria, saw her principal enemies in the Arab world. But those days were over. France now had no quarrel with the Arabs. She had good reason to hope that intelligent diplomacy and cultural prestige would restore her to the position of influence in the Arab world which she had failed to maintain by force of arms and which was likely to be denied her so long as she was associated with the Anglo-Americans. Early on in the crisis General de Gaulle had proposed consultations among 'The Big Four' to deal with the problem. Britain and the United States had expressed their readiness to try this solution, but the Soviet Union would not co-operate. Thereafter France affirmed her strict neutrality in the dispute. 'France is committed in no sense or on any subject to any one of the States involved', stated President de Gaulle on 2 June. 'The State which uses arms first, whatever that may be, would have neither France's approval nor its support'.[37]

In face of the hostility not only of the Soviet Union but of France, India, and a great part of the Afro-Asian world, there was thus little chance that Britain and the United States could gain a majority in the United Nations for action to secure the opening of the Straits. If the Western powers were to take action, they would have to do so on their own. The British proposed that this should be done by an appeal to all members of 'The International Maritime Community' to issue a Declaration that the Gulf of Aqaba was an international waterway into which and through which all nations should have right of passage, and to assert their intention of maintaining that right on behalf of their own and all other vessels. But there was to be no indication in the Declaration that force would be used, if necessary, to maintain that right: an omission deliberately contrived to secure the greatest number of signatories but one which robbed the document of much of its effectiveness as a guarantee. It was a point which did not escape the attention of the Israeli Foreign Office.

The State Department, however, was considering also a further proposal. An international naval force might be set up if all else failed, to patrol the Gulf and, it was hoped, by its mere presence deter the Egyptians from enforcing the blockade. With this went suggestions for testing the blockade. Israel had already considered doing this and was preparing vessels for the purpose when Mr Eban was despatched to Washington.

The support they could expect from the Western powers, in the event of their doing so, was one of the principal questions which Mr Eban had to explore. On 25 May Mr Dean Rusk and officials of the State Department explained to him the proposals which they had in mind. The following day he was received by the President. Mr Johnson, it is reported, was frank about the problems which he faced in persuading Congress to sanction any action which was likely – as had the famous encounter in the Gulf of Tonkin in August 1964 – to involve the United States in war. But he emphatically urged Israel not to take any unilateral action. He gave equally emphatic, if somewhat indefinite, assurances that so long as Israel did not act on her own, she could rely on the support of the United States. He only asked time for diplomacy to work.

With these assurances, for what they were worth, Mr Eban returned home. On 31 May Mr George Brown announced in the House of Commons the project of the Maritime Declaration, and the following day the State Department declared their support for this 'British initiative'. Little support came from anyone else. The French Minister for Information said drily on 2 June that 'it does not noticeably advance matters'. Canada, West Germany, and Italy were reported to be considerably less than enthusiastic. By 4 June positive reactions had been received only from Australia, New Zealand, the Netherlands, and Iceland. From this also the Israeli Government doubtless drew their own conclusions.

Useless as the Maritime Declaration proved as a measure either to restrain or to help Israel, it served to infuriate the Arab States. Since Arab propaganda had from the very outset of the crisis depicted Israeli actions as part of a general 'imperialist plot', it is doubtful whether any action taken by the Western powers could have convinced the Arab world of their dispassionate desire for a peaceful resolution of the conflict. Now that they had openly aligned themselves with Israel, there was an eruption of fury. 'It is now crystal clear', said Cairo Radio on 3 June, 'that the imperialist, mad, immoral Anglo-American plot is no different from the tripartite aggression against our glorious Egyptian people in 1956. … The rulers in London and Washington are dragging the Israeli rulers to annihilation and destruction to protect their exploitation, greed, and insatiable lust for power and dominion'. But the Arabs were in a good position to deter, or if necessary to punish, Israel's Western allies. On 29 May the Iraqi Government announced their intention of imposing a ban on all oil supplies to powers supporting Israeli 'aggression', and invited all other oil-producing States in the region to take similar action. They further summoned a conference of interested States to discuss ways and means, which met at Baghdad on 4 June. In the event, these States were able to take action which certainly damaged the economy of the United Kingdom, if of nobody else; but it had not the slightest effect on the war.

By the end of May a growing air of pensiveness, to use no stronger term, was becoming apparent in both Washington and London. It was pointed out in both capitals – and promptly denied by the Israeli Embassies – that anyhow no merchant vessels flying the Israeli flag had passed through the Straits of Tiran for the past two years. Official circles in Washington were beginning to discuss the cost of subsidizing Israel to enable her to do without the port of Eilat. A number of British newspapers – *The Economist*, *The Observer*, *The Financial Times* – pointed out that a commitment to the continuing existence of the State of Israel was a very different matter from risking a world war to enable Israeli ships to use the Gulf of Aqaba. And on Monday 5 June – a day more memorable for other events – *The Guardian* boldly suggested negotiations with President Nasser. 'Ultimately of course the right of free passage must be asserted. ... Immediately, however, it might be possible to accept President Nasser's formulation if he on his side were willing to let the case go to the International Court'.

The formulation referred to, which Nasser had outlined to U Thant in Cairo on 24 May, certainly looked moderate enough. President Nasser was reported to have made four points. The Straits of Tiran should be recognized as Egyptian territorial waters; Israel should fully accept the provisions of the 1949 armistice; the United Nations should police all frontiers and demarcation lines; and the Israelis should strictly observe the demilitarized zones. If access to the Gulf of Aqaba was really the only problem to be solved, a compromise solution might have been found. But President Nasser was quite frank in expressing his view that it was not; and his statements gave good ground for assuming that his intention was now to restore the *status quo ante bellum*, not of 1956, but of 1948.

His public announcements in fact contrasted very remarkably with the reasonable tones in which he talked to U Thant and envoys from the West.[38] 'The Arabs insist on their rights', he declared to the Pan-Arab Workers Federation on 26 May, in a speech repeatedly re-broadcast by Cairo Radio the following day, 'and are determined to regain the rights of the Palestinian people. The Arabs must accomplish this set intention and this aim. . . . If Israel embarks on aggression against Syria or Egypt the battle against Israel will be a general one and . . . our basic objectives will be to destroy Israel'. Two days later he reiterated this view at a large Press Conference. The Straits, he said, was only part of the major problem caused by Israel's aggression in simply existing. 'We do not accept any method for co-existence with Israel'. And the following day he told members of the Egyptian National Assembly, 'We have completed our preparations and are ready to confront Israel. We are ready to reopen the case of Palestine. The question today is not of Aqaba nor is it the Tiran Strait or the UNEF. It is the rights of the people of Palestine'. These pronouncements make it hard to believe that the conflict could have been resolved by a judgment of the International Court about rights of belligerency, innocent passage, or strategic goods. The most that such a judgment, at this stage, could have done would have been to deprive Israel of a clear *casus belli*.

Nevertheless President Nasser had assured U Thant, as he had assured the Soviet Ambassador, that he would not strike the first blow. Such an assurance had limited value. With forces in such close and direct confrontation, escalation from an incident was almost inevitable. For States armed with modern aircraft, the temptation to launch a pre-emptive attack was terrifyingly strong. In any case, Nasser had good reason to hope the Israelis would play into his hands. In a remarkably frank and perceptive article in *Al-Ahram* on 26 May his friend M. Mohammed Hasanein Haikal gave his grounds for supposing that they would.

> The closure of the Gulf of Aqaba ... [he wrote] means first and last that the Arab nation represented by the UAR has succeeded for the first time, *vis à vis* Israel, in changing by force a *fait accompli* imposed on it by force. ... To Israel this is the most dangerous aspect of the current situation – who can impose the accomplished fact and who possesses the power to safeguard it. Therefore it is not a matter of the Gulf of Aqaba but of something bigger. It is the whole philosophy of Israeli security. Hence I say that Israel must attack.[39]

This was not an unfair summary of the Israeli predicament. By the end of May the question of Eilat was secondary to the menace presented to Israel by an Arab world mobilized behind

Egypt, overtly bent on the destruction of the Jewish State and the restoration of the Palestinians to their lost lands. The Israelis had long before learned to live with the abuse directed at them from Radios Cairo, Damascus, and Amman. They might not have taken even President Nasser's speeches too seriously; it was still widely assumed that his involvement in the Yemen would make him unwilling to precipitate another war. But two developments convinced them that the crisis was at hand.

The first was the build-up of Egyptian forces in Sinai after the closing of the Straits. Within a week seven divisions had been rushed into the area, two of them armoured; and although their positions could indicate a defensive posture, many of them were concentrated too far forward on the frontier to be given the benefit of the doubt; and there was an armoured force poised in central Sinai in a position to strike across the Negev and sever communications with Eilat.[40] And the second, and far more alarming, development was the spectacular *rapprochement* of King Hussein of Jordan and President Nasser on 30 May.

Jordan's position was peculiarly unenviable. Although she posed the greatest strategic threat to Israel by her capacity to cut the country in two, the salient of the West Bank made her by far the most vulnerable of the Arab powers to Israeli attack. Her security lay only in close co-operation with the other Arab powers; but this would almost certainly involve accepting the forces of her Allies on her territory, which King Hussein was profoundly reluctant to do. The presence of Egyptian or Iraqi troops stationed among his Palestinian subjects was likely to cause irreparable damage to his precarious regime. Nevertheless, by the end of May, war seemed so imminent that the price had to be paid. On 30 May King Hussein flew to Cairo, was met and publicly embraced by President Nasser, and signed a defence pact which asserted that each country would react to an attack on the other as if it were an attack on itself. A

Defence Council and joint command was set up under General Fawzy. Five days later Iraq joined the pact. On 4 June Iraqi forces moved into Jordan, and General Riad of the Egyptian Army flew into Amman with two Egyptian commando battalions, to take over the new command.

The collapse of Hussein's moderating influence and the triumph of revolutionary-nationalist forces in Jordan had long been considered by the Israeli High Command to be an eventuality which, like the closing of the Straits of Tiran, would compel them to go to war. For the Israelis it came as the climax to the long week of tension which had begun with President Nasser's speech on the evening of 22 May.

We have seen how, on the 23rd, the Cabinet sent Mr Eban to sound out the intentions of the Western powers. It also authorized a general mobilization, which took place on the 24th. Men and vehicles suddenly disappeared from Israeli towns. Within twenty-four hours the army was deployed in full strength along the frontiers: troops trained to take the offensive and now longing for the order to do so. It was an open secret that the whole philosophy of the Israeli armed forces was one of attack: the principle of the offensive was ingrained even in the smallest sub-units. The small extent of Israeli territory, its absence of natural barriers, gave no serious strategic alternative. For men brought up in such a doctrine, the next few days were to be agonizing. From Arab radio stations all round them came a stream of hatred, threats, and vilification. One after another the States of the Arab League fell into line and mobilized forces for the explicit purpose of their destruction. Meanwhile their own government urged moderation, and Mr Eban negotiated in Europe and North America with distant powers whose will and capacity to bring effective and immediate help was not rated by the men in the Sinai Desert as highly as one might like to believe.

It is not surprising that under the circumstances confidence in Mr Eshkol's government began to ebb. Within the army, senior officers watched with professional apprehension as chances of mounting a successful surprise attack waned with the growth in the size and preparedness of the enemy forces. In the country as a whole – and once the army was mobilized, no valid distinction between country and army was really possible – pressure grew for the return to power of the heroic figures of the Rafi party, the venerable David Ben-Gurion, the spectacular Moshe Dayan. General Dayan, having placed himself at the disposal of the Chief of Staff, was acting as a sort of unofficial Inspector-General, visiting the units of the army in Sinai, discussing their operational roles and raising their morale. His invigorating presence made him increasingly appear as the man of the hour. Even senior officers loyal to the government and with no love for Dayan began to press for his appointment to the post of Minister of Defence.

Mr Eshkol hesitated. To abandon the portfolio of Defence, which since the time of Mr Ben-Gurion had always been held by the Prime Minister, would be a grave constitutional step as well as a humiliating personal sacrifice. If he had to take it, his candidate for the post, it was generally known, would have been his colleague Yigal Allon, a figure whose military achievements in the war of 1948 were at least equal to those of Dayan in 1956, and whose political ambitions he had less reason to mistrust. Moreover, between Dayan and his colleagues in the Rafi party on the one hand, and Mr Eshkol's own colleagues in Mapai on the other, there were bitter personal antagonisms which would make co-operation almost impossible. This disagreeable necessity might be avoided if the external pressure abated, so a decision was delayed until Mr Eban returned from Washington. This he did on the evening of 27 May, and his report was considered at a long Cabinet meeting the follow-

ing day. Mr Eban conveyed the assurances of support which
he had received from President Johnson and also his warnings
against Israel taking any initiative of her own. Several of his
colleagues found the assurances unconvincing. In any case the
question of the Straits, as President Nasser had made clear, was
now secondary to that of the survival of Israel: the presence
of an Egyptian detachment at Sharm-el-Sheikh was unimportant compared to the seven menacing divisions in Sinai. As for
the idea of Israel accepting the closure of Eilat and continuing
to exist as a pensioner of the West, it would only have to be
raised to be scornfully dismissed. There was still no majority
in the Cabinet in favour of taking the plunge into war, with
all the uncertainties and horrors which this might involve; but
the government was not persuaded that the destinies of the
country could be left entirely in American hands.

No decision was reached, but some announcement to the
country had to be made. Mr Eshkol broadcast that evening.
The whole nation was listening, waiting for a lead: civilians at
home and in cafes, the army in their messes or on transistor
sets in their tents in the desert. The performance was a disaster.
The Prime Minister was tired; he had a bad cold; he lost his
place in his script; and he had nothing particular to say. Israel,
he said, would try to resolve the crisis by diplomacy, but she
would defend herself if necessary. She would remain in a state
of readiness, and the army could be relied on to do its duty. No
trumpet could have been more uncertain. The worst suspicions
of the government's indecisiveness seemed to be confirmed.
There were rumours of direct action by army leaders – not a
Syrian-type *coup d'état* but a collective resignation by the High
Command which would be equally effective in bringing about
the fall of the government. Only one thing could now reassure
public opinion – the co-option of Moshe Dayan. Further negotiations were brief. On 1 June it was announced that General

Dayan and two other opposition leaders, Mr Menaghem Begin and Mr Joseph Saphir, would join the coalition in a Government of National Unity. Dayan would receive the portfolio of Defence.

Dayan's appointment was greeted in Israel with unanimous relief. Abroad, it was widely seen as a sign that the government had resolved on war. This was not quite accurate. The decision for war was taken only gradually. General Dayan brought to the Cabinet an expert knowledge of the military situation which did much to increase their self-confidence, but he proved more moderate in his views than had been generally expected. It was Mr Begin, an old leader of the extremist group Irgun Zwai Leumi, who brought the greatest access of strength to the 'hawks'. In so far as there was a clear-cut debate over the issue, the 'hawks' were able to present an increasingly strong case as the Egyptians moved up their forces in Sinai and as Iraqi troops began to enter Jordan. The arguments for delay rested on Mr Eban's reports from Washington; reports not simply of American assurances of support, but of American displeasure if Israel should be the first to resort to force. At the very least, he insisted, Israel must not seem to have acted 'with improper haste'.

American displeasure was still a powerful deterrent, but by Sunday 4 June it was the only one left. The Israeli High Command was in any case sceptical about it. They had reason to believe that an Israeli initiative would command sufficiently influential sympathy in Washington to counteract any pressure there might be for the imposition of serious sanctions. All depended on the speed and success of the attack, and on this score the military leaders were still confident. They reckoned they could inflict sufficient damage on the enemy forces to remove the threat to Israel's borders before the Great Powers intervened; and they knew that time was likely to be very short indeed.

The Cabinet met again on the morning of 4 June. At this meeting, it is reported, the High Command was able to present its arguments in a fashion which resolved the last doubts. Next morning the war began.

III. The war

The war opened at 7.45 on the morning of Monday 5 June, when the Israeli Air Force struck their first blow at the airfields of the UAR.[41] By the end of the week the Israeli armed forces had occupied the Sinai Peninsula, including the eastern bank of the Suez Canal and the western shores of the Tiran Straits; they had conquered the whole West Bank of the Jordan and with it the entire city of Jerusalem; and they had seized the heights from which the Syrian Army had for so long dominated the Upper Jordan Valley. The armies of Egypt and Jordan had been virtually destroyed, and that of Syria routed. There was nothing to stop Israel, if she so wished, from occupying the Suez Canal area, Amman, and Damascus. Military power had not only once again changed the map of the Middle East: it had transformed the pattern of international relations, with consequences which it is still impossible to foresee.

It was only the rapidity of this victory that surprised military specialists in the West. Most of them had assumed that once the war began, superior Israeli training, intelligence, and morale would compensate for any disadvantage in numbers and in strategic position. The total mobilized strength of the Israeli Army was some 275,000 men – and women – organized into 22 infantry brigades, eight armoured brigades, and one parachute brigade. In the south, they confronted an Egyptian force in the Sinai Peninsula of about 100,000 men; the total mobilized strength of the Egyptian Army was 240,000 men, of whom about 50,000 were in the Yemen. And in the east, Israel confronted a Jordanian force of 55,000; the Syrian Army, numbering 50,000; and an Iraqi division moving up through Jordan. Time did not permit the engagement of forces promised by other members of the Arab League. All these armies had been provided with up-to-date equipment by wealthier powers anxious to maintain their influence in the area and find markets for their armament industries. The Israelis had about 800 tanks, including British *Centurions*, American *Super Shermans*, and M48 *Pattons*, and French AMX-13s.[42] The Egyptian total was somewhat larger, with a nucleus of Soviet T-54s and T-55s, and many of the older T-34s. They also had a substantial number of tank destroyers. Jordan's 250 tanks were mainly *Pattons* and *Centurions*; the Syrian 400 (only 200 operational) were provided by the Russians; the Iraqis were equipped with both British and Soviet armour. In the air, Syria and Egypt relied on Russian MiG interceptors and fighter-bombers, of which Syria had about 100 and Egypt 400, Egypt possessing also a force of about 80 Tupolev and Ilyushin medium and light bombers which could have done serious damage to Israeli cities. Jordan had almost two dozen British *Hunter* fighter-bombers. The Israeli Air Force was equipped almost completely by the French aircraft industry: *Mirage* IIIC and *Super Mystère* fighters, *Mystère* IV fighter-bombers (about 140 in all), as well as 50 obsolescent *Ouragan* fighter-bombers, 60 *Magister* training aircraft, which could be – and were – used for ground support, and 25 *Vautour* light bombers. If the belligerent powers had been equal in all other respects, Israel would have been quickly crushed.[43]

But they were not equal. In the first place, the military establishments of Israel and of her adversaries reflected the basic difference in the social and economic structure of their societies. The Arab States were still basically agrarian communities with small political and technical élites. Their officer corps, as is usual in developing countries, contained a large proportion of the best-educated and most politically conscious elements in the nation. Many of the officers were skilled professionals, but there appear to have been many others, especially in the Syrian Army, who regarded political fanaticism as a substitute for military expertise and who were concerned more with the army's role in domestic politics than with national defence. Between the officers and their barely literate soldiers a great gap yawned, betraying the extent to which the Arab revolution remained a middle-class monopoly and showing how little it had as yet affected the peasants from whom the army was still recruited. The Arab soldiers fought with courage but with neither fanaticism nor skill. More important, they had not developed the qualities of intelligence and initiative in their NCOs and junior officers on which the effectiveness of modern armies so largely depends. When plans broke down, as plans invariably do in war, when no orders were available from superior authority, they collapsed; much as the armies of eighteenth-century Europe collapsed before the onslaught of revolutionary France.

Israel, by contrast, was a homogeneous and tightly integrated society, with a high level of general education and a lively realization of the importance of military efficiency to its very survival. It was indeed a garrison State of a kind almost unique in the modern world. Out of a population of 2.75 million, its regular armed forces numbered only some 10,000. The remainder of its standing army, 60,000 strong, consisted of national servicemen who served for two and a half years before being relegated to a reserve from which they were called up for annual training of varying length: two months for officers, five weeks for NCOs, and one month for other ranks. These were minimum periods: the army seldom had difficulty in extending training time if it needed to do so. Not until the age of 45 did this obligation cease, and then the Israeli citizen enrolled in the Civil Defence Force. Service in the technical branches was somewhat longer, and pilots in the Air Force enlisted for a minimum period of five years when they were 18 years old, and were operational after three years' training. Military units were drawn as far as possible from residents of a single neighbourhood, particular members being designated to ensure that mobilization instructions, broadcast in code over the radio, got round to everyone. Test mobilizations were frequent: at any time the reservist might be called out in the middle of the night to report to his unit, and be fully operational by dawn; while vehicles (like horses in Europe before 1914) were as subject to requisition as men.

Finally, the Israeli forces had the great advantage of knowing where they would have to fight. Every yard of their frontiers and the surrounding terrain had been studied from maps, from aerial photographs, and possibly from the reports of clandestine reconnaissance patrols. Terrain conditions were systematically analyzed. Israeli tanks and infantry held exercises over ground as similar as possible to that over which they would have to operate. As a result, when the Sinai campaign began, the Israeli forces showed themselves far more familiar with the conditions of the battlefield than did the Arabs, who had occupied it for so many years.

Full mobilization of the Israeli armed forces produced a quarter of a million men and women: 10 per cent of the total population. The strain which this imposed on the economy was obviously considerable, and during the 1967 crisis many Western experts believed that the impossibility of sustaining it for long would force Israel to seek a rapid settlement, whether by capitulation or by war. They exaggerated, much as their predecessors in 1914 had exaggerated in predicting that the strain of mobilization on the European powers would force them to conclude peace within a few weeks. People become very ingenious in wartime, and Israel's small size gave her mobilization arrangements a remarkable degree of flexibility. It certainly suited Israel's policy to have her friends believe that circumstances would compel her, failing their intervention, to force the issue one way or the other, within a few days. Privately, experts in Tel Aviv suggested that the economy even of a fully mobilized Israel would remain viable until the end of the year.

This pattern of military service was very similar to the model created by Prussia in the early nineteenth century; another small country needing to maximize her military resources against her more powerful neighbours. But whereas the Prussian system had resulted in the militarization of society, the Israeli resulted in the civilianization of the army. Israeli troops went about their work with a complete absence of the barrack-square discipline which the forces of other nations consider essential to the maintenance of disciplined obedience. The Israeli Army could do without it, and regarded it as a waste of time. Its units came together to do a particular job, which was examined, discussed, decided upon, and executed in a workmanlike manner. If they fell down on that job, they knew it would mean the end of Israel. Officers maintained their authority not by orthodox discipline but by personal example. Their function was to lead and if necessary to get killed, as many of them did. But if they did get killed, their men knew what to do – and even if they did not, their training and their *esprit de corps* enabled them to keep the initiative. The morale and efficiency of the Israelis was not the product of military indoctrination; it was rooted in their realization that they had escaped massacre once, and were unlikely to get a second chance.

There was another similarity between Israel and Prussia. States surrounded by openly hostile neighbours are strongly tempted to strike first and eliminate one of them, rather than wait until they choose their time to attack concentrically with superior forces. Such pre-emption is certainly the path of conventional military wisdom, although there may be strong political reasons against it. But Israel's territory was so minute that she could hardly afford to follow the path of political and legal rectitude by allowing her adversaries to strike the first blow and hope to recoup her losses in a counter-attack. Her airfields were too concentrated and vulnerable to a pre-emptive strike. On the ground she could within a few hours lose Eilat and the Upper Jordan Valley and have her country cut in two. No definition of 'aggression' had yet been devised to suit the circumstances of all States. Here it is enough to suggest that Dr Fedorenko's comparison, in the United Nations Security Council, of Israel's offensive in Sinai with Hitler's attack on the Soviet Union, was not one which commanded very wide agreement.

At 7.45 a.m. on 5 June, Israeli military authorities announced that Egypt had opened a land and air attack. Egyptian armoured forces, they contended, had moved at dawn towards the Negev, and Israeli radar had picked up numerous Egyptian aircraft approaching their borders. Later reports spoke of exceptionally heavy shelling of Israeli outposts from the Gaza Strip. One need neither take these reports at their face value nor dismiss them as complete fabrications. Egyptian air patrols probably were seen on Israeli radar screens. There was certainly shelling from the Gaza Strip. The Israeli command was naturally sensitive to the threat which the Egyptian armoured force in Central Sinai posed to Eilat, and its movements that morning may have looked particularly menacing. But it remains very doubtful whether there was anything so unusual about these Egyptian activities as to justify so shattering a riposte. The explanation – and if necessary the justification – for the Israeli offensive must be found in the realm of strategy rather than that of tactics. The decision to launch it was not based entirely on General Gavish's report from Beersheba.

At the moment when the above announcement was being made over Israeli radio stations, Israeli aircraft were opening their attack on nineteen Egyptian airfields in Sinai and the Nile Delta. In the battle to come, complete command of the air was necessary not only to give Israeli forces freedom of movement on the ground – especially in the Sinai Peninsula – but also to free the country of the nagging anxiety about the vulnerability of her cities. The time was well chosen. The Egyptian aircraft had already flown their dawn patrol and were grounded while their pilots had breakfast. They were not lined up in a state of complete unpreparedness wing-towing as has sometimes been alleged, but were dispersed at maximum readiness, and some-times even taxi-ing for take-off. The Israelis did not even give the Egyptians warning by first attacking their radar stations: they sent their aircraft in low over the sea, or sweeping behind the mountains of the Sinai Peninsula. They probably used elec-tronic deception measures as well. The attacks were so timed as to allow each pilot three passes at his allotted target; then he returned to base, refuelled, and attacked again. With inter-vals of only ten minutes, attacks against the airfields continued uninterruptedly for three hours. By noon the Egyptian Air Force had lost nearly 300 aircraft, and was of little further use as a fighting force.

The success of this blow was due to two factors alone: intel-ligence and training. Of the first little can be reliably said, but the results speak for themselves. Among the intelligence services of the world, that of Israel has a high reputation. The effectiveness with which it tapped enemy communications was surprisingly revealed a few days later, when it committed a remarkable breach of security by publishing an intercepted radio-telephone conversation between President Nasser and King Hussein. And the Israeli Air Force had carried out suffi-cient flights over Egyptian territory over the past few days to have a very exact knowledge of its targets. This knowledge was fed to a group of pilots who had received a gruelling course of training involving a weekly briefing on their targets, a major battle practice every four months, and once a year a full-scale exercise. There had never been any doubt in the minds of the Air Staff that their major function would be a pre-emptive strike. In the words of General Ezer Weizmann, the creator of the Air Force and its Chief of Staff until 1966, the only place where Israel could be defended was over Cairo. His successor, Brigadier-General Mordecai Hod, brought Weizmann's preparations to completion. He knew that this time, unlike 1956, he could expect no help from the Royal Air Force: but this was a handicap he saw no reason to regret.

Outsiders found it hard to believe that this astonishing and perhaps decisive success did not have some recondite cause, and they interpreted it in predictable ways. American and British commentators looked for a 'secret weapon' – some kind of air-to-ground homing missile which would explain the accuracy with which the Egyptian aircraft were destroyed on the ground. None existed. The only unexpected weapon the Israelis used, and one probably under development by most air forces, was a bomb fitted with retroactive rockets to give it a vertical descent to ensure maximum destruction of runways; a weapon naturally not used against the forward airfields in Sinai, such as El Arish, which the Israelis expected to capture and use themselves. Indeed one of the principal advantages of the Israeli aircraft lay in their comparative *lack* of sophistication, which simplified maintenance and refuelling, making possible the fast turn-arounds which enabled pilots to fly six or more sorties in a single day.

This capacity of the Israelis to get the utmost out of their machines and men took their adversaries completely by surprise. It was this that led President Nasser to assert on 9 June, 'If we say now that it was a stronger blow than we had expected, we must say at the same time . . . that it was bigger than the potential at his [the enemy's] disposal . . . the enemy was operating with an air force three times stronger than his normal force'. This assessment, combined with memories of 1956 and the *a priori* assumption of an 'imperialist-Zionist plot', predisposed the Arabs to believe in Anglo-American intervention even before King Hussein informed Nasser, early on the morning of 6 June, that a Jordanian radar station had detected approaching from the sea a large flight of aircraft which could only come from British or American carriers. This report was promptly and indignantly denied by both governments concerned. The British had no aircraft carriers nearer than Malta and Aden, a thousand miles from the scene of action. The American Sixth Fleet in the Mediterranean was, fortunately, being closely observed by units of the Soviet fleet, which no doubt reported to Moscow the absence of any unusual activity. Certainly the Soviet Government and press ignored the report. Later, King Hussein himself was to retract it. How it originated – whether in misreading of signals, Israeli spoofing, or the deliberate passing of false information – is still unknown and will probably remain so. But the damage was done. On 6 June Kuwait and Iraq announced the cessation of all oil supplies to the United Kingdom and the United States; Iraq, Syria, and the Sudan broke off diplomatic relations with these Western powers, and Syria and the Lebanon interrupted the flow of oil through the pipelines on their territories. The American and British invitation to the United Nations to send inspectors to their fleets and airfields, reiterated throughout the week, were disregarded. The belief remained that even if American and British aircraft were not taking part in the actual attacks – and the Syrians in fact reported that British aircraft had been identified over their territory – they were maintaining an 'air umbrella' over Israel itself, enabling the Israeli Air Force to exert its full strength in offensive operations.[44] Unfortunately it is likely to be many years before this belief is eradicated from the Arab mind.

In fact the reaction in Washington, London, and Moscow to the outbreak of war was one of unanimous consternation. The British feared for their oil supplies; the Russians and Americans dreaded the prospect of escalation to a greater cataclysm still. Mr Kosygin took the initiative in opening up the 'hot line' from Moscow to Washington with a personal message to President Johnson, in which he is reported as expressing his concern at the turn of events and urging joint action to secure a cease-fire. A cease-fire call from the United Nations was predictable; but in what terms should it be couched? From the beginning the United States and the United Kingdom advocated a cease-fire call without conditions. India, the Soviet Union, and a number of Afro-Asian States held out for a motion condemning Israel and demanding a withdrawal of all her forces to their original positions. They had a case for doing so: the experience of 1948 had shown that ceasefire lines usually harden into frontiers. Had they realized the extent of Israel's initial victories, it is unlikely that they would have prolonged matters as they did; but the delay of the Israeli High Command in issuing a definitive communiqué left them, perhaps designedly, in ignorance. When information about the extent of Egyptian aircraft losses began to leak out during the afternoon of 5 June, the Israeli Army spokesman denounced them as 'premature, unclear, and utterly unauthorized'. Not until two o'clock the following morning did General Hod make a statement, and then it was very precise. The Israeli Air Force had destroyed for certain 286 Egyptian, 52 Syrian, 27 Jordanian, and nine Iraqi aircraft, and claimed a further 34 probabilities. They had lost only twenty aircraft themselves.

Even if these figures did not immediately command the credibility they were later shown to deserve, they made it clear that any prolongation of the fighting was likely to be to the Arabs' disadvantage. At the United Nations the Soviet Union reversed its position. On the afternoon of Tuesday 6 June the Security Council unanimously called upon the governments concerned 'as a first step to take forthwith all measures for an immediate cease-fire and for a cessation of all military activity in the area'.

By that time a great deal had happened in the theatre of war. In their broadcasts the Arabs indicated neither surprise nor resentment at the Israeli attack, but rather relief that the expected battle had begun. 'The decisive moment has come', declared the announcer on Cairo Radio: 'The battle has come and be it welcome'. 'Today is the day of the great revenge', he exhorted the Palestinian Arabs, 'revenge against the criminal gang which violated your blood and freedom. Fight, my brother, with all the hate you have against imperialism and Zionism'. A statement broadcast by the Federation of Arab Oil Workers was remarkably frank. 'The Zionists', it announced, 'fell into the trap and started a treacherous aggression on the forward positions of the Arab armies'. No Arab nation could now ignore the call to the *jihad*, the Holy War. Lebanon, Syria, Iraq, Kuwait, the Sudan, Algeria, the Yemen, and Jordan all declared war on Israel. Morocco announced the despatch of troops to the Middle East; Saudi Arabia announced that its troops were entering Jordan; even in moderate Tunisia mobs attacked the embassies of Britain and the United States. Syrian artillery opened fire on Israeli settlements in the Upper Jordan Valley; Syrian aircraft bombed an airfield at Megiddo, attacked a number of villages near Haifa, and claimed to have left the Haifa oil refineries in flames. Iraq claimed, equally without foundation, that her aircraft had raided Tel Aviv. Jordanian artillery did actually begin a spasmodic long-range bombardment of the suburbs of Tel Aviv. At considerably closer range its guns began, at 8.30

a.m., to shell the Jewish quarter of Jerusalem, and soon firing had broken out at many other points on the Israel–Jordan border. There was now military action on three fronts.

The Israeli Air Force reacted against the Syrian and Iraqi air bases, with the results announced by General Hod early next

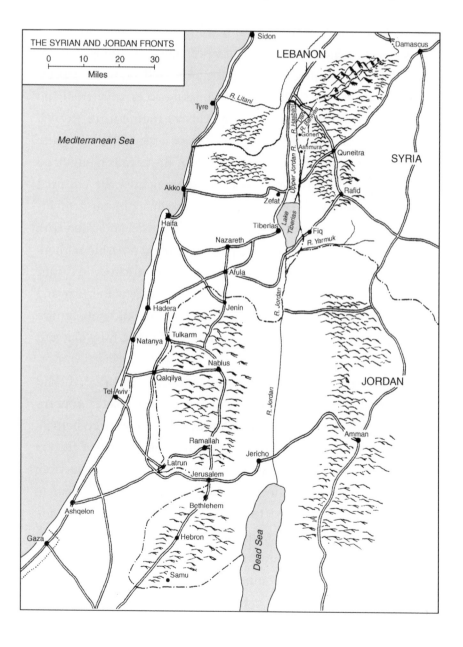

THE SYRIAN AND JORDAN FRONTS

0   10   20   30
Miles

Mediterranean Sea

Sidon
LEBANON
Damascus

R. Litani
Tyre

R. Hasbani
R. Banias
Gonen
Ashmura
Quneitra
SYRIA

Akko
Zefat
Rafid

Haifa
Tiberias
Lake Tiberias
Fiq
R. Yarmuk
Nazareth

Afula

R. Jordan

Hadera
Jenin

Natanya
Tulkarm

Nablus

Qalqilya
Tel-Aviv

R. Jordan
JORDAN

Amman

Ramallah
Jericho
Latrun
Jerusalem

Bethlehem

Ashqelon

Gaza
Hebron
Dead Sea

Samu

day. Jordan, however, was given a chance. Syria's hostility was accepted as inevitable in Tel Aviv, but it seemed possible that King Hussein might just be able to keep his country out of war. If he did so Israel would be spared a campaign on a second front against an adversary for whose military capacity she had a certain respect. Soon after the Jordanian shelling began, Mr Eshkol used the UNTSO headquarters in Jerusalem to pass a message to King Hussein assuring him that if Jordan did not open serious hostilities Israel would not retaliate. Shortly afterwards he reiterated this assurance, in more general terms, in a statement to the Knesset. King Hussein ignored it. Even if he had known the extent of the damage the UAR Air Force had suffered, it is doubtful whether he could have done anything else. The ink was hardly dry on his pact with the UAR; an Egyptian general was already in command of his armed forces; and his own army commanders were unlikely to have tolerated any hesitation. The shellfire on Jerusalem intensified and extended to the Israeli enclave at Mount Scopus; Jordanian forces occupied UNTSO Headquarters in the old Government House, a vantage point commanding the entire city of Jerusalem; and Jordanian aircraft raided Natanya and the Israeli air base at Kfar Sirkin.

Israel struck back heavily. By midday her air force had finished with the Egyptian airfields and was able to concentrate on the Jordanian bases at Mafraq and Amman, where all Jordan's first-line aircraft were quickly put out of action. On the ground, also, the Israelis swung over to the attack. With so few troops deployed on this front it was essential at least to 'fix' the Jordanian forces until reinforcements could be made available from the main battle in Sinai, and this could be most effectively done by the most ferocious offensive possible. In the words of a senior Israeli military expert, 'We were too weak to do anything else'. As it was, the Israelis were able, with the one brigade stationed in Jerusalem, an armoured brigade of reservists from the coastal plain, a parachute brigade detached from the southern front, and an armoured force intended for action against Syria, to drive the Jordanians across the Jordan before operations against Egypt were completed. Even the most optimistic planner would have been unwise to stake much on such an outcome. Its explanation lies almost entirely in Israel's command of the air. On the evening and night of 5 June the Jordanians fought stubbornly and well in the close country and suburbs around Jerusalem and Jenin, inflicting heavy casualties on their assailants. But by Tuesday the 6th movement in daylight was impossible. Israeli aircraft wiped out their convoys and repeatedly attacked their static positions. Israeli armoured columns penetrated deeply behind their defences. By the night of the 6th, the Jordanian Army had collapsed.

The Israeli attacks on Jordan were largely improvised. On the Jerusalem front, while Colonel Amitai's brigade attacked south of the Old City during the afternoon of the 5th and recaptured Government House, the area commander, Brigadier-General Narkiss, prepared to attack to the north with infantry and armour. His infantry consisted of Colonel Gur's parachute brigade, which had been rushed up from the southern front and most of whose members had never seen the terrain over which they were to fight. Fighting at night in a closely built-up area, against troops defending positions they had been preparing for years, the parachutists had to force their way through to seize the heights which dominated the Old City, from the Sheikh Jarah quarter in the north to the Augusta Victoria Hospital on the Mount of Olives to the east. It was a bloody soldiers' battle in which the Israelis did not have the advantage of surprise and the forces of the Arab Legion opposed to them fought tenaciously. By daybreak on 6 June the Israeli forces had somehow struggled through to Sheikh Jarah and controlled most of the area to the north of the Old City. Meanwhile, to their left, Colonel Ben-Ari's armoured force had advanced northward to clear the hills between Jerusalem and Ramallah, frontally attacking heavily fortified positions with excellent fields of fire. By the morning of the 6th it had broken the crust of the Jordanian defences. In the west, another unit of the brigade had stormed the town of Latrun, which for eighteen years had blocked the road from Jerusalem to Tel Aviv. Both parts of his command converged on Ramallah, and cleared it that night. Next day, Wednesday the 7th, against purely sporadic opposition, Ben-Ari's armour pushed on to Jericho; and later that morning it was on the banks of the Jordan.

Meanwhile in Jerusalem the parachute brigade, fighting throughout the day and night of Tuesday the 6th, had consolidated its hold on the heights to the north-east, while Colonel Amitai's troops cleared the Abu Tor district south of the city in bitter fighting. By the morning of Wednesday the 7th the two Israeli pincers had almost closed round the Old City, and General Dayan ordered them to seize it before the cease-fire agreement reached at the United Nations the previous evening could come into effect. They attacked at 8.30 a.m.; by 2 p.m. the city was in their hands. Dayan himself, Rabin, and Narkiss made their way to the Wailing Wall of the Temple and gazed in silence. The Jews had returned to Jerusalem, after nineteen hundred years.

Meanwhile the rest of the West Bank had fallen into Israeli hands, as a result of the attack launched from the north by the force detached from Brigadier-General Elazar's northern command. Elazar received the order to attack at noon on 5 June, primarily to silence the heavy Jordanian fire on the Israeli positions. The attack which he actually launched at 5 p.m. was rather more ambitious in scope. His objective was the town of Nablus in the very centre of the West Bank. He launched his principal

attack with a mechanized brigade, supported by tanks, against
Jenin, where heavy fighting continued throughout the night.
He also launched a feint attack in the Jordan Valley down the
right bank of the river, which effectively distracted Jordanian

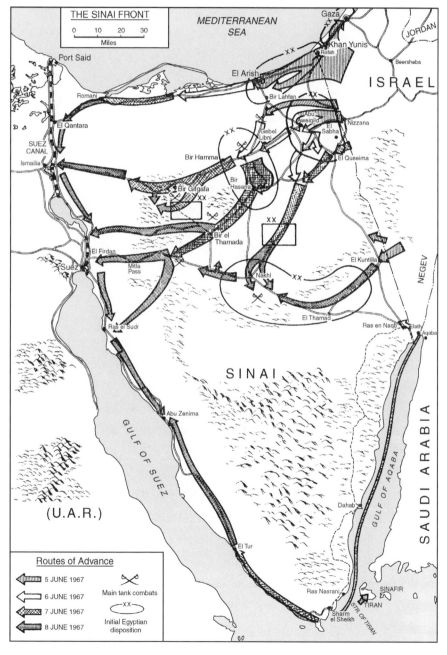

THE SINAI FRONT

0   10   20   30
Miles

Routes of Advance

5 JUNE 1967
6 JUNE 1967
7 JUNE 1967
8 JUNE 1967

Main tank combats

Initial Egyptian
disposition

forces from the main thrust. Next day all attempts by the Jordanians to move over the mountain roads, forward or backward, were defeated by the Israeli Air Force, which attacked their convoys with a terrible mixture of high explosive and napalm. By the 7th Jordanian resistance was broken. Elazar's forces joined hands at Nablus with a detachment of Ben-Ari's brigade advancing from the south. Israeli forces stood along the length of the Jordan from Dan to the Dead Sea, while over the bridges poured a stream of terrified Arab refugees, some of them going into exile for the second time in their lives. An Arab population of 900,000, however, including 500,000 Palestinian refugees, remained. It remains to be seen how far the superb success of General Elazar's armoured thrust has created for Israel rather more problems than it solved.

While the Israelis were wresting Jerusalem and the West Bank from the Jordanians, the decisive battle of the war was fought in the sands and hills of Sinai. Here the Egyptians had concentrated seven divisions. That in the Gaza Strip, the 20th Division, consisted mainly of the Palestine Liberation Army. The 7th Division lay to the west of it, from the international frontier at Rafah to El Arish. South of the 7th was the 2nd Division, covering the vital road junction at Abu Aweiqila. The 3rd Division was in second line, in the area of Gebel Libni, Bir Hamma, and Bir Hasana. The 6th was stationed in the centre of the peninsula on the route from Suez to Eilat, between Nakhl and El Thamad. The principal armoured division, the 4th, lay well back, between Bir Gifgafa and Bir el Thamada. Another armoured force of something less than divisional strength was said by the Israelis to be moving in Central Sinai in the general direction of Kuntilla – the force which they believed to be threatening the Lower Negev. The 7th and 2nd Divisions were dug into strong positions barring the three roads which led across the Sinai Peninsula to the Canal at El Qantara, Ismailia, and Suez. The Israeli forces had to breach this line and the one behind it held by the 3rd Division, bring the armour to battle, and destroy the fighting force of the Egyptian Army – their first objective. Their second was to seize and hold Sharm-el-Sheikh, where there was a small Egyptian force; and their third, to provide security for that position, was to clear and occupy the Sinai Peninsula. It was at first an open question whether they should press on to that passage of ill-omen, the Suez Canal.

To achieve these objectives General Gavish had three divisional groups, under Brigadier-Generals Tal, Joffe, and Sharon.[45] Though numerically outnumbered, his forces had an armoured strength almost comparable to the Egyptian; and whereas about half the Egyptian tanks were allocated to infantry divisions, the Israeli tank force was concentrated in all-armoured units which packed a very considerable punch. The contrast between the two patterns of organiza-tion was interesting. The Israeli was that which had brought the Germans their victories in the early years of the Second World War, and which the British had adopted in the Western Desert and, initially, in Normandy. The Egyptians, under Russian tutelage, modelled themselves on the mixed units which were generally adopted in Europe in the latter years of the war, when all-armoured units had proved highly vulner-able to resolute infantry armed with anti-tank weapons. In close country the advantage overwhelmingly lies with mixed units, but in this desert the older formations again proved their worth. It is anyhow doubtful whether the Russians fully appreciated the problems of desert fighting, which they had themselves never had to face. The Egyptians were not trained for the quicksilver mobility of operations without flanks and virtually without supply lines. They sat in ponderous hedge-hogs – not unlike the Eighth Army 'Boxes' in front of Tobruk in summer 1942 – from which they refused to be drawn. Given their standard of training, this may well have been the wisest course for them to follow.

Gavish attacked at 8.15 a.m. on 5 June. Tal struck in the north against the 7th Division. Sharon, based on Nizzana, attacked the 2nd Division before Abu Aweiqila. Joffe, whose force consisted entirely of reservists (he himself in civil life was head of Israel's Nature Conservancy Board), passed between them, threading his way through sand dunes generally held to be impassable, till at about 4 p.m. he reached the road from Abu Aweiqila to El Arish, where he sat intercepting Egyptian forces moving forward to reinforce their front or, next morning, hurrying rearwards in retreat. Farther south a brigade advanced from Kuntilla, more as a feint to draw Egyptian forces southward than as a serious threat.

Tal attacked in broad daylight, but avoided 7th Division's well-mined front. He divided his forces into two. The brigade on the left wing, like Joffe's force, crossed territory which the Israelis had discovered, by careful tests, to be less impassable than the Egyptians had supposed. They took the Egyptians in the flank, achieving complete surprise, and destroyed, after heavy fighting, a force double their strength. The brigade on the right had a harder time. They had little difficulty in breaking through to the coast at Khan Yunis and cutting off the Palestinians in the Gaza Strip; who were then dealt with by a brigade from General Gavish's reserve. But when they turned west to attack Rafah, they encountered strong prepared positions – fortifications, anti-tank guns, entrenched tanks – manned for the most part by extremely resolute troops. No surprise, no indirect approach was possible. The left-wing brigade, with the divisional reserve, had now come up on their right, and the whole division battered its way grimly forward down the road towards El Arish. By now the air force was available to take part in the ground battle, and air strikes helped to overwhelm the strongest positions.[46]

A battalion reached El Arish before midnight; but it was dawn before the last Egyptian stronghold was overcome.

At Abu Aweiqila General Sharon also had a very tough nut to crack: an entrenched position protected by minefields and antitank guns, held by four battalions of infantry, six regiments of artillery, and about 90 tanks. He attacked by night – the night of 5 June, which also saw Tal's armour break through to El Arish, Narkiss's parachute troops seize the heights of Sheikh Jarah outside Jerusalem, and Elazar's forces battle their way through Jenin. During the afternoon his infantry and armour closed up to the main Egyptian positions, driving in their outposts.

Flanking forces were sent round the position to north and south, cutting the roads to Quseima, Gebel Libni, and El Arish. Tanks established themselves north-west of the position, six artillery regiments on the east, while a parachute battalion was landed by helicopter to attack from the north. At 10.45 p.m. the barrage began, and half an hour later, their objective illuminated by searchlights, the infantry and armour went in to the attack. The battle went on all night. By six o'clock next morning the last resistance had collapsed.

The main Egyptian defences were now shattered. There were still two Egyptian infantry and two armoured divisions intact, whereas the Israelis had only two brigades – one in General Joffe's division, one in the south at Kuntilla – which had not been fighting uninterruptedly for twenty-four hours. But the Egyptians now had to conduct a mobile war, of a kind for which they had not been trained, against an enemy who enjoyed complete command of the air and whose morale, always high, was now raised by victory to a pitch of exhilaration at which physical fatigue was almost forgotten. Only these factors can explain the remarkable achievements of the Israeli Defence Force during the next two days.

Much of Tuesday 6 June had to be devoted to consolidation, mopping up, and planning for the next stage. General Gavish's reserve brigade completed the clearing of the Gaza Strip; General Tal's troops smashed the last Egyptian positions south of El Arish at Bir Lahfan, and while a task force set out along the coast road towards the Suez Canal, the rest of his division turned south to make contact with General Joffe's second brigade, which had come up through Abu Aweiqila and was clearing resistance round Gebel Libni. At Gebel Libni, Tal and Joffe laid their plans for the advance. Large Egyptian forces still lay before them, but those forces depended on two roads: one to Ismailia through Bir Hamma and Bir Gifgafa, one to Suez through Bir el Thamada and the Mitla Pass. By a rapid advance these roads could be blocked and the entire Egyptian Army trapped in the desert. Farther south, a thrust by General Sharon could block the retreat of the Egyptian right wing at Nakhl. Speed was essential before the enemy could recover and regroup, and the Israelis wasted no time. The advance began at once and continued through the night.

By the evening of Wednesday 7 June Joffe's leading brigade under Colonel Iska was in position at the eastern end of the Mitla Pass, barring the road to Suez. Behind them the Pass itself was already blocked by a huge tangle of wrecked vehicles destroyed by the Israeli Air Force. Iska's brigade fought all night against the Egyptian forces bearing down on them, and somehow held their ground until relieved next day by Joffe's second brigade, which forced its way through the wreckage in the Pass to reach the banks of the Canal at 2 a.m. on the morning of Friday 9 June. Tal and Sharon also successfully blocked their roads; but to reach Bir Gifgafa and Nakhl, respectively, they had to pass through the main forces of the enemy armour. For both this involved thirty-six hours of continuous and confused fighting as the armoured forces of both sides streamed in the same direction along the same tracks. Sharon came upon the tanks of an Egyptian armoured brigade abandoned intact by their crews. The commander was taken prisoner and explained to his astonished captors that he had been ordered to withdraw but nothing had been said about taking the tanks with him – and that to blow them up would make too much noise. Both at Nakhl and at Gifgafa the Israeli tanks established ambushes which trapped the retreating Egyptians.

Throughout the three days of Tuesday, Wednesday, and Thursday the Israeli Air Force roved the desert at will, where necessary co-operating in the land battle but mainly seeking out and destroying enemy forces wherever they saw them. By Friday morning, when the cease-fire at last came into effect, hardly an Egyptian unit remained intact. The desert was littered with the debris of thousands of vehicles, including over 700 Russian tanks. Egyptian soldiers in tens of thousands, for the most part abandoned by their officers, had cast away arms, equipment, and boots and were hopelessly making their way across the waterless desert in the direction of home. The *jihad* was over. In the course of it, on 7 June, a small force of patrol boats had sailed down the Gulf of Aqaba and, landing unopposed, hoisted the Israeli flag at the Straits of Tiran.

Meanwhile, in New York, Mr Abba Eban was fighting his country's battles at the Security Council. Although the sympathy of the Western world had not, on the whole, been forfeited by Israel's apparent action in striking the first blow, it was not likely to extend to any blatant violation of a cease-fire resolution by the United Nations. Support from public opinion in the United States, so long as no American involvement was required, was overwhelmingly strong – so strong that Mr Dean Rusk felt it necessary to soften the statement of one of his officials that the United States was 'neutral in thought, word, and deed' by explaining that neutrality was a concept in international law which did not imply indifference. But for Britain, much as she sympathized with the Israeli cause, the prospect of prolonged conflict in the Middle East, with all that this implied for her relations with the Arab world, was intensely disagreeable. The French Government, to the fury of most articulate French public opinion, reaffirmed its position of glacial neutrality; while the Soviet Union could only view the humiliation of her clients in the Arab world with alarm and despondency.

The refusal of the Soviet Union to intervene on their behalf, which must have been made clear to the Arab leaders at the very beginning of the conflict, made it the more necessary for her to sponsor their cause at the United Nations; not only to salvage her own reputation with them but to save them from the consequences of their own folly. Dr Fedorenko found himself in a difficult position. On the one hand, he had to get a cease-fire as quickly as possible. On the other, he had to read into the record the maximum abuse of Israel's aggression and the iniquity of her supporters in the West. Mr Eban and Mr Gideon Raphael, Israel's Permanent Representative at the United Nations, may have consoled themselves for the hours of abuse which they had to endure from Dr Fedorenko and his Communist and Arab colleagues with the reflection that every hour thus spent was being put to good use by the Israeli High Command.

But it was not in the interests of the Western powers to see the Arabs and their Russian sympathizers reduced to complete despair. Besides, the longer the conflict lasted, the greater was the risk of its spreading. An example of how this might happen occurred on the afternoon of Thursday 8 June, when Israeli aircraft attacked the US Navy vessel USS *Liberty* some 14 nautical miles north of El Arish. The circumstances leading up to this attack have not been made public, any more than the real reasons for the presence of this vessel so close to the battle zone; but the Israelis were able to convince the United States Government that the bombing was due to a genuine error of identification, and it seems highly probable that *Liberty*, an electronic intelligence vessel, was monitoring the wireless traffic of both sides. Whatever the facts of the case, this attack led to a reaction in the US Sixth Fleet, whose aircraft flew off to investigate. Realizing that the Russians in their turn might react to this move, a direct explanation was sent over 'the hot line'. The affair in fact was very competently handled; but it must have increased the general anxiety for a cease-fire.

The Security Council, it will be remembered, had already on the afternoon of 6 June called upon the governments concerned 'as a first step to take forthwith all measures for an immediate cease-fire and for a cessation of all military activities in the area'. Mr Abba Eban at once informed the Security Council that his country welcomed the cease-fire appeal, but that its implementation 'depended on the acceptance and co-operation of the other parties'. Syria and Iraq, whose forces were as yet only marginally engaged in the war, rejected the appeal. The UAR remained silent. Only Jordan, whose forces on the West Bank were at their last gasp, responded immediately, but the Israelis were not yet ready to leave her alone. Pointing out that, since the Jordanian Army was under Egyptian command, this decision was of doubtful validity, they continued to fight – in Jerusalem, as we have seen, with redoubled vigour. On 7 June a wrathful Dr Fedorenko sponsored a more strongly worded motion, adopted unanimously by the Security Council, which '*demand*[*ed*] that the Governments concerned should as a first step cease fire and discontinue all military activities at 20.00 hours GMT on 7 June 1967'. This the Israelis accepted. By then the Old City of Jerusalem was securely in their hands.

On the Sinai front, the obstinacy of the UAR Government played straight into the hands of Israel. It was not until the evening of Thursday 8 June that their delegate conveyed to the Security Council their acceptance of the cease-fire. By then General Gavish's forces had completed the rout of the Egyptians in Sinai and had only to close up to the Suez Canal. Only Syria now remained.

Up till now the Israeli forces opposite Syria had remained on the defensive, while the Syrians confined themselves to occasional raids in battalion strength and frequent, heavy shelling of the *kibbutzim* in the Jordan Valley below them. It is not clear at what point the Israeli Government took the decision to attack Syria, but the decision is not likely to have caused much controversy. Israeli public opinion would have found it difficult to understand or forgive a campaign which, having disposed of Egypt and Jordan, left intact the enemy whose hostility to Israel had been most implacable, whose activities had been directly responsible for the war, and whose forces still dominated one of the most fertile stretches of Israeli land. But the problems of launching an attack were considerable. The Syrian heights above the Upper Jordan Valley are a steep escarpment rising 1,000 feet to the bare plateau which stretches eastwards to Damascus and beyond. The Syrian Army had not only constructed positions from which they could dominate the valley, but also fortified the plateau to a depth of some ten miles with a continuous zone of wire, minefields, trenches, gun emplacements, pill-boxes, and tanks. Constructed under Russian direction, it was a masterpiece of defensive fortification, and suitably equipped with artillery, machine-guns, anti-aircraft batteries, and rocket-launchers. Viewing the ground afterwards, it seemed impossible that any army in the world could have taken it, except by a campaign lasting for weeks.

It took the Israelis about twenty-four hours. Their attack was preceded by heavy air attacks which began on the morning of Thursday 8 June and went on all day and all night. There was great pressure to launch the assault that day, before the Syrians could take advantage of the United Nations' demand for a cease-fire, but there were strong reasons against doing so; including the need to bring up forces from other fronts and the value of giving the air barrage time to take effect. As a result the attack was forestalled by a Syrian request for a cease-fire to begin at 3.20 a.m. GMT on Friday 9 June. The Israelis ignored this (as indeed did the Syrian artillery) and attacked at 11.30 that morning. General Elazar struck in the extreme north of the Jordan Valley up the slopes near the Baniyas head waters with a force of infantry, armour, and parachute troops. There was no cover: the way was led by bulldozers carving out tank-able tracks under heavy fire. It took three hours and about 700 casualties to gain the crest. At the same time subsidiary attacks were delivered farther down the valley opposite Gonen and Ashmura; and early next morning another mixed force attacked Syria in the far south, tanks and infantry clambering up from the Yarmuk valley, helicopters dropping parachute troops on the escarpment, and moved north-west over the plateau towards Boulmiye and Rafid.

Astonishing as the Israelis' achievement was in getting up on to the escarpment at all, this might have been only the beginning of their task. A considerable part of the Syrian defences still stretched before them. Yet on Saturday 10 June they had little more to do except advance. After the first few hours of resistance the Syrian troops collapsed and fled. This was not due entirely to the efforts of the Israeli forces; the Syrian Government itself took a hand. Early on the Saturday morning Damascus Radio announced the fall of Qnaitra, Syrian Army headquarters and the only major town between the frontier and Damascus. It did so, it has been suggested, in order to strengthen the hand of their representative at the United Nations, who for the past twenty-four hours had been trying to persuade the Security Council to force Israel into accepting the cease-fire. Hearing that their main base had fallen, the Syrian forces panicked. The Israelis were able to walk over positions which might have held them up for weeks. By 2.30 on the afternoon of 10 June they really were in Qnaitra. Two hours later the cease-fire came into effect.

The Third Arab–Israeli War was over. The only prisoners taken by the Israel Defence Force were about 5,500 officers and NCOs. It had inflicted an unknown number of casualties, including perhaps as many as 15,000 killed. It had destroyed or captured 430 combat aircraft and 800 tanks. Its own losses totalled 40 aircraft and just over 3,000 men, of whom 676 were dead. Henceforward there was not likely to be very much difficulty about Israeli rights of passage through the Straits of Tiran.

IV. Conclusion

The Third Arab–Israeli War is likely to be studied in staff colleges for many years to come. Like the campaigns of the younger Napoleon, the performance of the Israeli Defence Force provided a text-book illustration for all the classical Principles of War: speed, surprise, concentration, security, information, the offensive, above all training and morale. Airmen will note with professional approval how the Israeli Air Force was employed, first to gain command of the air by destruction of the enemy air forces, then to take part in the ground battle by interdiction of enemy communications, direct support of ground attacks, and finally pursuit. The flexibility of the administrative and staff system will be examined, and the attention of young officers drawn to the part played by leadership at all levels. Military radicals will observe how the Israelis attained this peak of excellence without the aid of drill-sergeants and the barrack-square. Tacticians will stress the importance they attached, in this as in previous campaigns, to being able to move and fight by night as effectively as they did by day.

Above all it will be seen how Israel observed a principle
which appears in few military text-books but which armed
forces neglect at their peril: the Clausewitzian principle of
Political Context, which the British ignored so disastrously in
1956. The Israeli High Command knew that it was not operat-

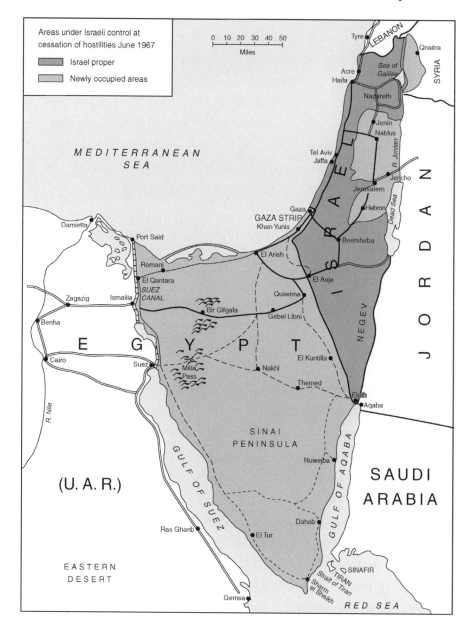

Areas under Israeli control at
cessation of hostilities June 1967

Israel proper

Newly occupied areas

ing in a political vacuum. It worked on the assumption that it would have three days to complete its task before outside pressures compelled a cease-fire. In fact it had four, and needed five. The general disapproval even in the West when Israel ignored the United Nations' cease-fire call and opened its offensive against Syria showed how narrow was the margin on which it had to work. The lesson is clear. So long as there remains a tacit agreement between the super-powers to co-operate in preventing overt conflicts which threaten international peace and security, a nation using open force to resolve a political problem must do so rapidly, if it is to succeed at all. Once it *has* succeeded, the reluctance of the Great Powers to countenance a second conflict means that it is likely to preserve its gains. The lesson is a sombre one, placing as it does a premium on adventurism and pre-emption.

Could the war have been prevented? And has it in fact resolved the political problems which led to the military confrontation? The answers to these questions will differ according to the level at which one examines the situation, and there are, broadly speaking, three: the basic hostility between Israel and the Arab World; the closing of the Straits of Tiran; and the immediate threat to Israel's security posed by the Arab political and military measures taken in the last days of May.

It has been widely assumed in the West – and perhaps in the Soviet Union as well – that the first of these situations was one which, even if it could not be peacefully resolved, was decreasingly likely to erupt into open war: that, as with the East–West confrontation, cold war would give place to peaceful co-existence and ultimately to mutual toleration. This confidence in the power of time and enlightened self-interest to solve all problems, doubtfully warranted as it is by past experience, is perhaps the only thing that keeps diplomats from despair; but there was little ground for such confidence in the history of

Israeli-Arab relations over the past twenty years. The trauma inflicted on the Arab consciousness by the establishment of Israel and the expulsion of a million native Palestinians was likely to grow more rather than less acute as Arab national self-consciousness increased. What could be taught about the event to generations of Arab schoolboys, except that it was a monstrous and intolerable injustice? The situation might have been more tolerable if the Israelis had not been, in spite of their absorption of many Middle Eastern Jews, so evidently a *Western* people, with Western skills, standards, and affiliations. The Arab and Soviet accusations against Israel of being an outpost of Western imperialism are, at the level at which they are made, self-evidently absurd. Yet they reflect a deeper reality. 'Imperialism' does not necessarily indicate a deliberate intention to conquer and subjugate other peoples. The dominance of Europe over much of the world in the nineteenth century, and of the United States in the twentieth, derived from the ascendancy gained by more energetic, self-confident, and ingenious peoples over less effectively organized and dynamic cultures. The Israelis, more than any indigenous Middle Eastern people, display the qualities of hard work, technical expertise, and self-confidence which historians once mistakenly associated with the Protestant religion and the spirit of capitalism. They may have gone to Palestine, as an earlier generation of refugees from persecution went to New England, to seek sanctuary from the storms of the outside world; but their sanctuary is not, any more than was New England, a quiet and contemplative retreat. The Israelis have pressed relentlessly on their neighbours in the cultivation of land. Plans are on foot for turning the Negev Desert into a great industrial complex by desalination – assisted by nuclear energy. Tel Aviv has become a major conurbation, Haifa a leading Mediterranean port, and Eilat's future is now assured. All this economic expansion the West naturally regards with admiration and approval. The Arabs see it with different eyes. Who, they are bound to ask, is by the end of the twentieth century likely to dominate the Middle East?

Time was not, and is not, likely to assuage the conflict between an Israel waxing in self-confidence, wealth, and economic activity and an Arab world whose political and cultural progress seems to involve the kind of nationalistic self-assertion usually associated with the States of Europe in the nineteenth century. The most that one could ask is that outside powers should do nothing to make the conflict worse; but even this is asking a great deal. Short of a policy of total non-involvement in Middle Eastern affairs, economic, military, cultural, or political, it is difficult to visualize how any party in the area can be helped, however innocently, without increasing its power to harm the others. The apparent callousness with which the Great Powers put arms into the hands of these sworn enemies is only a symptom of the way in which encouraging the development of two antagonistic parties is unlikely to reduce the antagonism. Whether they adopt, like the French Government since 1962, a dispassionate commercial approach, or like the British and Russians openly espouse the cause of specific regimes, the policy of external powers will be simply one factor – and not necessarily a very important one – in a situation which local conditions will ultimately determine. Britain, the United States, and no doubt the Soviet Union have all been through demiurgical phases in which they believed they had the power and the responsibility to mould the Middle East. Their statesmen now are sadder, wiser, and considerably more modest men.

Could external powers have done more to head off or to resolve the crisis which led to this war? The State Department has been criticized for failing to take note of the crisis until it was too late; the unspoken assumption being that it was in the power of the United States, by timely action, to save the situation. This assumption is a considerable one. The crisis was precipitated by local circumstances: primarily the revolutionary fervour of Syria and the political predicament of the UAR, working on the growing pressure of national self-assertiveness within Israel. The Soviet Union did not help matters by its warning of imminent Israeli attacks against Syria, but they were warnings for which the Israelis themselves had, perhaps deliberately, provided enough evidence to alert the Syrians without Soviet aid. Soviet intervention was incidental to the pattern of mutual warnings seen as mutual menaces, leading to explosive armed confrontation. By the time the crisis erupted, the Western powers were firmly classed as adversaries by the revolutionary Arab States. The worst construction was put on all their actions. Any pressure they could bring to bear on President Nasser – and after the withdrawal of American aid this was not considerable – would have been automatically discounted as part of the general imperialist-Zionist-reactionary conspiracy. And even the least paranoic Arab statesmen could hardly regard as impartial powers which, while taking a strong stand on Israeli rights of navigation in the Gulf of Aqaba, had nothing whatever to say about the rights of a million Palestinian Arabs dispossessed of their lands.

From 15 May onwards the initiative was in the hands of President Nasser, and about his decisions, to evict UNEF and close the Straits, much remains to be learned. About the first, the Western powers were in a position to do very little. The United Nations are not an embodiment of abstract International Justice as visualized in London and Washington, but a political body composed of numerous mutually antagonistic members, all of whose views have to be taken into account by the Secretary-General; and over the question of UNEF the Western powers, for a number of reasons, were almost certainly in a minority. Had U Thant appealed on the issue to the General Assembly, he is likely to have received an overwhelming vote of confidence. But the Straits were a different matter. The point at issue here was not one of international law: it was that of the credibility of a solemn and explicit Western guarantee. In reimposing his blockade President Nasser was, whether consciously or not, placing in jeopardy not only the economic future of Israel but also the reliability of the United States and Great Britain as allies. The implications of that for the world as a whole were very grave indeed.

The assurances which the United States and Britain had given to Israel over this issue were so inescapable that failure to implement them would have involved both powers in a humiliation as public as that suffered by France and Britain in 1956 – or indeed in 1938. The Western powers naturally attempted to gain world support by invoking international law and maritime rights, but found little backing anywhere for their position. They faced, therefore, the prospect of a lonely and prolonged confrontation with the Arab world which, whatever the outcome, could only cause them serious economic and political damage and in which they would enjoy very little neutral sympathy. Once President Nasser closed the Straits, in fact, Britain and America no longer had the status of external powers: they were up to their necks in the crisis themselves.

It was their good fortune, paradoxically, that within a few days the crisis had moved on to a graver stage and become a matter, not of Israel's economic future, but of her survival. The massing of Egyptian troops in Sinai, the creation of the United UAR-Jordanian Command, the movement of Iraqi forces into Jordan, created a situation for Israel in which it was immaterial whether the United States guaranteed passage through the Tiran Straits or not. War could now only be prevented by an assurance to Israel by the Western powers that they would react to an attack on Israeli territory as they would to one on their own. The President of the United States was in no position to issue such an assurance, and without the United States Britain could do nothing. The Israelis realized this very well.

Wars, it used to be said, settle nothing. Unfortunately the statement was untrue: they can settle many problems, and are sometimes, regrettably, the only way of settling them. But they also create new ones, sometimes so grave that one may look back to the old almost with nostalgia. Israel's victories have eliminated many of the points in dispute over the past twenty years. Whatever now happens, Syrian guns will not fire down on the Upper Jordan Valley, the City of Jerusalem will not be divided, and the future of Eilat is assured. The anomaly of the Gaza Strip is likely to be eliminated, and wherever the new frontier is drawn between Israel and Jordan, it will not run within twelve miles of the coast. But the Israelis may well look back with regret to the days when Israel was almost as homogeneous a Jewish State as its Zionist founders intended; for it will never be that again. Two and a half million Jews now control territory containing nearly a million and a half Arabs, and whatever settlement is made on the West Bank, Arabs are likely in future to make up at least a quarter of Israel's population. Israel will be confronted with all the problems of a multiracial society, in which the minority group is potentially hostile and sustained by powerful consanguineous supporters beyond the frontier.

On her ability to solve this problem Israel's future security will depend. If the Arab States have learned anything from their defeat, it should be the folly of challenging Israel to the kind of war which only fully developed societies can effectively fight. The re-equipment of their armies and air forces with modern weapons will not restore their military efficiency; it would be like fitting another heavy suit of armour on to a half-grown boy who has already proved unable to bear its weight. But half-grown boys, as the Israelis will recall, can be handy shots with slings and smooth pebbles from the brook. The weapon of revolutionary peoples, as Colonel Boumedienne among others has pointed out, is revolutionary war. There was not much scope for guerrillas in the Sinai Desert; but among a large, discontented Arab population in Israel herself, who knows?

We do not suggest that events in Israel will take the course of those in, for example, southern Africa, Algeria, or Vietnam. The Jewish population will still be in a majority, and a policy of apartheid based on religion is likely to be even less workable than one based on race. The advantages of terrain enjoyed by guerrillas in North Africa and South-East Asia are not to be found in the Sinai Desert or the restricted area of the West Bank, although Jordan, Syria, and the Lebanon could still provide sanctuary for the forces of a new 'Liberation Front'. But a renewal of the kind of inter-communal friction – the sniper at the upper window, the grenade lobbed into the coffee house – that was so common under the Mandate is by no means to be ruled out. If a fourth Arab–Israeli war occurs, this is the shape it is likely to take; and the military brilliance recently displayed by the Israeli nation and its leaders will not be very relevant to its conduct. If Israeli statesmanship does not match up to her military achievements, her victories may, like so many victories in the past, bear very bitter fruit.

Israel thus faces a dilemma to which her military talents provide no solution, and to which even nuclear weapons will be irrelevant. A strategically secure frontier, in the south and the east, will give her a strategically insecure population. There are no doubt hawks in the Cabinet who would gladly see the Arabs expelled again or at least encouraged, by very firm methods, to leave; but they are fortunately unlikely to carry the day. Barring that solution, the Arabs must be absorbed; and however hard the Israelis work to absorb them, Arab nationalist propagandists will work equally hard to inflame their grievances. The Israelis can congratulate themselves on their success in reconciling the small Arab population for twenty years within their borders, but the change in the dimensions of their task is likely to transform its entire nature. It is hard, indeed, to see how it can be accomplished at all, unless the Israelis abandon many of their Zionist ideals and revert to the older concept of a Palestine shared peacefully between Arab and Jew.

Such a policy would certainly make easier the task of moderate statemen within the Arab world. At present they enjoy a precarious ascendancy. The war so clamorously demanded by the revolutionary nationalists has taken place and ended in disaster. King Hussein's stock stands high. Not only was his policy vindicated by events, but he emerged from a war he did not want with as great credit as any of his allies. But no amount of statesmanship will incline the Arabs to accept a settlement which does not dispose once and for all of their fundamental grievance – the status of the Palestinian refugees. So long as that question remains unsettled, Hussein may fight a losing battle against Colonel Boumedienne. And if Boumedienne wins, there will be a fourth Arab–Israeli war. It will not be so short as the third; and there can be no assurance that this time Israel will win.

Notes

I. THE CONFLICT

1 Publication of the Sykes-Picot Agreement by the Bolsheviks after the October Revolution failed to stir Hussein, who expressed no opposition to Jewish settlement; Hussein's son, Feisal, even concluded an agreement on the Jewish National Home with the Zionist Chaim Weizmann. Their sentiments changed, however, when Feisal was turned out of Damascus in 1920, and the political ambitions of the Zionists began to be apparent.

2 The Mandate provided that 'the administration of Palestine, while ensuring that the rights and position of other sections of the population are not prejudiced, shall facilitate Jewish immigration under suitable conditions and shall encourage . . . close settlement by Jews on the land' (Article 6). Jewish immigration during those years

was as follows: 1923: 7,991; 1924: 13,553; 1925: 34,641; 1926: 13,910; 1927: 3,595; . . . 1931: 5,533; 1932: 11,289; 1933: 31,977; 1934: 44,143; 1935: 64,147.

3   *Palestine: Statement of Policy*, May 1939, Cmd. 6019.

4   In order to secure agreement in the General Assembly, the Jewish Agency even accepted the transfer to the Arab State of a large area of Palestine along the Egyptian frontier.

5   These raids followed a terrorist attack by the Jews on a village near the Syrian border in December 1947.

6   Jon and David Kimche, *Both Sides of the Hill* (London, 1960).

7   Soon after the campaign began to link up the body of the State of Israel with the Negev pocket, Israeli forces drove the remaining elements of the Arab Liberation Army from the area north-west of Lake Tiberias.

8   Although Egypt was awarded provisional control over the Gaza Strip by the General Armistice Agreement, it remained part of Palestine. Egypt has observed this legal distinction, which has enabled her, unlike Jordan, to deny Egyptian citizenship to the Arab refugees.

9   Iraq and Saudi Arabia did not conclude Armistice Agreements with Israel, but gave separate undertakings that they would accept terms agreed upon by Palestine's Arab neighbours and the Arab League, respectively. Jordan assumed responsibility for all Iraqi forces in Palestine.

10 Like all statistics on the Arab refugees, these can only be rough approximations, since many refugees are not registered, some

live in Iraq and Kuwait, and there is no systematic method for eliminating numbers of refugees who have died. There is also no indication here of the refugees' relative standard of living, which has been far higher in the Lebanon, for example, than in the Gaza Strip.

11 Following the 1948–49 war, Egypt contended that Israel had illegally occupied Eilat after their Armistice of 24 February. Israel replied that the southern Negev had not been contested by forces of Egypt and Israel. The movement of Israeli forces into Eilat was against nominal Jordanian opposition, and occurred the day before the Israel–Jordan truce.

12 Terence Prittie, *Israel* (London, 1967).

13 Egypt and Syria formed a Joint Military Command in October 1955. Jordan joined the command just before the 1956 war.

14 See Appendix I.

15 Since the involvement of the Great Powers in the Middle East has been exhaustively dealt with elsewhere, little is said about them in this paper. The reader is referred particularly to the ISS publication, *Sources of Conflict in the Middle East*, Adelphi Paper 26, March 1966.

16 The Israeli Government now argues, perhaps partly to allay Arab fears, that diversion of sweet water from the Jordan will not permit large areas of the Negev to be brought under cultivation, chiefly because of a fall in the water table elsewhere in Israel and an increase in industrial demands for water. The future of the Negev will depend upon new desalination techniques.

17 See Appendix 2.

[18] For most of the period since the Second World War, the United States has been the leading supplier of Egyptian imports, primarily in the form of foodstuffs sold for local currency. Relations between the United States and the UAR deteriorated during 1964, however, following the burning of the USIS library in Cairo; US aid was suspended. The two Governments managed to negotiate a $55-million aid agreement covering the first half of 1966, but this was not renewed, largely because of American concern over the Yemen war and Egyptian attacks on American policy in Vietnam.

[19] Although the UAR was immediately concerned in the confrontation, she elected to contribute funds rather than receive them under this scheme.

[20] Nasser accused Feisal of granting a military base to the British; this was perhaps a round about way of expressing his displeasure at the British agreement to supply Saudi Arabia with *Lightning* fighter aircraft.

[21] Throughout her long confrontation with her Arab neighbours, Israel has chosen to meet provocation with stronger response – as in the reprisal raids before the wars of 1956 and 1967. This is a policy that has often served to escalate conflict. Her strategic vulnerability has also led her, in three wars, to believe her choice to be between 'death by a thousand cuts' and major military action.

[22] The Armistice Demarcation Line between Israel and Syria was drawn between the Israeli Truce Line and the International Frontier, where the two were not the same. The area of Palestine between the Armistice Line and the Frontier was designated a demilitarized zone, of three sections, including areas on the eastern shores of Lake Tiberias and Lake Huleh that were on the Israeli side of the Armistice Line.

[23] UNTSO was the successor of the Truce Commission established by the Security Council in April 1948. The Chief of Staff of UNTSO was made chairman of the four Mixed Armistice Commissions.

[24] By October 1966, there were 66,085 complaints outstanding: 35,485 by Israel and 30,600 by Syria.

[25] The Es Samu attack illustrated the strategic advantage which Syria held over Jordan, *vis-à-vis* Israel. The nature of the terrain meant that Israel could mount reprisal attacks much more easily against Jordan than against Syria.

[26] Between 25 January and 28 March, 1967, the Israeli-Syrian Mixed Armistice Commission received 790 formal Israeli complaints.

II. THE CRISIS

[27] The date of Israel's Independence Day – 14–15 May 1948 – is reckoned by the Hebrew calendar; therefore by the Gregorian calendar it falls on a different date each year. In 1967 it again fell on 14–15 May.

[28] According to *Al-Ahram* on 12 May, the Egyptian Government had barred units of the Sixth Fleet from visiting Egyptian ports. The ostensible reason appeared to stem from an interview given in April by Israel's Premier Eshkol to the magazine *US News and World*

Report, in which he said: 'We ask the United States for arms and are told, "Don't spend your money. We are here. The Sixth Fleet is here"'.

29 'To your information, I gave my instructions to all UAR Armed Forces to be ready for action against Israel the moment it might carry out any aggressive action against any Arab country. Due to these instructions our troops are already concentrated in Sinai on our eastern borders. For the sake of complete secure [sic] of all UN troops which install OPs along our borders, I request that you issue your orders to withdraw all these troops immediately. I have given my instructions to our Commander of the eastern zone concerning this subject. Inform back the fulfillment of this request. Yours, Farik Awal (M. Fawzy), COS of UAR Armed Forces'.

30 On the afternoon of 17 May, U Thant handed two *aide-mémoires* to the UAR Permanent Representative. The first recapitulated the events of the previous twenty-four hours, and ended with a stern warning that UNEF 'cannot now be asked to stand aside in order to become a silent and helpless witness to an armed confrontation between the parties'. It either had to stay where it was, or depart entirely. U Thant added that the Chief of Staff of UNTSO had seen 'no recent indications of troop movements or concentrations along any of the lines which should give rise to undue concern'. The second *aide-mémoire* reviewed the 'Good Faith Agreement' of November 1956. See Appendix 1.

31 See Appendix 1.

32 *Ibid.*

33 The Yugoslav platoon at Sharm-el-Sheikh had withdrawn from the actual positions commanding the Straits of Tiran, at Ras Nasrani, on 19 May. The UAR probably could have imposed a blockade at any time from then on.

34 Unconfirmed reports from Israel after the war have indicated that David Ben-Gurion was considerably less willing to entertain military action than he had been eleven years earlier, as Prime Minister. He reportedly was concerned that Israel should have the support of at least one major Western power. Premier Eshkol, on the other hand, is reported to have been more inclined towards military action from the early stages of the crisis.

35 The previous evening the United States Government had also counselled the UAR to exercise restraint.

36 Mr Eshkol, in his reply on 1 June, stated that a settlement must be founded on 'the territorial independence and integrity of all States of the region; resistance to revanchism and attempts to change the situation by force; abstention from acts of hostility, including acts of sabotage carried out by infiltrators across the border and the imposition of a maritime blockade; and non-interference in the internal affairs of States'.

37 The rejection by President de Gaulle of Israel's bid for French support met with strong opposition in France, both within the ruling Gaullist party and without. There have been recurrent reports that armaments shipments, including a few aircraft, continued to flow to Israel, until the French Government formally declared an arms embargo on the first day of the war. After that, according to widespread reports in

Western capitals, some aid reached Israel through third countries.

38 The latter image was presented in two television interviews given by President Nasser to Messrs. Anthony Nutting and Christopher Mayhew, M.P., a few days before the war.

39 For a considerable segment of public opinion in Israel, this article was too accurate in analyzing Israel's position to permit further doubts that Nasser had calculated the consequences of closing the Straits of Tiran.

40 One division in the Gaza Strip was that of the Palestine Liberation Army, and cannot be accorded equal weight in the order of battle with the other Egyptian forces. This division was in position when the crisis began.

III. THE WAR

41 Israel time, which is an hour behind Cairo time.

42 Israel's *Sherman* tanks were relics of the 1940s, while the *Centurions* had long been obsolescent and the *Pattons* were cast-offs from the Bundeswehr. Their excellent performance in this war was unexpected, and was due almost entirely to the high maintenance and training standard of the Israeli Defence Forces.

43 These figures for armaments are those at present available to the Institute for Strategic Studies. A full presentation is given in Appendix 3. Their accuracy, particularly in relation to the Israeli forces, cannot be guaranteed. Israeli security is excellent, and the precise size of her armed forces remains one of her most closely guarded secrets.

44 The Israelis are reported to have held back no more than twelve operational aircraft for defensive operations over Israel.

45 The largest regular formation in the Israeli Army was the brigade. Larger formations were, like Army Corps in the British Army, created *ad hoc* of whatever combination was suitable to the task in hand. Thus General Tal's division contained a preponderance of armour; General Joffe's was entirely armoured; General Sharon's was a balanced force of infantry, armour, and parachute troops.

46 It was afterwards emphasized by General Hod that two-thirds of all sorties flown were 'taking part in the land battle', mostly in striking Egyptian armour and vehicles behind the battle zone. Israeli ground forces had been warned to expect little air co-operation in the earlier phases of operations. But aircraft which could not be used in the main air battle, such as the Fouga *Magister* trainers, were placed at General Gavish's disposal from the very beginning.

Appendixes

1. The United Nations Emergency Force

The United Nations Emergency Force (UNEF) was initially established by a series of three General Assembly Resolutions adopted between 4 and 7 November 1956. The first requested the Secretary-General to present 'a plan for the setting up, with the consent of the nations concerned, of an emergency international United Nations Force to secure and supervise the cessation of hostilities. In accordance with all the terms of the [cease-fire resolution, of 2 November]'.

Mr Hammarskjöld lost no time, and the following day the General Assembly accepted his recommendation to establish 'a United Nations Command for an emergency international Force', and authorized recruitment of officers. On 7 November the General Assembly accepted Hammarskjöld's final report and approved his plans. In addition it created an Advisory Committee of seven countries to assist the Secretary-General. He was required to consult this Committee on a number of matters, including regulations and instructions essential to the effective functioning of the Force. The Advisory Committee, in turn, had the right at any point to request a meeting of the General Assembly to consider any matter that in the Committee's opinion was of 'urgency and importance'. Nothing was said about the Security Council. Indeed, it had no standing with regard to the operation of UNEF other than its continuing mandate under the UN Charter to consider threats to the peace.

From the beginning, there were three interrelated questions to be answered. What were UNEF's functions? How long was it to remain in being? And what would happen if there were a disagreement between the United Nations and the host state over the answers to the first two questions?

Hammarskjöld's statement about the functions of UNEF (quoted in the text) seemed straightforward enough. But there was a difference of opinion from the first. The three occupying powers wished the Force to be a means of pressuring Egypt to reach some political settlements. The Arab States, on the other hand, conceived the role of the Force to be the limited one of overseeing the cease-fire and withdrawal of British, French, and Israeli troops. The latter view prevailed within the General Assembly at the time, partly because of the need to gain Egypt's consent to the Force, and partly because neither the United States nor the Soviet Union was inclined to support the former view. The Russians argued then and later that the Assembly had no power to create an international peace force, but did not vote against the resolutions establishing it after Egypt agreed to Hammarskjöld's plan.

However, the Secretary-General had given certain assurances to Britain and France on 7 November to secure their agreement to a cease-fire; in particular, he agreed that the peace force 'would be competent to secure the objectives' of the General Assembly's cease-fire resolution of 2 November. Later, these assurances and the resolutions establishing UNEF formed the basis of a widely held view that UNEF's role properly went beyond the temporary one of supervising the cease-fire and troop withdrawals; in part, the cease-fire resolution had urged the parties to the Armistice Agreements 'to desist from raids across the armistice lines into neighbouring territory, and to observe scrupulously the provisions of the armistice agreements'. Did this mean that UNEF would remain on Egyptian soil until these injunctions were observed?

This provision gained its importance from subsequent developments. Immediately after the UN troops arrived in Egypt on 15 November, Hammarskjöld flew to Cairo to achieve an understanding with President Nasser on the functioning of the

Emergency Force. They concluded an *aide-mémoire* that included what has come to be known as the 'Good Faith Agreement': they agreed that with regard to UNEF, both the UN and the Egyptian Government would be guided, in good faith, by the General Assembly resolutions establishing the Force, and the Force would be maintained 'until its task is completed'.

But what did the phrase 'until its task is completed' mean? Since there was a difference of opinion concerning the nature of the roles originally assigned to UNEF, there was bound to be controversy over the meaning of the Good Faith Agreement as well. In a statement released on 19 June 1967, U Thant specifically endorsed the narrower view, although on 17 May he had recalled this Agreement to the attention of the Egyptian Government. The UAR was certainly not prepared to accept any but the most narrow view.

Whatever the relative merits of the different arguments in this dispute, the matter did not rest there. On 2 February 1957, the General Assembly adopted a further resolution with regard to the Emergency Force, formally broadening its functions. The resolution provided that, 'after full withdrawal of Israel from the Sharm-el-Sheikh and Gaza areas, the scrupulous maintenance of the Armistice Agreement requires the placing of the United Nations Emergency Force on the Egyptian-Israel armistice demarcation line and the implementation of other measures as proposed in the Secretary-General's report [of 1 February 1957]'. The 'other measures' were deliberately left ambiguous; they were later stretched to embrace the establishment of UNEF posts at Sharm-el-Sheikh and Ras Nasrani, controlling the Straits of Tiran.

This resolution provided the most widely accepted basis for the stationing of UNEF on Egyptian territory; significantly, the resolution came after the Good Faith Agreement and, it has been argued, was not subject to it.

These considerations touch on a central problem that was evident from the beginning: what would happen if Egypt asked UNEF to leave. She clearly had the right to do so: the Force was in Egypt on sufferance, since enforcement action could only be taken by the Security Council under Chapter VII of the UN Charter. At the very least, such an Egyptian request would have to come to the Secretary-General, since the Force had been established in Egypt under an agreement between Mr Hammarskjöld and President Nasser. And the Secretary-General, in turn, would have to consult the Advisory Committee, which, if it chose to do so, could ask for a meeting of the General Assembly. But should more be done than this?

During the crisis of May 1967, U Thant was criticized for ignoring a memorandum written by Hammarskjöld in August 1957, concerning the conditions under which UNEF was to remain in Egypt, which indicated that, in case of disagreement between the Secretary-General and the Government of Egypt, 'the matter would at once be brought before the General Assembly'. But U Thant correctly stated that this so-called 'Hammarskjöld Memorandum' had no standing because it was not an official UN document and had never been conveyed to the Egyptian Government.

But U Thant overlooked a more substantial interpretation by Hammarskjöld of the procedure to be followed, which was contained in his 1958 Summary Study of experience derived from the establishment and operation of the Force (A/3943). Hammarskjöld had not challenged the 'sovereign right of the host government' but he did lay down firmly that, 'were either side to act unilaterally in refusing continued presence or deciding on withdrawal, and were the other side to find that such action was contrary to a good-faith interpretation of the purposes of the operation, an exchange of views would be called for towards harmonizing the positions' (Para. 158). This interpretation went unchallenged, and may fairly be considered to have met with the approval of the principals involved.

In any event, the problems that would arise if and when Egypt asked UNEF to leave had not been ignored over the years; the issue was widely discussed in the standard texts on United Nations peace-keeping operations, and had been a central concern of the Israeli Government when deciding to withdraw its forces from Sharm-el-Sheikh.

In conclusion, it should be noted that considerable thought had also been given to the problems that could arise if one or more of the countries contributing forces to UNEF decided to withdraw them, as did Yugoslavia and India in 1967. There had been some difference of opinion on this issue, although the agreements between the participating States and the United Nations indicated that 'adequate prior notification' must be given. Hammarskjöld himself had been aware of the political risks inherent in becoming too dependent upon any single State's contribution to the Force, and had adopted a policy of balancing the relative sizes of different contingents.

2. The Jordan Waters

The Upper Jordan River is formed by the confluence of three principal rivers: the Dan, which has its source in Israel; the Hasbani (Lebanon); and the Baniyas (Syria). The average annual flow of these three sources was estimated in 1953 to be 258 million cubic metres a year (mcm/year) for the Dan, and 157 mcm/year for each of the other two rivers. Thus the Upper Jordan is a plentiful source of sweet water until it reaches Lake Tiberias, where salt springs increase the salinity of the water to the point at which it must be mixed with fresh water to be suitable for irrigation. But below Lake Tiberias, the Lower Jordan is joined by another fresh water source, the Yarmuk River (475 mcm/year), flowing into Israel from the east, where it forms part of the Syria–Jordan border. The Lower Jordan flows south into the Hashemite Kingdom, finally reaching the Dead Sea.

The Jordan Valley Unified Water Plan of 1955, negotiated by Ambassador Eric Johnston, proposed to divide these waters among the riparian States according to the use they could effectively make of them, in the following manner:

Jordan: 100 mcm/year from the Jordan; 377 mcm/year from the Yarmuk; and 243 mcm/year from side wadis of the Jordan.

Lebanon: 35 mcm/year from the Hasbani.

Syria: 22 mcm/year from the Jordan; 90 mcm/year from the Yarmuk; and 20 mcm/year from the Baniyas.

Israel: The balance of the Jordan waters after the other riparian States had satisfied their needs. This amount has been variously calculated to be between 400 and 490 mcm/year (about one-third of the total), including 25 mcm/year specifically allocated from the Yarmuk.

Among the Arab countries, Syria has been using about 68 mcm/year of water from the Yarmuk River, and a small amount from the Baniyas, while the Lebanon has made some use of the Hasbani. But it is Jordan that has been most enterprising in the use of water, and since 1958 has been developing plans to use the Yarmuk, beginning with irrigation of the East Ghor region just east of the Jordan. Although this diversion scheme will raise the salinity of the Lower Jordan, it has not been a serious point at issue between Jordan and Israel, because the latter accepts that under the Johnston Plan the great bulk of the Yarmuk waters was intended for use by Jordan.

For the same reason, one would not expect Israel to be unduly concerned about a limited diversion of the Baniyas and Hasbani Rivers before they reach the Israel frontier. Indeed, much of the annual flow of these two rivers is in the form of flash floods, and it is open to question whether the flood waters could be effectively dammed without an engineering feat far beyond what the Arabs have contemplated. But the Arab diversion schemes of 1964 were undertaken with a view to thwarting the development of Israel, and this must seem to the Israeli Government to be a serious challenge, whether or not it is likely that the Arabs could do Israel significant damage.

The dispute has been further complicated by evidence that there is less water available than was believed in 1953, and by inefficient use of the total water resources of the Jordan Valley system because of separate national development. As a result, the withdrawal of the Johnston Plan quotas by all the riparians is no longer possible, a factor destined to increase anxiety on both sides of the dispute.

Until June 1967, development of the Arab diversion projects had progressed only sporadically, since the Baniyas River works were repeatedly shelled by the Israel Defence Forces. The Lebanon was particularly reluctant to proceed without credible assurances that Israeli military action could be met in kind by forces of the Unified Arab Command.

Having occupied the Syrian Heights during the recent war, Israel now holds the Baniyas River, and is in a position to hold hostage the Jordanian projects on the Yarmuk River.

3. Armed forces of the belligerents (4 June 1967) *
ISRAEL
Army
- Total strength: 275,000 (fully mobilized).
- 8 armoured brigades (3,500 men each).
- 22 infantry brigades (4,500 men each).
- 1 parachute brigade (4,000 men).
- 800 tanks, including 250 *Centurions*, 200 *Super Shermans*, 200 M48 *Pattons*, and 150 AMX-13s.
- 250 SP guns, including 155mm howitzers on *Sherman* chassis and 105 mm howitzers on AMX chassis.

- Anti-tank weapons included the 106mm recoilless rifle mounted on jeeps, and SS-10 and SS-11 missiles mounted on weapons carriers.
- Separate regional defence units in the border areas.

Navy
- Total strength: 3,000 (regulars).
- 2 destroyers.
- 1 anti-aircraft frigate.
- 4 submarines.
- 1 patrol vessel.
- 3 landing craft.
- 14 patrol craft of less than 100 tons.

Air Force
- Total strength: 8,000 men; about 280 combat aircraft (including armed trainers).
- 25 *Vautour* light bombers.
- 72 *Mirage* IIIC interceptor fighter-bombers.
- 20 *Super Mystère* interceptors.
- 45 *Mystère* IV fighter-bombers.
- 50 *Ouragan* fighter-bombers (obsolescent).
- 60 *Magister* trainers (can be armed).
- About 40 *Noratlas*, C-47, and *Stratocruiser* transports.
- 25 helicopters, including S-58 and *Alouettes*.
- Some light aircraft, including *Piper Cubs*.
- 2 battalions of *Hawk* surface-to-air missiles.

UNITED ARAB REPUBLIC
Army
- Total strength: 180,000 (including mobilized reservists).
- 2 armoured divisions (with 350 medium and heavy tanks each).

- 4 motorized rifle divisions (with about 150 medium tanks each).
- 1 parachute brigade.
- 12 artillery regiments.
- About 1,200 tanks and assault guns, including 350 T-34, 50 PT-76, 500 T-54 and T-55, 60 JS-3, and 150 Su-100.
- 100 surface-to-surface missiles with ranges of between 200 and 450 miles were believed not to be operational.
- Army reserves total a further 60,000. There was a para-military National Guard of about 60,000.
- Forces in the Yemen were probably less than 50,000.
- The Palestine Liberation Army (PLA) consisted of about 30,000 irregular troops trained by the Egyptians, a large proportion of whom (about 10,000) were stationed in the Gaza Strip.

Navy
- Total strength: 11,000.
- 8 destroyers (6 ex-Soviet *Skory* class, 2 ex-British 'Z' type).
- 11 submarines (ex-Soviet 'W' class).
- 6 escort vessels.
- 6 coastal escorts.
- 18 missile patrol boats (10 *Osa* class, 8 *Komar* class, both with *Styx* short-range cruise missiles).
- 10 minesweepers.
- About 50 small patrol vessels.

Air Force
- Total strength: 20,000 men; 500 combat aircraft.
- 30 Tu-16 medium jet bombers.
- 40 Il-28 light jet bombers.
- 120 MiG-21 C/D jet interceptors.
- 80 MiG-19 all-weather fighters or fighter-bombers.

- 200 MiG-15, MiG-17, and Su-7 fighter-bombers.
- About 60 transports, including Il-14 and An-12, and 60 helicopters, including 8 Mi-6 *Hook*.
- Training aircraft, some of which could be armed, made up another 120 aircraft.

Air Defence
- Was provided both by conventional anti-aircraft guns and by 150 SA-2 *Guideline* surface-to-air missiles deployed in 25 batteries of six launchers each. These missiles were supported by a recently installed radar network and by the six squadrons of MiG-21 interceptors.

JORDAN
Army
- Total strength: 55,000.
- 6 infantry brigades.
- 3 armoured brigades.
- 250 tanks, including 150 M48 *Pattons*. Also some *Centurion* tanks and 155mm howitzers.

Navy
- A few patrol craft in the Dead Sea and Gulf of Aqaba.

Air Force
- Total strength: 2,000.
- 21 *Hunter* Mk. 6 fighters and fighter-bombers.
- F-104s not operational.

SYRIA
Army
- Total strength: 50,000.
- 2 armoured brigades.

- 2 mechanized brigades.
- 5 infantry brigades.
- About 400 Soviet tanks, of which only 200 were operational
- Soviet artillery up to 155mm.
- 10 SA-2 *Guideline* sites.

Navy
- Total strength: 1,500.
- 6 coastal escorts.
- 2 minesweepers.
- 4 missile patrol boats (*Komar* class).

Air Force
- Total strength: 9,000 men; 120 combat aircraft.
- 6 Il-28 light bombers.
- 20 MiG-21 jet interceptors.
- 20 MiG-19 jet interceptors.
- 60 MiG-17 fighter-bombers.
- Transports, trainers, and helicopters.

IRAQ
Army
- Total strength: 70,000.
- 1 armoured division.
- 4 infantry divisions.
- About 600 tanks, of which 400 were operational: mostly T-54 and T-34 with some *Centurions*.

Navy
- Total strength: 2,000.
- Small number of MTBs and patrol vessels.

Air Force

- Total strength: 10,000 men; 200 combat aircraft.
- 10 Il-28 jet bombers.
- 60 MiG-21 interceptors.
- 50 *Hunter* Mk. 9 ground-attack.
- 30 MiG-17 and MiG-19 jet fighters.
- 20 T-52 jet *Provost* light-strike.
- 2 *Wessex* helicopter squadrons.
- About 40 Soviet and British medium transports.

Note

* The authors are indebted to Mr David Wood, of the ISS, for permission to quote these figures, which were released to the press on 6 and 7 June.

CHAPTER ELEVEN

The classical strategists

From Adelphi Paper 54, 1969

I

It may help to begin with a definition of 'classical' strategy. Liddell Hart has provided us with one which is as good as any, and better than most: 'The art of distributing and applying military means to fulfil the ends of policy'.[1] Whether this remains adequate in the nuclear age is a matter of some controversy. André Beaufre, for example, has adumbrated the concept of an 'indirect strategy', to be considered later, which embraces more than purely military means;[2] but even he still gives as his basic definition of the term 'the art of the dialectic of two opposing wills using force to resolve their dispute'.[3] It is this element of *force* which distinguishes 'strategy' from the purposeful planning in other branches of human activity to which the term is often loosely applied. When other elements such as economic pressure, propaganda, subversion and diplomacy are combined with force, these elements may also be considered as 'strategic'; but to apply this adjective to activities unconnected with the use, or threatened use, of force would be to broaden it to such an extent that it would be necessary to find another word to cover the original meaning of the term as defined by Liddell Hart, and as considered in this paper.

It need hardly be said that students of strategy have generally assumed that military force is a necessary element in international affairs. Before World War I, there were few who questioned even whether it was desirable. After 1918, many regretted its necessity and saw their function as being to ensure that it should be used as economically, and as rarely, as possible. After 1945, an even greater proportion devoted themselves to examine, not how wars should be fought, but how they could be prevented, and the study of strategy merged into that of arms control, disarmament and peace-keeping. There the 'classical strategists' found themselves working with scholars of a different kind; men who believed that the element of force was *not* a necessary part of international intercourse, but could be eliminated by an application of the methodology of the social sciences. The work of that group is considered by Dr Kenneth Boulding (see pp. 33–40). This paper will, therefore, concern itself solely with the thinkers who assume that the element of force exists in international relations, that it can and must be intelligently controlled, but that it cannot be totally eliminated. Further, it is confined to the men who have primarily used the methodology of history or traditional political science; though it includes such figures as Schelling and Morgenstern, who have made considerable contributions in the newer disciplines as well.

The art* of strategy remains one of such complexity that even the greatest contributors to its study have been able to do little more than outline broad principles; principles which nevertheless must often be discarded in practice if the circum-

---

* The term seems appropriate. Strategy deals with too many imponderables to merit the description 'science'. It remains, as Voltaire described it two hundred years ago, 'murderous and conjectural'.

stances are inappropriate, and which must never be allowed to harden into dogma. Even when these principles appear self-evident, it may be extraordinarily hard to apply them. In World War II 'command of the sea' as advocated by Mahan and 'command of the air' as advocated by Douhet were certainly necessary preliminaries to the military victory of the Western powers. The problem was how to obtain them with resources on which equally urgent calls were being made for other purposes. The academic strategist could not help the Chiefs of Staff much, for example, in deciding how to allot a limited number of long-range aircraft between the conflicting needs of the strategic offensive against Germany, the war against German submarines, interdiction bombing of German railways, the requirements of the Pacific theatre and support for guerrilla activities in occupied Europe. Operational research and systems-analysis could simplify the problem without ever eliminating it. In the last resort the quality termed by Blackett 'the conventional military wisdom'[4] remained the basic factor in making the decision; and that decision was determined by what could be done rather than by what ideally should. The military commander is always primarily conscious of the constraints under which he operates, in terms both of information and of resources. He is, therefore, likely to be impatient with the advice of the academic strategist which may appear to him either platitudinous or impracticable. His decisions must be based at best on educated guesses.

But the academic strategist does have one vital role to play. He can see that the guesses *are* educated. He may not accompany the commander to battle, as Clausewitz expressed it, but he forms his mind in the schoolroom, whether the commander realizes it or not. In World War II the Allied High Command did operate in accordance with certain very definite strategic principles. It is tempting to link these principles with the names of specific theorists: General Marshall's desire for concentration against the enemy army with Clausewitz, General Brooke's desire to enforce dispersal on the enemy with Liddell Hart, the doctrine of the Allied air forces with Douhet: tempting, but difficult to prove. The name of Douhet was virtually unknown in the Royal Air Force.[5] The most eminent thinkers sometimes do no more than codify and clarify conclusions which arise so naturally from the circumstances of the time that they occur simultaneously to those obscurer, but more influential figures who write training manuals and teach in service colleges. And sometimes strategic doctrines may be widely held which cannot be attributed to any specific thinkers, but represent simply the consensus of opinion among a large number of professionals who had undergone a formative common experience.

Of this kind were the doctrines which were generally held in the armed forces of the Western world in the mid-1940s as a result of the experiences of World War II. It was considered, first, that the mobilization of superior resources, together with the maintenance of civilian *morale* at home, was a necessary condition for victory; a condition requiring a substantial domestic 'mobilization base' in terms of industrial potential and trained manpower. It was agreed that, in order to deploy these resources effectively, it was necessary to secure command of the sea and command of the air. It was agreed that surface and air operations were totally interdependent. And it was agreed that strategic air power could do much – though *how* much remained a matter of controversy – to weaken the capacity of the adversary to resist. The general concept of war remained as it had been since the days of Napoleon: the contest of armed forces to obtain a position of such superiority that the victorious power would be in a position to impose its political will. And it was generally assumed that in the future, as in the immediate past, this would still be a very long-drawn-out process indeed.

II

The advent of nuclear weapons, to the eyes of the layman, transformed the entire nature of war. But certain eminent professionals suggested that they made remarkably little difference, at least in a conflict between two powers of the size of the United States and the Soviet Union. These weapons obviously would make it possible to inflict with far greater rapidity the kind of damage by which the strategic bombing offensive had crippled Germany and Japan. But the stockpiles of bombs were small – how small is still not known. The bombs were vulnerable to interception; and they had to operate from bases which had to be protected by land armies which would have in their turn to be supplied by sea. All this was pointed out to the general public by, among others, two scientists with long experience in military planning – the British Professor P. M. S. Blackett and the American Dr Vannevar Bush. Blackett, on the basis of careful calculations from unclassified material, concluded in 1948 that 'a long-range atomic bombing offensive against a large continental Power is not likely to be by itself decisive within the next five years'.[6] Bush, a figure closely associated with the American military establishment, described in 1949 a conflict barely distinguishable from the last.

> The opening phases would be in the air soon followed by sea and land action. Great fleets of bombers would be in action at once, but this would be the opening phase only ... They could undoubtedly devastate the cities and the war potential of the enemy and its satellites, but it is highly doubtful if they could at once stop the march of great land armies. To overcome them would require a great national effort, and the marshalling of all our strength. The effort to keep the seas open would be particularly hazardous, because of modern

submarines, and severe efforts would be needed to stop them at the source. Such a war would be a contest of the old form, with variations and new techniques of one sort or another. But, except for greater use of the atomic bomb, it would not differ much from the last struggle.[7]

It was along these lines that planning went forward when the framework of the North Atlantic Treaty Organization was established at the end of the 1940s. Such ideas were legitimate deductions from the then 'state of the art'. NATO planners had to think what could be done with the weapons they had available, not with those which might or might not be developed in ten years' time. But many scientists and academic strategists, particularly in the United States, were already thinking ahead. Because their views appeared to have no immediate relevance, or because of the pressures of inter-service politics, they had little immediate influence on Western policy; and they were usually set out in papers or articles which enjoyed only a limited circulation within the academic world.[8] An adequate account of these seminal discussions would require a separate paper. We can, however, salvage and admire the shrewd insights shown by two thinkers who had already established their reputation in the pre-nuclear era: Bernard Brodie and Sir Basil Liddell Hart. Both of them, in works published in 1946, made prophecies which twenty years later were to be commonplaces of strategic thinking.

In the final chapter of *The Revolution in Warfare*,[9] Liddell Hart suggested that, failing disarmament, attempts should be made 'to revive a code of limiting rules for warfare – based on a realistic view that wars are likely to occur again, and that the limitation of their destructiveness is to everybody's interest'. 'Fear of atomic war', he wrote, 'might lead to indirect methods of aggression, infiltration taking civil forms as well as military, to which nuclear retaliation would be irrelevant. Armed forces would still be required to fight "sub-atomic war", but the emphasis should be on their mobility, both tactical and strategic.'

The great armies of the past would be irrelevant to the needs of the nuclear age. Liddell Hart did not, at this stage, consider the problems and contradictions of limited war, including the possibility which emerged fifteen years later, that it might be necessary to have large conventional forces precisely in order to keep war limited.

Neither did he explore the implications and requirements of deterrence. Brodie, however, with his collaborators in the Yale Institute of International Studies' publication *The Absolute Weapon*, did exactly this, and with remarkable prescience. Much that he wrote was to become unquestionably valid only with the development of thermonuclear weapons, but his insights were none the less remarkable for that. He rejected, for example, the whole concept of a 'mobilization base'. 'The idea', he wrote, 'which must be driven home above all else is that a military establishment which is expected to fight on after the nation has undergone atomic bomb attack must be prepared to fight with the men already mobilized and with the equipment already in the arsenals.'[10] More important, he outlined the concept of a stable balance of nuclear forces.

> If the atomic bomb can be used without fear of substantial retaliation in kind, it will clearly encourage aggression. So much the more reason, therefore, to take all possible steps to assure that multilateral possession of the bomb, should that prove inevitable, be attended by arrangements to make as nearly certain as possible that the aggressor who uses the bomb will have it used against him ...

Thus, the first and most vital step in any American programme for the age of atomic bombs is to take measures to guarantee to ourselves in case of attack the possibility of retaliation in kind. The writer in making that statement is not for the moment concerned about who will *win* the next war in which atomic bombs are used. Thus far the chief purpose of our military establishment has been to win wars. From now on its chief purpose must be to avert them. It can have almost no other useful purpose.[11]

Not until thermonuclear weapons had been developed and the Soviet Union had shown itself to possess an inter-continental delivery system did the US Joint Chiefs of Staff accept Brodie's logic; though it is significant that shortly after the publication of this work Brodie joined the newly formed RAND Corporation, where with the support of the US Air Force the full implications and requirements of his ideas, and others current in the United States academic community, were to be exhaustively studied. The first western government to adopt the concept of 'deterrence' as the basis of its military policy was that of the United Kingdom in 1952; very largely thanks to the thinking of Marshal of the Royal Air Force, Sir John Slessor, the then Chairman of the Chiefs of Staff.[12]

Giving a late account of his stewardship at Chatham House in 1953, Slessor was to say:

The aim of Western policy is not primarily to be ready to win a war with the world in ruins – though we must be as ready as possible to do that if it is forced upon us by accident or miscalculation. It is the prevention of war. The bomber holds out to us the greatest, perhaps the only hope of that. It is the great deterrent.[13]

This doctrine of 'the great deterrent' was to unleash within the United Kingdom a debate which foreshadowed that set off in the United States by the comparable 'New Look' strategy which Mr Dulles was formally to unveil there in January 1954. Among its earliest and ablest critics were the men who, four years later, were to be primarily responsible for the foundation of the Institute for Strategic Studies: Rear-Admiral Sir Anthony Buzzard, Mr Richard Goold-Adams, Mr Denis Healey, and Professor P. M. S. Blackett. In its public presentation by Ministers and senior officers, the doctrine of 'massive retaliation' provided its critics in England with an even easier target than it did in the United States. No official distinction was made between the use of Bomber Command as a first-strike force in response to a Soviet 'conventional' invasion of Western Europe and as a second-strike force to retaliate after a Soviet nuclear attack. In face of the growing strength of Soviet nuclear-strike forces, the first role appeared to lack political, the second technical, credibility. Liddell Hart had already pointed out in 1950 that defence against nuclear weapons would be credible only if accompanied by massive civil-defence measures of a kind which no government showed any sign of being prepared to carry out.[14] Britain's military leaders indeed at first assumed that the civilian population might be induced to grin and bear the nuclear holocaust as cheerfully as they had endured the German blitz. The inhabitants of areas which contained no protected installations, suggested Slessor, 'must steel themselves to risks and take what may come to them, knowing that thereby they are playing as essential a part in the country's defence as the pilot in the fighter or the man behind the gun'.[15] This attitude presumably remained the basis of British official thinking until the acquisition of the *Polaris* missile system gave the United Kingdom a second-strike weapon which was technically if not politically credible. The validity of this thesis however gave rise to widespread doubts, and not only among the members of the Campaign for Nuclear Disarmament. In a famous lecture to the Royal United Service Institution in November 1959, after Mr Duncan Sandys had, in two Defence White Papers, laid yet greater stress on the importance of 'the deterrent', Lieutenant-General Sir John Cowley was to ask a question unusual for a senior serving officer:

> The choice of death or dishonour is one which has always faced the professional fighting man, and there must be no doubt in his mind what his answer must be. He chooses death for himself so that his country may survive, or on a grander scale so that the principles for which he is fighting may survive. Now we are facing a somewhat different situation, when the reply is not to be given by individuals but by countries as a whole. Is it right for the Government of a country to choose complete destruction of the population rather than some other alternative, however unpleasant that alternative may be?[16]

As a coherent theory of strategy in the traditional sense, the doctrine of deterrence by the threat of massive retaliation, in the simple form in which it was set out by the British and American governments in the early 1950s, is not easy to defend, and its exponents tended at times to use the vocabulary of exhortation rather than that of rational argument in their attempts to justify it. But three points should be noted if we are to appreciate their standpoint. First, the British Chiefs of Staff from the beginning saw Bomber Command as a supplement to rather than a substitute for the United States Strategic Air Command, with the task of striking at targets of particular significance for the United Kingdom. Its strategic utility and its credibility as a deterrent were thus to be judged within the context of the Western deterrent force as a whole.[17]

Second, it was an attempt, like the American 'New Look' two years later, to solve the problem – and one far more difficult for the United Kingdom than for the United States – of maintaining an effective military force in a peace-time economy. The burden of rearmament assumed in 1950 had proved not only economically crippling but politically unacceptable; and since the political objective of the United Kingdom was the maintenance, *virgo intacta*, of the *status quo* in Europe, a policy which imposed the maximum penalty for *any* violation of that *status quo* was not so irrational as it appeared. For the United Kingdom not one inch of Western Europe could be considered negotiable.

Third, as British officials repeatedly said later in the decade, 'The Great Deterrent' existed not to fight but to deter war: 'If it is used, it will have failed.' This argument was open to the rejoinder that a strategy which was not militarily viable was not politically credible, but this rejoinder is by no means conclusive. The concept of 'deterrence' takes us out of the familiar field of military strategy into the unmapped if not unfamiliar territory of political bargaining, where total rationality does not invariably reign supreme. Schelling and others were only then beginning their studies of 'the strategy of conflict'; but even without the help of game-theory techniques, it could be reasonably argued that, even if there was only one chance in a hundred that a political move would really be met by the threatened nuclear response, that chance would be an effective deterrent to any responsible statesman.** 'The most that the advocates of the deterrent policy have ever claimed for it', said Slessor in 1955, 'is that it will deter a potential aggressor from undertaking total war as an instrument of policy, as Hitler

** This of course begs the whole question so carefully examined by Stephen Maxwell in Adelphi Paper 50: *Rationality in Deterrence* (London: ISS).

did in 1939, or from embarking upon a course of international action which obviously involves a serious risk of total war, as the Austrian Government did in 1914.'[18]

Certainly the British advocates of the 'deterrent policy' in the 1950s did not underrate the continuing importance of conflicts which would *not* be deterred by nuclear weapons. Liddell Hart repeatedly pointed out that nuclear stalemate would encourage local and indirect aggression which could be countered only by conventional forces; a lesson which British armed forces tied down in operations from Cyprus to Malaya had no need to learn. Faced with the double burden of deterring total war and fighting small ones, it was natural enough for British strategists to adopt the doctrine later termed 'minimal deterrence'. This was stated with uncompromising clarity by Blackett in 1956:

> I think we should act as if atomic and hydrogen bombs have abolished total war and concentrate our efforts on working out how few atomic bombs and their carriers are required to keep it abolished. In the next few years I see the problem not as how many atomic bombs we can afford but as how few we need. For every hundred million pounds spent on offensive and defensive preparations for global war, which almost certainly will not happen, is so much less for limited and colonial wars, which well may.[19]

British strategic thinkers in fact – even Slessor after his retirement – tended to take the existence of stable deterrence very much for granted. In view of the highly classified nature of all information relating to Bomber Command and the absence of any serious intercourse at that time between Ministry of Defence officials and freelance strategic thinkers, this was not altogether surprising. It enabled them to concentrate, not only on problems of limited wars (Liddell Hart) but on graduated deterrence and restraints on war (Buzzard) and, in the atmosphere of *détente* which followed the Geneva Summit Meeting of 1955, on 'disengagement', disarmament and arms control (Blackett and Healey). When a few years later American thinkers questioned the validity of the doctrine of 'minimal deterrence' they evoked from Blackett a forceful rejoinder,[20] in which he expressed the fear that to depart from such a policy would only lead to an endless and increasing arms race. But by the end of the 1950s it was becoming clear that any doctrine of deterrence depended for its validity on technical calculations which stretched far beyond the orthodox boundaries of strategic thinking; and on which it was difficult for thinkers who did not enjoy access to the facilities available in the United States to pronounce with any degree of authority.

III

Within the United States the controversy was now well under way. It had been got off to an excellent start by Mr John Foster Dulles, whose definition of the doctrine of 'massive retaliation' in January 1954 had been far more precise and dogmatic than the statements emanating from Whitehall to the same effect during the past two years. This, it will be remembered, announced the intention of the United States Administration to place its military dependence 'primarily upon a great capacity to retaliate, instantly, by means and at places of our own choosing', thereby gaining 'more basic security at less cost'.[21] The rationale behind this policy was of course political and economic: American weariness with the Korean War, and the desire of the Republican Party to return to financial 'normalcy' after what they regarded as the ruinous spending spree of the last four years.[22] It should perhaps be judged, not as a coherent strategic doctrine, but as a political expedient – or even as a diplomatic communication, itself a manoeuvre in a politico-military strategy of 'deterrence'. By these criteria the policy must be pronounced not ineffective. But its logical fallacies were too glaring to be overlooked. The assumption of American invulnerability to a pre-emptive or a retaliatory strike was unconvincing in the year in which the Soviet Union first unveiled her inter-continental bombers. Even when that assumption had been justifiable four years earlier, American nuclear monopoly had not deterred the Korean conflict; and in that very year American nuclear power was to prove irrelevant to the conflict in Indo-China. These, and other points, were rapidly made with force and relish by Democrat politicians and sympathizers out of office, by academic specialists, and by members of the armed services which were being cut back to provide greater resources for the Strategic Air Command.

There has perhaps never been a strategic controversy which has not been fuelled by political passions and service interests. It is entirely understandable, and for our purposes quite unimportant, that the US Air Force should have sought every argument to justify the doctrine of massive retaliation while the US Army powerfully supported its opponents. What is significant, however, is that the latter included every strategic thinker of any consequence in the United States; and the failure of the present writer to find any serious academic defence of the doctrine may not be entirely due to unfamiliarity with the literature. Among the first critics was that pioneer of deterrence theory, Bernard Brodie, who published in November 1954 one of the earliest analyses of the place of 'limited war' in national policy;[23] but the first really formidable public broadside was fired by a group of scholars at the Princeton Center of International Studies under the leadership of William W. Kaufmann, in a collection of essays published in 1956 under the innocuous-sounding title *Military Policy and National Security*. In this work Kaufmann himself stressed the need for the United States to have the capacity to meet, and therefore deter, Communist aggression at every level;[24] that 'spectrum of deterrence', in fact, which Mr Robert McNamara was to develop, not without some assistance from Dr Kaufmann himself, when he became Secretary for Defense four years later. In the same work Dr Roger Hilsman discussed the actual conduct of nuclear war; both making the distinction between counter-force and counter-value targets in total war, and considering the tactics of war with nuclear weapons fought on the ground;[25] and Professor Klaus Knorr gave one of the earliest published estimates of the kind of civil defence policy which might be feasible and necessary if the United States were really to employ the kind of nuclear strategy implied in Mr Dulles's statement.[26] Finally Mr Kaufmann emphasized the necessity for ensuring that military force should be tailored to the actual requirements of foreign policy: a point which was to be expanded more fully in two important books published the following year.

These were Dr Robert Osgood's study of *Limited War* and Dr Henry Kissinger's *Nuclear Weapons and Foreign Policy*.[27] Neither author had any significant experience of military operations or operational research. Their intellectual training was in the disciplines of history and political science; but with the shift of strategic thinking from the problem of waging war to that of its prevention, this background was at least as relevant as any more directly concerned with military affairs. Both analysed the traditional rigidity of the American attitude towards war and peace, contrasting it with the flexibility of Communist theory and, as they saw it, practice. Both emphasized the irrelevance of strategic nuclear weapons to the conduct of foreign policy in peripheral areas. Both stressed, as had Kaufmann, the need to provide the appropriate forces for the fighting of limited wars;

and both considered that tactical nuclear weapons should be regarded as appropriate for this purpose – a view shared by Mr Dulles himself,[28] and by the Joint Chiefs of Staff under the Chairmanship of Admiral Radford.

Osgood based his belief in the need to use nuclear weapons in limited wars largely on the difficulty of preparing troops to fight with both nuclear and conventional weapons.[29] Kissinger, whose study developed out of panel discussions at the Council on Foreign Relations in which a number of professional soldiers took part, went into the question more deeply, discussing both the possible *modus operandi* of tactical nuclear forces and the kind of limitations which might be agreed between two bellig-erents anxious not to allow their military confrontation to get out of hand.[30] In doing so he aligned himself with the views of Rear-Admiral Sir Anthony Buzzard, who was energetically canvassing before British audiences both the value of tactical nuclear weapons in making possible graduated deterrence at acceptable cost, and the feasibility of negotiating agreed limita-tions on the conduct of war.[31] But Buzzard's views were hotly contested in England. Slessor gave them general support, but Liddell Hart was highly sceptical (believing the capabilities of conventional forces to be unnecessarily underrated) and Blackett, after some hesitation, came out flatly against them.[32] In the United States the same controversy blew up. Brodie, writing in 1959, was prepared to admit only that there might be *some* circumstances in which tactical nuclear weapons might be appropriate, but considered that 'The conclusion that nuclear weapons *must* be used in limited wars has been reached by too many people, too quickly, on the basis of too little analysis of the problem'. Schelling the following year suggested that the break between conventional and nuclear weapons was one of the rare 'natural' distinctions which made tacit bargaining possible in limiting war.[33] By this time Kissinger himself had

had second thoughts, and agreed that, though tactical nuclear weapons were a necessary element in the spectrum of deterrence, they could not take the place of conventional forces.[34] Within a year Mr McNamara was to take the debate into the council chambers of NATO, where the advocates of tactical nuclear weapons had already found staunch allies among officials grimly conscious of the unpopularity and expense of large conventional forces. Throughout the 1960s the debate was to continue, in three major languages, about the place of tactical nuclear weapons in the defence of Europe.[35] Only the sheer exhaustion of the participants keeps it from continuing still.

It will be seen that the major American contributions to strategic thinking published in 1956–67 were distinguished by two main characteristics. They attempted to reintegrate military power with foreign policy, stressing, in contradiction to the doctrine of massive retaliation, the need for 'a strategy of options'. And they tended to be the work of academic institutions; Kaufmann's group at Princeton, Osgood from Chicago, Kissinger working with the Council on Foreign Relations. Their authors were thus concerned less with the technicalities of defence (Hilsman at Princeton, a former West Pointer, was an interesting exception) than with its political objectives. Over what those objectives should be, they had no quarrel with John Foster Dulles. Although British thinkers, like British statesmen, had been exploring possibilities of *détente* ever since 1954, in the United States the cold war was still blowing at full blast. The Soviet Union was still, in the works of these scholars, considered to be implacably aggressive, pursuing its objective of conquest in every quarter of the globe, its machinations visible behind every disturbance which threatened world stability. As Gordon Dean put it in his introduction to Kissinger's book, 'Abhorrent of war but unwilling to accept gradual Russian enslavement of other peoples around the world, which we know will eventually lead to our own enslavement, we are forced to adopt a posture that, despite Russian military capabilities and despite their long-range intentions, freedom shall be preserved to us'.[36] The strategy of options which they urged had as its object, not the reduction of tensions, but the provision of additional and appropriate weapons to deal with a subtle adversary who might otherwise get under the American guard.

IV

Two years later, in 1959–60, the major works on strategy in the United States showed a slight but perceptible change of emphasis. As it happened, the most significant of these were the work, not of full-time academics in universities, but of men drawn from a wide variety of disciplines – physicists, engineers, mathematicians, economists and systems analysts – who had been working in defence research institutes on classified information, particularly at RAND Corporation. As a result they analysed the technical problems of deterrence with an expertise which earlier works had naturally lacked. These problems appeared all the more urgent to the general public after the launching of the Sputnik satellite in 1957; which revealed the full extent of the challenge which the United States had to meet from Soviet technology. For the first time in its history the United States felt itself in danger of physical attack, and the question of civil defence, which had for some time agitated academic specialists, became one of public concern. Yet at the same time there was beginning to emerge in some quarters a new attitude to the Soviet Union. This saw in that power not simply a threat to be countered, but a partner whose collaboration was essential if nuclear war through accident or miscalculation was to be avoided. It recognized that Soviet policy and intentions might have certain elements in common with those of the United States, and that its leaders faced comparable problems. This attitude was by no means general. For scholars such as Robert Strausz-Hupé and William Kintner the conflict still resembled that between the Archangel Michael and Lucifer rather than that between Tweedledum and Tweedledee. But the concept, not only of a common interest between antagonists but of a joint responsibility for the avoidance of nuclear holocaust became increasingly evident after the new Administration came into power in 1961.[37]

The view which commanded growing support among American strategic thinkers was, therefore, that the 'balance of terror' was a great deal less stable than had hitherto been assumed, but that if it could be stabilized (which involved a certain reciprocity from the Soviet Union) there would be reasonable prospects of lasting peace. The technical instability of the balance was described by Albert Wohlstetter in the famous article which appeared in *Foreign Affairs* at the beginning of 1958, describing on the basis of his classified studies at RAND Corporation, the full requirements of an invulnerable retaliatory force: a stable 'steady-state' peace-time operation within feasible budgets, the capacity to survive enemy attacks, to make and communicate the decision to retaliate, to reach enemy territory, penetrate all defences and destroy the target; each phase demanding technical preparations of very considerable complexity and expense.[38]

The following year the mathematician Oskar Morgenstern was to suggest, in *The Question of National Defense*, that the best answer to the problem as defined by Wohlstetter, and the best safeguard against accidental war, was to be found in the development of seaborne missiles; and that it would be in the best interests of the United States if such a system could be developed by both sides. 'In view of modern technology of speedy weapons-delivery from any point on earth to any other,' he wrote, 'it is in the interest of the United States for Russia to have an invulnerable retaliatory force and vice versa.'[39] Whether Morgenstern reached this conclusion entirely through applying the game-theory in which he had made so outstanding a reputation is not entirely clear. Professor Thomas Schelling, who also brought the discipline of game-theory to bear on strategy, reached the same conclusion at approximately the same time;[40] but even by cruder calculations its validity seemed evident, and the concept of a 'stable balance' was central to Bernard Brodie's *Strategy in the Missile Age*, which also appeared in 1959.[41] This study pulled together all the threads of strategic thinking of the past five years and set them in their historical context. Brodie reduced the requirements of strategy in the missile age to three: an invulnerable retaliatory force; 'a real and substantial capability for coping with local and limited aggression by local application of force'; and provision for saving life 'on a vast scale' if the worst came to the worst.[42] About how, if the worst did come to the worst, nuclear war should be conducted, he did not attempt to offer any guidance beyond suggesting that the most important problem to study was not so much how to conduct the war, but how to stop it.

Not all of Brodie's colleagues at the RAND Corporation were so modest. The following year, 1960, saw the publication of Herman Kahn's huge and baroque study *On Thermonuclear War*;[43] the first published attempt by any thinker with access to classified material to discuss the action which should be taken if deterrence *did* fail. The horrible nature of the subject, the broad brush-strokes with which the author treated it, his somewhat selective approach to scientific data and the grim jocularity of the style, all combined to ensure for this study a reception which ranged from the cool to the hysterically vitriolic. Many of the criticisms, however, appear to arise rather from a sense of moral outrage that the subject should be exam-

ined at all than from serious disagreement with Kahn's actual
views. In fact Kahn basically made only two new contributions to the strategic debate. The first, based on the classified
RAND *Study of Non-Military Defense* for which he had been
largely responsible, was that a substantial proportion of the
American population could survive a nuclear strike, and that
this proportion might be considerably increased if the necessary preparations were made. The second was that the United
States should equip itself with the capacity to choose among a
range of options in nuclear as well as in non-nuclear war; that
rather than relying on a single spasm reaction (von Schlieffen's
Schlacht ohne Morgen brought up to date) the United States
should be able to conduct a controlled nuclear strategy, suiting
its targets to its political intentions – which would normally
be, not to destroy the enemy, but to 'coerce' him.[44] Kahn in fact
reintroduced the concept of an operational strategy which had
been almost entirely missing, at least from public discussion,
since the thermonuclear age had dawned ten years earlier. For
smaller nuclear powers any such notion, as applied to a conflict
with the Soviet Union, was self-evidently absurd. Between the
super-powers it was – and remains – a perfectly legitimate
matter for analysis. Kahn may have exaggerated the capacity of the social and political structure of the United States to
survive a nuclear holocaust; certainly many of his comments
and calculations were oversimplified to the point of naïveté.
But it is hard to quarrel with his assumption that that capacity,
whatever its true dimensions, could be increased by appropriate preliminary measures; while the position adopted by some
of his critics, that even to contemplate the possibility of deterrence failing might increase the possibility of such failure, is
hardly one that stands up to dispassionate analysis.

At the beginning of 1961 President Kennedy's new
Administration took office and Mr Robert McNamara became

Secretary of Defense. Not entirely coincidentally, the great period of American intellectual strategic speculation came to an end, after five astonishingly fruitful years. The military intellectuals were either drawn, like Kaufmann and Hilsman, into government, or returned to more orthodox studies on university campuses. Most of them continued to write. Kahn has produced two further works refining some of the views expounded in *On Thermonuclear War*.[45] Kissinger has remained a sage observer of and a prolific commentator on the political scene, and is at the moment of writing President Nixon's adviser on international security affairs. Osgood, Wohlstetter and Brodie have all produced notable work of synthesis or criticism. Perhaps the most interesting work has been that of Knorr and Schelling, who have broadened their studies to embrace the whole question of the role of military power in international relations;[46] a remarkably little-explored field in which a great deal of work remains to be done. It would be absurdly premature to suggest of any of these scholars – many of them still comparatively young men – have no more substantial contributions to make to strategic studies; but they are unlikely to surpass the intellectual achievement for which they were individually and jointly responsible in the 1950s. Between them they have done what Clausewitz and Mahan did in the last century, during times of no less bewildering political and technological change: laid down clear principles to guide the men who have to take decisions. Like Clausewitz and Mahan they are children of their time, and their views are formed by historical and technological conditions whose transformation may well render them out of date. Like those of Clausewitz and Mahan, their principles are likely to be misunderstood, abused, or applied incorrectly, and must be subjected by each generation to searching examination and criticism. Debate will certainly continue; but at least we now have certain solid issues to debate about.

The principles established by the thinkers of the 1950s were to guide Mr McNamara in his work of remoulding American defence policy during the eight years of his period of office in the Department of Defense. 'The McNamara Strategy' had a logical coherence – almost an elegance – which may have commanded rather more admiration among academics than it did in the world of affairs.[47] An invulnerable second-strike force was built up on a considerably larger scale than that considered adequate by the believers in 'minimal deterrence'. These forces were endowed with the capability, even after a surprise attack, of retaliating selectively against enemy forces rather than against his civilian population, so that 'a possible opponent' would have 'the strongest imaginable incentive to refrain from striking our own cities'.[48] Forces for 'limited wars' at all levels were created, armed both with nuclear and with conventional weapons. This involved an increase in expenditure, but it was an increase which was not grudged by Congressmen alarmed by an alleged 'missile gap' and happy to see fat defence contracts being placed within their home states; and the techniques of systems analysis which had also been developed at RAND Corporation were employed to keep this increase within bounds.[49] Overtures were made, official and unofficial, to the Soviet Union to establish arms-control agreements based on the principle of a stable balance resting on invulnerable second-strike forces on either side. And plans were put in hand for civil defence projects on a massive scale.

McNamara was able to carry out much of his programme, but not all. The Russians were remarkably slow to absorb the reasoning which appeared so self-evident to American academics. The American public was even slower to co-operate in the sweeping measures necessary to provide effective insurance against holocaust. The ideal of a second-strike counter-force strategy seemed to many critics to be one almost intrinsically impossible of realization. And America's European allies flatly refused McNamara's requests that they should increase their conventional forces to provide the necessary 'spectrum of deterrence'. The Germans saw this as a diminution of the deterrent to any invasion of their own narrow land, and besides had their own not particularly enjoyable memories of 'conventional war'. The British, struggling to maintain a world presence on their obstinately stagnant economy, could not afford it; while the French had ideas of their own. None of them, perhaps, could produce a coherent theoretical framework to sustain them in their arguments, but they remained unconvinced. Several of Mr McNamara's emissaries received, in consequence, a somewhat gruelling introduction to the refractory world of international affairs.

For the American strategic programme was based on two assumptions which were not accepted by all the major allies of the United States; first, that America was the leader of 'the Free World' and had both the right and the power to shape its strategy; and second, it was in the interests of the world as a whole that the United States and the Soviet Union should enter into an ever closer dialogue. Neither of these assumptions was challenged by the British; though not all their countrymen admired the assiduity with which successive British Prime Ministers set themselves up as 'honest brokers' between the super-powers the moment they set foot inside Downing Street. Indeed the most substantial British contribution to the strategic debate in the early 1960s, John Strachey's *On the Prevention of War*, quite explicitly advocated a Russo-American diarchy as the best guarantee of world peace.[50] But on the Continent reactions were different. The Chancellor of the Federal German Republic took a glum view of a Russo-American *détente* which could only, in his view, confirm the division of his country and might even threaten the position of Berlin; and long before Mr McNamara had appeared on the scene the President of the French Fifth

Republic had made clear his own attitude to the American claim to act as leader and the spokesman of 'The Free World'.

V

Too much should not be made of the personality of General de Gaulle in shaping the French contribution to the strategic debate which began to gain in importance towards the end of the 1950s. French military experience during the past twenty years had been distinctive and disagreeable. They had their own views on the reliability of overseas allies as protectors against powerful continental neighbours – neighbours who might in future comprise not only Russia but a revived Germany or, in moments of sheer nightmare, both. The decision to develop their own nuclear weapons had been taken before De Gaulle came into power, though perhaps it took De Gaulle to ensure that they would not be integrated, like the British, in a common Western targeting system. General Pierre Gallois, the first French writer to develop a distinctive theory of nuclear strategy,[51] advanced the thesis that nuclear weapons rendered traditional alliance systems totally out of date since no state, however powerful, would risk nuclear retaliation on behalf of an ally when it really came to the point. In a world thus atomized (in the traditional sense of the word) the security of every State lay in its capacity to provide its own minimal deterrence. The more States that did, indeed, the greater the stability of the international system was likely to be.

Extreme as Gallois's logic was, it probably reflected the sentiments of a large number of his countrymen and a substantial section of the French Armed Forces. In spite of innumerable official expressions to the contrary, there is every reason to suppose that many influential members of the British governing establishment felt very much the same about their own nuclear force. A more subtle variant of this doctrine was presented by General André Beaufre, who argued powerfully in his work, *Deterrence and Strategy*, that a multipolar nuclear balance in fact provided greater stability than a bipolar, since it reduced the area of uncertainty which an aggressor might exploit. So far from atomizing alliances, argued Beaufre, independent nuclear forces cemented them, 'necessarily covering the whole range of their vital interests'.[52] He was careful to distinguish between multipolarity and proliferation. 'The stability provided by the nuclear weapon' he argued, 'is attainable only between *reasonable* powers. Boxes of matches should not be given to children';[53] a sentiment which one can endorse while wondering what Beaufre would define, in international relations, as the age of consent. As for the Russo-American diarchy welcomed by Strachey, Beaufre specifically identified this as a danger to be avoided. 'The prospect of a world controlled by a *de facto* Russo-American "condominium" is one of the possible – and menacing – results of nuclear evolution' he wrote. 'Looked at from this point of view, the existence of independent nuclear forces should constitute a guarantee that the interests of the other nuclear powers will not be sacrificed through some agreement between the two super-powers.'[54]

The doctrine of 'multipolarity' was thus one distinctive contribution by French theorists to the study of strategy in the nuclear age. The second was their analysis of revolutionary war: a subject virtually ignored by American strategic thinkers until the Vietnam involvement brutally forced it on their attention. For the French it had been inescapable. For nearly ten years after World War II the flower of their armies had been involved, in Indo-China, in operations of far larger scope than the various 'imperial policing' activities which absorbed so much of the attention of the British Armed Forces, and one which imposed on the French nation a longer and perhaps even more severe a strain than the Korean War imposed on the United States. The war in Indo-China was lost. It was followed by six years of struggle in Algeria which ended, for the French Armed Forces, no less tragically. The outcome of these wars significantly altered the balance of power in the world, but the strategic concepts being developed in the United States appeared as irrelevant to their conduct as those which guided – or misguided – the French armies during the two world wars. The concepts which *were* relevant of course were those of Mao Tse-tung; those precepts evolved during the Sino-Japanese struggles of the 1930s and developed into a full theory of revolutionary warfare whereby a strongly-motivated cadre operating from a position of total weakness could defeat a government controlling the entire apparatus of the state.

The theories of Mao lie outside the scope of this study, though there is little doubt that he is among the outstanding strategic thinkers of our day. Certainly the French paid him the compliment of trying to imitate him. The literature on the subject is so considerable that it may be only by hazard that the earliest French study to receive widespread recognition was Colonel Bonnet's historical analysis, *Les guerres insurrection-nelles et révolutionnaires*.[55] Bonnet in this work gave a definition which has since been generally accepted: 'Guerre de partisans + guerre psychologique = guerre révolutionnaire.' 'Poser cette équation', he went on to claim, 'c'est formuler une loi valable pour tous les mouvements révolutionnaires qui, aujourd'hui, agitent le monde.'[56] On the basis of this definition and their own experiences, French military thinkers, true to their national intellectual traditions, attempted to formulate *une doctrine*. (It is interesting to note that the pragmatic British, whose cumulative experience in counter-insurgency campaigning was certainly no less than that of the French, thought more modestly in terms of 'techniques'.)[57] As worked out by such writers as

Bonnet himself, Hogard, Lacheroy, Nemo, and Trinquier,[58] this *doctrine* set out the object, both of revolutionary and counter-revolutionary war, as the gaining of the confidence and support of the people, by a mixture of violent and non-violent means directed both at 'military' and at 'non-military' targets. It was not enough to suppress guerrillas: it was necessary to destroy the basis of their support among the population by eliminating the grievances which they exploited, by giving protection against their terroristic activities and, insisted the French writers, by a process of intensive indoctrination to combat that of the revolutionary cadres themselves.

It would be painful to record in detail where and why these excellent recommendations went wrong. The use of undifferentiated violence by legitimate authority undermines the basis of consent which is its strongest weapon against revolutionary opponents. Indoctrination of a population can be done only by men who are themselves indoctrinated; and since the whole essence of the 'open societies' of the West is virtually incompatible with the concept of ideological indoctrination, the men thus indoctrinated rapidly found themselves almost as much at odds with their own society as the revolutionaries they were trying to combat. In Algeria the French Army applied its doctrines with a fair measure of at least short-term success, but in so doing it alienated the sympathies of its own countrymen. The main fault of its theorists – and of their imitators in the United States – was to overlook the element of simple *nationalism* which provided such strength for the insurgent forces: a curious failing in the country which was the original home of that immensely powerful force. They accepted the propaganda of their adversaries, and saw the conflict simply in terms of a global struggle against the forces of world Communist revolution. Marxist categories of thought make it impossible for their theorists even to consider that the most potent revolutionary force in the world may be not the class struggle but old-fashioned 'bourgeois' nationalism. The French theorists were no doubt equally unwilling to take into account a consideration which boded so ill for their own side. But there is good reason to suppose that the FLN won in Algeria, not because they were Marxist but because they were *Algerian*, and the French were not. *Mutatis mutandis* the same applied – and applies still – in Indo-China. Marx and Lenin may provide the rationale of insurgency warfare; Mao Tse-tung may provide the techniques; but the driving power is furnished by the ideas of Mazzini. It is therefore difficult for foreign troops, however well-intentioned, to apply counter-insurgency techniques among a people which has awoken to a consciousness of its national identity with any chance of success.

In addition to the doctrines of multipolarity and revolutionary war, France has produced yet a third contribution to strategic thinking: the doctrine of indirect strategy. This was not totally novel. A group of American thinkers based on the Center for Foreign Policy Research at the University of Pennsylvania had long been working on the assumption that 'The Free World' and the Communists were locked in a protracted conflict which could end only in the victory of one side or the other and in which force was only one element out of many which might be used.[59] It was an assumption that could certainly be justified by reference to the works of Marx–Leninist theoreticians. But the publications of these writers tended to be as emotional and tendentious as those of the Marxists themselves. Certainly they had never formulated their theories with the clarity, reasonableness and dispassionate precision of General André Beaufre and his colleagues at the Institut d'Études Stratégiques in Paris.[60] For Beaufre the whole field of international relations constituted a battefield in which the Communist powers, thwarted in the use of force by the nuclear stalemate, were attacking the West by indirect means. Strategy had progressed from the 'operational' (Clausewitz and Jomini) through the 'logistic' (the great build-ups of World War II) to the 'indirect'. Political manoeuvres should therefore be seen as strategic manoeuvres. The adversary attacked, withdrew, feinted, outflanked, or dug in, using direct force where he could and infiltration where he could not. The West should respond accordingly, devise a single overall political strategy and use economic, political, and military means to implement it.

The trouble with this is that it is not simply a theory of strategy but also a theory of international relations. If it is correct, Beaufre's recommendations follow naturally enough; but Beaufre states his assumptions rather than argues them, and to most students of international relations they are not self-evident. Such a view leaves too many factors out of account. The world is not really polarized so simply. Communist leaders do not control events so firmly. Whatever the ideologues may say, in practice interests are not so implacably opposed. Strategy must certainly be shaped by the needs of policy; but policy cannot be made to fit quite so easily into the Procrustean concepts of the professional strategist.

Perhaps the most significant conclusion to be drawn from this survey is the extent to which the quality of strategic thinking in the nuclear age is related to an understanding of international relations, on the one hand, and of weapons technology on the other. There is of course nothing new in this dependence. Clausewitz emphasized the first, though he never fully adjusted his purely strategic thinking to take account of the political environment whose overriding importance he quite rightly stressed. The second has been evident, particularly in naval and air operations, at least since the beginning of the twentieth century. But strategic thinkers, from the pioneers of the eighteenth century to Liddell Hart in his earlier writings, were able to assume a fairly simple model of international relations within which armed conflict might occur, as well as a basically stable technological environment. Neither assumption can now be made. No thinking about deterrence is likely to be of value unless it is based on a thorough understanding of 'the state of the art' in weapons technology. Any thinking about limited war, revolutionary war, or indirect strategy must take as its starting point an understanding of the political – including the social and economic – context out of which these conflicts arise or are likely to arise. Inevitably the interaction works both ways. Strategic factors themselves constitute an important element in international relations: the statesman can never be a purely despotic law-giver to the strategist. Similarly, strategic requirements have inspired scientists and technologists to achievements they would normally consider impossible. Increasingly the three fields overlap. That is why strategic studies owe at least as much to the work of political scientists at one end of the spectrum, and of physical scientists, systems analysts and mathematical economists at the other, as they do to the classical strategist. One may indeed wonder whether 'classical strategy', as a self-sufficient study, has any longer a valid claim to exist.

Michael Howard is Fellow in Higher Defence Studies, All Souls College, Oxford

Notes

1 B.H. Liddell Hart, *Strategy: The Indirect Approach* (London: Faber, 1967), p. 335.

2 André Beaufre, *An Introduction to Strategy* (London: Faber, 1965), *passim*, esp. pp. 107–130.

3 *Ibid.*, p. 22.

4 P.M.S. Blackett, *Studies of War* (London: Oliver & Boyd, 1962), p. 128.

5 Sir John Slessor, 'Air Power and the Future of War', *Journal of the Royal United Service Institution*, August 1954.

6 P.M.S. Blackett, *The Military and Political Consequences of Atomic Energy* (London: The Turnstile Press, 1948), p. 56.

7 Vannevar Bush, *Modern Arms and Free Men* (New York: Simon and Schuster, 1949), pp. 115–16.

8 As for example Jacob Viner's paper on 'The Implications of the Atomic Bomb for East–West Relations', the influence of which is acknowledged by Brodie and many others. Albert Wohlstetter gave an impromptu account, at the ISS Conference, of the main lines along which these discussions ran. Some account will also be found in Richard G. Hewlett and Oscar E. Anderson, *The New World* (Vol. I of the History of the United States Atomic Energy Commission, Pennsylvania, 1962), and in the early issues of the *Bulletin of the Atomic Scientists*.

9 B.H. Liddell Hart, *The Revolution in Warfare* (London: Faber, 1946), p. 87.

10 Bernard Brodie (ed.), *The Absolute Weapon* (New York: Harcourt, Brace, 1946), p. 89.

11 Brodie, *op. cit.*, pp. 75–76. He did not, however, deal with the problem of vulnerability of retaliatory forces, and the consequent dependence of stability on an effective second-strike capability.

12 Richard N. Rosecrance, *The Defense of the Realm* (New York and London: Columbia University Press, 1967), p. 159.

13 'The Place of the Bomber in British Policy'. Reprinted in *The Great Deterrent* (London: Cassell, 1957), p. 123.

14 B.H. Liddell Hart, *The Defence of the West* (London: Cassell, 1950), pp. 97, 134, 139, 140.

15 Sir John Slessor, *Strategy for the West* (London: Casseli, 1954), p. 108

16 Lt-Gen. Sir John Cowley, 'Future Trends in Warfare', *Journal of the Royal United Service Institution*, February 1960, p. 13.

17 Rosecrance, *op. cit.*, pp. 160–61.

18 Slessor, Lecture at Oxford University, April 1955, reprinted in *The Great Deterrent*, p. 181.

19 P.M.S. Blackett, *Atomic Energy and East–West Relations* (Cambridge: Cambridge University Press, 1956), p. 100.

20 P.M.S. Blackett, 'Critique of Some Contemporary Defence Thinking'. First published in *Encounter* in 1961, this article is reprinted in *Studies of War*, *op. cit.*, pp. 128–46. See also Blackett's dissenting note in Alastair Buchan: *NATO in the 1960's* (London: Chatto & Windus, 1960).

21 Text in *The New York Times*, 13 January 1954

22 See the analysis '"The New Look" of 1953' by Glenn H. Snyder, in Warner R. Schilling, Paul Y.

Hammond and Glenn H. Snyder, *Strategy, Policy and Defense Budgets* (New York: Columbia University Press, 1962), pp. 379–524.

23 Bernard Brodie, 'Unlimited Weapons and Limited War', *The Reporter*, 18 November 1954. For an indispensable annotated bibliography of the whole controversy, see Morton H. Halperin: *Limited War in the Nuclear Age* (New York and London: John Wiley, 1963).

24 William W. Kaufmann, ed. *Military Policy and National Security* (Princeton, N.J.: Princeton University Press, 1956), pp. 28, 38, 257.

25 *Ibid.*, pp. 53–7, 60–72.

26 *Ibid.*, pp. 75–101.

27 Robert E. Osgood: *Limited War: the Challenge to American Strategy* (Chicago: University of Chicago Press 1957). Henry A. Kissinger, *Nuclear Weapons and Foreign Policy* (New York: Houghton Mifflin, 1957).

28 J.F. Dulles, 'Challenge and Response in United States' Policy', *Foreign Affairs*, October 1957.

29 Osgood, *op. cit.*, p. 258.

30 Kissinger, *op. cit.*, pp. 174–202.

31 Anthony Buzzard *et al.*, *On Limiting Atomic War* (London: Royal Institute of International Affairs, 1956); and 'The H-Bomb: Massive Retaliation or Graduated Deterrence', *International Affairs*, 1956.

32 Slessor: 'Total or Limited War?' in *The Great Deterrent*, pp. 262–84. Liddell Hart, *Deterrent or Defence: a Fresh Look at the West's Military Position* (London: Stevens, 1960), pp. 74–81. Blackett, 'Nuclear Weapons and Defence', *International Affairs*, October 1958.

33 Brodie, *Strategy in the Missile Age* (Princeton, N.J.: Princeton University Press, 1959), p. 330. Thomas C. Schelling, *The Strategy of Conflict* (Cam., Mass.: Harvard University Press 1960), pp. 262–66. But the debate continued. Brodie in *Escalation and the Nuclear Option* (Princeton, N.J.: Princeton University Press, 1966) was to argue strongly against what had by then become known as the 'firebreak' theory, and emphasize the deterrent value of tactical nuclear weapons.

34 Kissinger, *The Necessity for Choice* (London: Chatto & Windus, 1960), pp. 81–98.

35 The literature is enormous, but three outstanding contributions are Helmuth Schmidt, *Verteidigung oder Vergeltung* (Stuttgart, 1961); Alastair Buchan and Philip Windsor, *Arms and Stability in Europe* (London: Chatto & Windus, 1963); and Raymond Aron, *Le Grand Débat* (Paris: Calmann-Lévy, 1963).

36 Kissinger, *Nuclear Weapons*, p. vii.

37 For an analysis of the various attitudes of American strategic thinkers to the question of *détente* see Robert A. Levine, *The Arms Debate* (Cam., Mass.: Harvard University Press, 1963), *passim*.

38 Albert Wohlstetter, 'The Delicate Balance of Terror', *Foreign Affairs*, January 1958. The article is reprinted in Henry A. Kissinger, (ed.) *Problems of National Strategy* (New York and London: Praeger and Pall Mall, 1965). The principal relevant studies were *Selection and Use of Air Buses* (R-266, April 1954) and *Protecting US Power to Strike Back in the 1950s & 1960s* (R-290, April 1956) by Albert

Wohlstetter, F.S. Hoffman, and H.S. Rowen. Wohlstetter in a private communication to the present writer has stressed also the significant part played in these studies by experts in systems-analysis such as J.F. Pigby, E.J. Barlow, and R.J. Lutz.

39 Oskar Morgenstern, *The Question of National Defence* (New York: Random House, 1959), p. 75

40 See particularly his 'Surprise Attack and Disarmament' in Klaus Knorr, (ed.), *NATO and American Security* (Princeton, N.J.: Princeton University Press, 1959). Schelling's whole work on the problem of dialogue in conflict situations is of major importance. His principal articles are collected in *The Strategy of Conflict* (Cam., Mass.: Harvard University Press, 1960).

41 Brodie, *Strategy in the Missile Age*, *op. cit.*, Chapter 8. Brodie and Schelling, like Wohlstetter, were at the time working at RAND Corporation, as also was Herman Kahn. All have acknowledged their mutual indebtedness during this formative period in their thinking.

42 *Ibid.*, pp. 294–97.

43 Herman Kahn, *On Thermonuclear War* (Princeton, N.J.: Princeton University Press, 1960).

44 *Ibid.*, pp. 301–2.

45 *Thinking the Unthinkable. On Escalation: Metaphors and Scenarios* (London: Pall Mall, 1965).

46 Knorr, *On the Uses of Military Power in the Nuclear Age* (Princeton, N.J.: Princeton University Press, 1966). Schelling, *Arms and Influence* (New Haven: Yale University Press, 1966).

47 William W. Kaufmann, *The McNamara Strategy* (New York: Harper & Row, 1964) provides

a useful if uncritical account. It should be read in association with Bernard Brodie's dry commentary 'The McNamara Phenomenon', *World Politics*, July 1965.

48 McNamara speech at the University of Michigan at Ann Arbor, 16 June 1962. Kaufmann, *op. cit.*, p . 116.

49 See Charles Hitch and Roland McKean, *The Economics of Defense in the Nuclear Age* (Cam., Mass.: Harvard University Press, 1960) for the promise. The performance was examined in *Planning – Programming – Budgeting: Hearings before the Subcommittee on National Security and International Operations of the Committee on Government Operations*, United States Senate, 90th Congress, 1st Session (US Government Printing Office, 1967).

50 John Strachey, *On the Prevention of War* (London: Macmillan, 1962).

51 Pierre Gallois, *Stratégie de l'Age nucléaire* (Paris: Calmann-Lévy, 1960).

52 André Beaufre, *Deterrence and Strategy* (London: Faber, 1965), p. 93.

53 *Ibid.*, p. 97.

54 *Ibid.*, p. 140. Beaufre's experience as commander of the French land forces in the Suez operation of 1956 may have had some relevance to his views on this point.

55 Gabriel Bonnet, *Les guerres insurrectionnelles et révolutionnaires de l'antiquité a'nos jours* (Paris: Payot, 1955). Important unpublished studies by Colonel Lacheroy were in circulation at the same time.

56 *Ibid.*, p . 60.

57 See, for example, Julian Paget, *Counter-Insurgency Campaigning* (London: Faber, 1967) and Sir

Robert Thompson, *Defeating Communist Insurgency* (London: Chatto & Windus, 1966).

[58] For a good select bibliography see the excellent and highly critical study by Peter Paret, *French Revolutionary Warfare from Indo-China to Algeria* (London: Pall Mall, 1964).

[59] Robert Strausz-Hupé, *et al.*, *Protracted Conflict; A Challenging Study of Communist Strategy* (New York, 1959) and *A Forward Strategy for America* (New York, 1961).

[60] André Beaufre, *An Introduction to Strategy* (London: Faber, 1965); *Deterrence and Strategy* (London: Faber, 1965); *Strategy of Action* (London: Faber, 1967).

CHAPTER TWELVE

Obituary: B.H.L.H., 1895–1970

Survival 12-3, 1970

Among the exalted godparents who presided over the chris-
tening of the Institute for Strategic Studies in 1958, the most
appropriate, if not indeed the most eminent, was Sir Basil
Liddell Hart, who died on 30 January 1970 at the age of 74.

When the Institute was founded, Liddell Hart's reputation
was only just beginning to recover from nearly twenty years
of neglect and mis-representation; which itself had followed
twenty years of dazzling success. While still in his early twen-
ties, at the end of the First World War, he had been invited to
redraft the British Army infantry training manual. His writings
on armoured warfare a few years later made him a world-wide
reputation; and as a military correspondent, first with *The Daily
Telegraph* and then with *The Times*, his prestige eclipsed that
of all his contemporaries and outshone even that of his prede-
cessor Colonel Repington. During this period he wrote some
twenty books, some of them authoritative military history, the
rest elaborating a theory of war for the guidance of all involved
in it from lance-corporal to Prime Minister. In 1937 he reached
the apogee of this first stage of his career when he became
for a year the unofficial adviser to the Secretary of State for

War. In this capacity he not only saw through a large number of overdue reforms in the British Army. He also defined the defence policy which the British Government was to follow in the early stages of the coming war: one of major reliance on naval and air power and 'limited liability' on the continent of Europe; where a well-planned defensive, he expounded in his book *The Defence of Britain* (1939) would hole any attacks the Germans might be rash enough to launch.

The position Liddell Hart occupied at the War Office, of power without responsibility, irritated even those regular officers who most admired his writings. By 1939 he was a highly unpopular figure in official circles, and a year later he was no less unpopular with the country as a whole. It was poor consolation to know that the author of the reassuring *Defence of Britain* was the author also of those doctrines of armoured warfare and the 'expanding torrent' method on which General Guderian had trained the German panzer divisions. The personal dislike of Churchill provided all that was needed to send Liddell Hart's reputation into total eclipse for the duration of the war, and for many years after it.

This period in the wilderness left an enduring mark on Liddell Hart. He continued to write prolifically. The profound respect in which he was held by the Germans enabled him to enhance his reputation as a historian yet further by his pioneer study of the German conduct of the war, based on his interviews with the captured German Generals, *The Other Side of the Hill* (1948). Ten years before the first American pundits, he was urging the need to set limitations on war in the nuclear age. But he felt with reason that he was a prophet honoured everywhere save in his own country, and he treasured, a little pathetically, every tribute to his influence that came his way. In the last ten years of his life these were to be many. Foreign statesmen paid homage to him, from President Kennedy to Moshe Dayan. The government of his own country honoured him in public and the senior officers of the Armed Forces consulted him often in private. And to his home in the Thames Valley there came an unending stream of disciples and pilgrims and a vast flood of correspondence. No letter went without a full and detailed answer. No visitor went empty away.

Members of the ISS will recall him most vividly at their annual conferences, holding court at the best available hotel; whisky in one hand, pipe in the other, the one warm, the other unlit; his spare figure set off by a gorgeous brocade waistcoat; beaming benevolently, talking endlessly, until his long suffering wife sent him to bed. To the end he never spared himself, or indeed anyone else. May his generous spirit now rest in peace.

MICHAEL HOWARD

Book Review: The roots of war: the men and institutions behind US foreign policy

The roots of war: the men and institutions behind US foreign policy, by Richard J. Barnet (New York: Atheneum, 1972)

Survival 15-6, 1973

Mr Barnet has written an honest and therefore a very confused book. He obviously started out with the intention of expounding, with a wealth of damning documentation, what is now the orthodox neo-Populist critique of American foreign policy since the World War II. 'The roots of war' he sees as three: the power of an elite bureaucracy with values and perceptions different from those of the American people as a whole; the capitalist economy and the business ethic that sustains it; and the manipulation of public opinion by the first in the interests of the second. William Jennings Bryan would have wholeheartedly agreed with all this, but that does not mean that Mr Barnet is necessarily wrong. What it does mean is that Mr Barnet and the large number of articulate intellectuals who think like him are representative of a powerful stream in American culture which has run largely underground for the past thirty years and has now burst into the open again with a vigour which may considerably affect American foreign policy over the next decade, and of which foreigners must take careful account. It is the mid-West reasserting itself against the East Coast, and Mr Barnet's denunciation of the wealthy Ivy-League lawyers and corporation men who have run America since the war – the Lovetts, the Achesons, the Cliffords, the McCloys, the Kennedys, the Bundys – echoes rather more articulately the passionate verbal assault on Mr Acheson by the extreme Republican Senators in the early 1950s. 'Get out! Get out! You stand for everything that has been wrong with this country for years!'

Yet Mr Barnet is far too good a scholar to perpetrate the Populist myth of a peace-loving and virtuous American people who would, if not misled by these East-Coast cookie-pushers, discern their interest by a kind of inner light. The East Coast establishment may have overreacted to 'the Communist menace', but vast sections of the American people were even more violent in their response. Mr Barnet does indeed document most damningly the terrible oversimplifications that informed American policy in the 1950s and 1960s, and the brash self-confidence of the young men who believed that all the problems of the world would yield to technology and systems analysis. But he also says something of the even worse oversimplifications that guided whole tracts of influential public opinion, and of the public impatience with the 'pussy footing' which went on in Washington. He also shows the extent to which electoral considerations influenced foreign policy decisions, of which the Cuba crisis was only one example. The Kennedy Administration's handling of that affair may indeed have been an exercise in 'coolness' and 'toughness' of the kind on which the Establishment prided itself and Mr Barnet excoriates; but if it had handled matters any less toughly it would have been out on its ear in 1964. The mass of the American press was basically conservative, hysterically anti-Communist, and clamouring for dramatic action; and in doing so it reflected public attitudes which sometimes *had* to be 'managed' if the United States were not to blunder into world war.

On the second of his two points, the relationship between 'the capitalist economy' and American foreign policy, Mr Barnet's honesty gets him into an even worse muddle. He discards the Marx–Leninist equation of capitalism and imperialism, agreeing rather with Schumpeter in believing their American expansion was not the result of economic pressures and to assume that it was would be to rationalize the irrational: 'the real decisions may be made for such costly uneconomic reasons as glory, honour, fear, or the sheer fun of winning'. Yet he concludes that 'the primary reason military power is projected abroad is to buy influence, which has been thought essential to the maintenance of the American standard of living'. But thought essential by whom? At one moment it seems to be those favourite devils of the neo-Populists, the corporations: the case is indisputable, states Mr Barnet, 'that corporations play the crucial role in the making of foreign policy'. But almost at once he backtracks: although corporations, he says, exercise 'the dominant *influence* in the society, the *power* keeps passing to the state'. Indeed he agrees that 'the impact of government security policies on the future of the corporation is in many cases so uncertain that the corporation managers do not even know what they should be for'. When they do know, corporation interests frequently conflict with the state interest as perceived by the bureaucracy and with one another. Altogether Mr Barnet does a pretty effective demolition job on his own thesis, and ends up by leaving us as confused as he is.

What Mr Barnet nowhere indicates is that 'the roots of war' may to some extent at least have lain *outside* the United States: that the international environment may have presented the government of the United States with certain problems to which the range of possible solutions would have seemed equally limited whatever the economic and cultural background of the men who had to deal with them; that 'the national security managers' may have been at least as much moulded by their situation as they moulded it. The message is implicit throughout: with a different lot of people in charge in the United States all this need never have happened. *Which* different lot Mr Barnet does not say, though he has kind words for anyone, from Robert Taft to Chester Bowles, who dissented from the conventional wisdom. He concludes however with an inspiring recipe for the future:

> A politically effective peace party would have to artic-ulate a new role for America – neither number one nation ... nor a self-pitying helpless giant ... It would have to develop a vision of a new world economy based on a fairer distribution of resources and power across the planet and to discuss candidly what sacri-fices in standard of living Americans must make and what isolationist assumptions we must give up to make such a vision a reality.

Yes indeed. But first it would have to win a few elections; and then it would have to learn how to deal with foreigners, who are a very much more complicated and bloody-minded lot of people than Mr Barnet seems to think.

MICHAEL HOWARD
All Souls College, Oxford

CHAPTER FOURTEEN

Obituary: P.M.S. Blackett

Survival 16-5, 1974

Patrick Blackett was a highly professional naval officer, a natural radical and a brilliant scientist: an unusual combination which made him outstanding as a strategic thinker. After a naval career in which he saw service both at the Battle of the Falkland Islands and at Jutland, he joined the Cavendish Laboratory at Cambridge to do the pioneer work on nuclear physics which was to bring him a Nobel Prize. In 1935 he was co-opted by Sir Henry Tizard on to the Committee for the Scientific Study of Air Defence which presided over the development of radar. For ten years thereafter, he was deeply involved in preparations for and the conduct of World War II, as a scientific adviser both to the Royal Air Force and to the Royal Navy. In this capacity he took the lead in developing concepts of operational research which are now commonplace, but forty years ago were revolutionary. Under his aegis the Services acquired a respect for scientific advice of a kind which had hitherto been notably absent from their make-up.

This respect was only partially reciprocated. Blackett never underrated the importance of 'conventional wisdom' in the conduct of war, but his experience of stupidity, prejudice, complacency and bureaucratic inertia in policy-making did not diminish this naturally critical attitude towards government. His book *The Military and Political Consequences of Atomic Energy* (1948) was the first serious critique, both of allied conduct of the war and of the development of strategic thinking after it. Little attention was paid to it in official circles, but six years later Blackett returned to the charge with his Lees Knowles lectures at Cambridge on *Atomic Weapons and East–West Relations*: the first serious analysis on this side of the Atlantic of the doctrine of 'Massive Retaliation' on which the British no less than the American Government was basing its strategic planning. His critical reflections on this topic led him to join the seminal study group on 'Graduated Deterrence' at Chatham House whose other members were Rear-Admiral Sir Anthony Buzzard, Richard Goold-Adams and Denis Healey; and it was from this body that the idea originated of the Brighton Conference in 1957 at which the IISS was founded.

Blackett was a member of the original Council of the Institute and his practical flair as well as his immense prestige played a large part in overcoming its initial teething troubles and establishing its international reputation. It was, for example, entirely due to Blackett that the Institute was able to establish itself in its highly convenient premises in Adam Street. Once he was satisfied that the Institute was a going concern he resigned as a member of the Council, although he was always ready, when needed, with help and advice. Strategic problems interested him only intermittently, but when they did it was as if the beam of a lighthouse had settled on them, clarifying their obscurities before sweeping on to illuminate other fields. He brought to strategic problems not so much technical expertise as hard common sense and powerful reason – qualities not always evident in the contributions of some other eminent scientists and *savants* to the subject. These talents, which had so powerfully contributed to victory in war, were to make just as important a contribution to the maintenance of peace. Scientists, scholars and strategists throughout the world will mourn his death.

MICHAEL HOWARD

CHAPTER FIFTEEN

Order and conflict at sea in the 1980s

From Adelphi Paper 124, 1976

Order at sea, the recognition of laws and conventions which enable ships to pass on their lawful occasions, is a basic part of the world political and economic order. A convention of experts on strategic questions is not particularly well equipped to discuss it, for our speciality comes into demand primarily when order breaks down. In our thinking we naturally tend to concentrate on the weaknesses of the system rather than its strength. For a more balanced view we would need to be reinforced by a greater number of international lawyers, shipping experts, insurance brokers, merchant bankers and government experts on trade – to say nothing of the men of the mercantile marine whose activities make possible the orderly functioning of the world economy.

Such a group would have much to tell us about the difficulties of operating this world system, but we would gain from them a good idea of its scale, continuity, and effectiveness. It is a system which has to be continually re-adjusted to meet the demands of change: political change as new sovereign states come into being, economic change as new products come on the market and demand fluctuates, technological change affecting transport and communication. On the whole I believe that we would be impressed by the success with which these challenges have been met; success due not simply to the ingenuity of the men operating the system but to the advantages derived from the revolution in communications and computer technology since World War II. In spite of economic recession and local conflicts, in spite indeed of such major disturbances as that caused by the Korean War, industrial and commercial activity throughout the world has expanded continuously, and the use of the seas with it. The system has shown itself at once stable and flexible. At present it is, admittedly, under very heavy strain indeed, but only the extreme pessimist – or, depending on one's viewpoint, the extreme optimist – would maintain that it is on the verge of total collapse.

Order at sea, the peaceful regulation of commerce and communications between states of diverse cultures and political structures, is the central element in this world system. It is the law of the sea, the co-operative maintenance of communications, harbours, and trade facilities, the entire activity of a trans-national maritime community, that makes it possible for our economies and our societies to function at all. And this order, it is important to realize, is the creation of the West. 'The West' in fact is the highly inaccurate term we apply to the community of maritime and trading nations, inclusive of Australia, Singapore and Japan, scattered throughout the world. It was brought into being by the expansion of the states of Western Europe: states which five hundred years ago constituted only one system among many in the world and by no means the most wealthy or the most powerful. The maritime activity of these nations had by the beginning of this century created a single world economy, of which Europe, and in particular Great Britain, was the unchallenged centre. Two world wars destroyed the European hegemony, and the system has become diversified; loosely but by no means exclusively centred on the United States. But the ground rules of the system which enable it to function, the rules of procedure in transport and communications, the conventions of maritime and commercial law, are those which have been developed by the European powers in their co-operation and conflict from the age of the 'great discoveries' until today. Grotius and Selden, as Hedley Bull reminded us,[1] hammered out the fundamentals of our problems more than three hundred years ago. And to these ground rules for the use of the seas and international commerce every other nation in the world, with one exception only, has almost unquestioningly conformed.

The exception is not the Soviet Union. The Soviet Union, like the Russian Empire which it replaced, has maintained an ambiguous relationship with the maritime nations, rooted in the cultural dichotomy so strikingly exemplified in the two cities of Leningrad and Moscow. On the one hand is a great world port, Western in appearance and culture, built by a tsar who was determined to make Russia a member (if possible the leading member) of the maritime community. (There is nothing either novel or unnatural in the Russian desire, as part of this process, to have a great ocean-going navy.) On the other is the centre of Old Russia, a culture weighted down by, yet drawing strength from, its land mass, conscious of and anxious to emphasize its difference from the corrupt and decadent West, the true inheritor of the cultural leadership of Rome and Byzantium. Russian history, literature and politics have shown to this day a continual interplay between these two tendencies. But the requirement for economic development, her inability to create an autarkic system of her own, have been bringing the Soviet Union into ever closer relations with the Western maritime system. She needs to import from the West; she needs fish to feed her growing population; she needs a merchant marine to earn hard currency. In all these activities she appears as a formidable – even alarming – competitor with the traditional maritime nations, but she has by and large accepted their ground rules. She operates within the framework of the system they have created – which indeed in the nineteenth century, as a participant in all the major international conferences on the subject, she helped to create. Soviet vessels, merchant or naval, are as meticulous as any other in observing the laws and conventions of the sea. Soviet commercial negotiators work hard to create the reputation that they are good people to do business with. Such friction as arises is more likely to result from inefficiency (not an exclusively Soviet characteristic) than from ill-will. Soviet theologians may continue to denounce capitalism as ferociously as Catholic theologians in the sixteenth century denounced usury, but that does not prevent the Russians, today, any more than it prevented pious Genoese, Florentine and Roman bankers then, from co-operating to make it work and deriving great benefit from the process.

Whether this co-operation will continue is naturally a matter of doubt. It is subject to all the unpredictable fluctuations of a secretive and arbitrary polity. But it is not unreasonable to suggest that this increased Soviet participation in and dependence on the Western maritime system has acquired a momentum that it would now be difficult permanently to arrest or reverse, even given the worst will in the world, and that any attempt to do so would create serious difficulties for the Soviet economy. The Soviet Union has in fact acquired a vested interest in the maintenance of the existing international order, including order at sea, and there is no *a priori* reason to suppose that this will not continue into the 1980s. If it does so continue, it will constitute a considerable factor in Soviet political planning and a powerful disincentive to adventurism and irresponsibility on the part of their leaders.

Does a greater threat to this system of international trade and communication arise from the Third World – if indeed one can still group so many disparate nations under that single heading? In his lucid and magisterial introduction to this conference Hedley Bull spoke of the 'alienation' of the Third World from the existing system, but I think we must analyse this rather more closely. There are aspects of the system which many Third World states understandably resent. The distribution within it both of resources and of power appears to them intolerably inequitable, and their representatives naturally do all they can by word and deed to redress it. But with the exception of one or two 'crazy states', whose ill-will is usually matched by their impotence, there does not seem to be any general desire on the part of Third World states to wreck a system upon the effective functioning of which their own economies are, on the whole, almost totally dependent. I would suggest indeed that, so far from being alienated from the existing order, the governing elites of most Third World states wish to assimilate to it as fast as possible; to learn the skills of the maritime powers in order to function, and be rewarded, as full members of the system rather than as apprentices. If one wants a 'counter-culture' one must seek it in Greenwich Village or Berkeley, California, rather than in New Delhi, or Cairo, or Jakarta. Whatever their rhetoric, the leaders of Third World states are reluctant to play the destructive revolutionary role for which they have been cast by intellectuals in both the Western and the Communist worlds.

The exception to which I referred earlier is China. China has never been a member of the world maritime community. Her leaders have always treated its representatives with disdain, and the latter replied in the nineteenth century with a brutality that has certainly not been forgotten and is unlikely to have been forgiven. (The Japanese war in China from 1931 to 1945 was only the last, if the most terrible, of the outrages which have been committed against China by the maritime powers during the past hundred years.) Today the People's Republic of China provides the only real example of doctrinaire abstention from the world economic system. But even that abstention is tempered by the tolerated anomaly of Hong Kong. One may wonder for how long the economic needs of China will permit her thus to insulate herself; and even if they do, whether her continued abstention will offer a serious threat to our maritime system, or any serious alternative to it for the discontented.

I am suggesting therefore that the overwhelming majority of states in the world have a continuing interest in the continuing stability of the world order which would, if they behaved rationally, keep that order in a state of stable equilibrium, capable of surviving severe shocks, interruptions and conflicts without being irretrievably upset. But, lest you think that Dr Pangloss has come again, let me rapidly add that the same kind of analysis could have been made on the eve of the French Revolution, and in 1914, and in 1939. At all these moments the nations of the world seemed to have everything to gain by continuing in a state of amicable mutual intercourse which was enhancing the wealth and well-being of all. Yet they took apparently irrational decisions then, and they could do so again. The capitalist system may indeed be entering the last agonies so frequently and confidently predicted by Marxist eschatologists. Even if it is not, its malfunctioning may bring into power, as it did in the 1930s, extremist or adventurist regimes which will ignore the advice of their experts and take decisions which will gravely harm the successful functioning of a world order on which they themselves ultimately depend. There can be no guarantee whatever that this will not occur during the next fifteen years. One can say only that such events are of their very nature unpredictable, and that there is no more reason to assume their inevitability than to assume the inevitability of traffic accidents in bad road conditions. The world order may break down again, as it has in the past, but that is no cause for assuming that it will.

Order at sea, the first topic I was invited to discuss, must thus be seen as a dimension of world order as a whole, and the future of the former will depend on the future of the latter. The seas are not so discrete and isolated an element that conflict can rage on them while the nations of the world are in every other respect at peace. By 'conflict' I presume that we here mean 'armed conflict'; normal conflicts of interest, at sea as on land, are an inevitable part of international politics, and so long as they can be settled by peaceful means they can be subsumed under the rubric of 'order'. And in discussing such armed conflict we need to distinguish between two overlapping categories: (1) the sea as a *cause*, or *occasion* for conflict; and (2) the sea as an *arena* for a conflict which has started elsewhere.

It has emerged very clearly at this conference that the seas are likely to provide increasing occasions for conflict as their resources become more eagerly sought after and as territorial frontiers are extended to include greater stretches of the sea bed. But the question here is whether these disputes are likely to lead to armed conflict, and that is more difficult to answer. The key, I suggest, lies not so much in the occasion of the conflict as in the nature of the competitors; that is, less in external than in domestic considerations.

The historical precedents are not encouraging. When the nations of Europe became aware, four hundred years ago, of the economic prizes which lay beyond the seas, they fought over them for the best part of three centuries. But we must remember that they were very bellicose societies. Their ruling classes were warriors, and war had been their business for a thousand years. If they were not fighting over colonies they were fighting over religion or over inheritance or over honour. As the structure of European society changed, so the more easily did European states find peaceful settlements for their differences. Today armed conflict between them is almost unthinkable. They divided the resources of the North Sea with barely a whisper of contention escaping from the committee rooms; and if the Baltic presents greater and so far unresolvable problems, it is as unlikely that these will lead to armed conflict as it would have been unthinkable that they should not have led to it in the days of Gustavus Adolphus or Peter the Great.

But there are still plenty of bellicose societies in the world, and bellicosity is as common in democracies as in dictatorships. A country may be pushed to the brink of war by popular outcry, as was Iceland during the 'Cod War'; or by the *machismo* of a national leader; or, as was the case with Egypt in 1967, by a combination of both. A skilful and unscrupulous leader might indeed provoke a war over such a maritime issue, or welcome the opportunity to fight one, as a deliberate device in 'nation-building'. But even if such cases did arise, it is hard to conceive of any such conflict being initiated except on the assumption that it could be kept limited, nor of the international community having any interest except in keeping it limited and terminating it as quickly as possible.

In this respect the experience of the Conference on the Law of the Sea seems on balance to be encouraging. When the conference was first convened diplomats and lawyers looked forward to it almost with despair. How could any order be created out of this confusion of conflicting claims? Could any common interest possibly be identified and defined? The conference sessions have indeed been as tumultuous and confusing as any in diplomatic history. Yet some kind of shape is beginning to emerge, and, more important, there seems a general desire that some shape should emerge. It now seems possible that, piecemeal, an acceptable order will be created, although a very imperfect one; certainly that the more gloomy prophecies of anarchy will be belied. Disputes will continue, but there is a world of difference between conflict, even armed conflict, over the interpretation and implementation of an accepted law, and an anarchic struggle of all against all to grab or defend resources.

Gloomy prognostications have also been made about terrorism and piracy on the seas, especially in relation to oil rigs. If terrorism is endemic on land there is no reason why it should not extend to the sea as well. But the resources needed to make terrorism effective at sea would be rather considerable. It is easier to sabotage an oil pipeline than an oil rig, or to hijack an aircraft than a ship at sea. And if such actions were attempted they would be more likely to create a sense of solidarity among the maritime community than to disrupt it. In the suppression of piracy all sea-going nations have dropped their quarrels in the past, and there is no cause to suppose that they would not do the same in the future.

There is even less reason to suppose that responsible governments will sponsor or engage in acts of piracy themselves, such as the seizure of sea-bed resources or the sinking of oil tankers on the high seas (as distinct from such hostile actions in conditions of quasi-war as the seizures of the *Pueblo* and the *Mayaguez*). Isolated acts against the shipping of wealthy nations by small, angry powers are always possible, but the dependence of all maritime powers on the security of such shipping is so great that it is hard to visualize such attacks as being anything but impulsive and spasmodic. On any larger scale they would anyhow constitute acts of war and provoke an appropriate response. Such acts by major powers, with yet greater interest in the flow of trade, are even more unlikely. In the past it was possible for the edges of piracy, privateer-

ing and official belligerence to be conveniently blurred, and
for Dutchmen, Spaniards, British and Frenchmen to fight one
another in the Caribbean or the South Seas while their governments at home were officially at peace. But improvement in
communications, if nothing else, has made this kind of activity impossible for well over a hundred years. The difference
between bellicose and peaceful acts, and the attribution of
responsibility for them, has become not more blurred, but
increasingly precise. Acts of violence against the shipping or
the possessions of a sovereign power on the high seas are acts
of war, and only powers prepared to engage in war, or at the
very least to submit to acts of retaliation in kind, are likely to
commit them.

In this connection I should like to refer to a point raised
in the course of the conference; the possibility that it may be
easier to cross the nuclear threshold at sea than on land; for a
sailor than for a soldier to take the decision to initiate the use
of nuclear weapons. In purely tactical terms this is no doubt
true. A nuclear strike at sea would carry none of the appalling
implications of one on the crowded plains of Central Europe.
But it is neither sailors nor soldiers who take the decision to
use nuclear weapons, but statesmen. If statesmen did devolve
the decision on to their military agents, this would amount to
nuclear release. The use even of the smallest nuclear weapon
in even the most insulated of conditions would have not only
operational but immense political significance. It is certainly
possible that a statesman might decide to initiate the use of
nuclear weapons, if he felt compelled to do so, by authorizing
limited nuclear release against a maritime target. But he could
not expect that such actions would necessarily remain confined
to the sea for very long.

This brings us to the seas as a *theatre* of conflict. If there
are wars in future the seas will figure in them for the same

reasons that they have in the past; as areas of communication to be controlled or interrupted, and as areas from which power can be deployed against the land. It is no part of my task to discuss the future of naval warfare as such, but the nature of naval forces is relevant to maritime order in peacetime, so to that extent it is appropriate to discuss them here.

The only prophecy that one can safely make about the future of naval warfare is that naval action in the 1980s will be as different from operations in World War II as those were different from the battles of Hampton Roads and of Lissa in the 1860s. The cause of the difference would be the same; the improvement of the range, the magnitude and the accuracy of firepower. Maximally effective fire-power no longer depends on heavy guns or manned aircraft which, in their turn, depend on massive floating platforms – battleships or aircraft carriers. The long-range precision-guided missile operated from small craft or even from submarines has introduced a radically new element into the situation. The manner and extent to which naval warfare has been transformed is still difficult to foresee. Those who use the analogy of the victory of the longbowmen over the French heavy cavalry at Creçy should remember that heavy cavalry remained indispensable on the battlefield for centuries after the longbow had been relegated to military museums. The continuing value of the aircraft carrier in, for example, projecting power from sea to land, appears self-evident. But the concept of the 'capital ship' is now more likely to confuse than to clarify thinking about naval strategy. The discussion as to whether the carrier or the nuclear submarine will be the capital ship of the future is singularly fruitless. There will probably not be any capital ships in the future – that is, any massive units of power which constitute the core of one's fleet and the principal instruments of one's strategy, and provide accurate indicators of one's naval strength. Their place is being taken by broad-based systems of surveillance and strike power built up from a complex of vessels, large and small. For these systems larger vessels may continue to furnish necessary centres for command and control, but their vulnerability and expense is likely to promote a constant search for more economical alternatives, a search which sooner or later is bound to be successful.

This development has important implications for peacetime. The systems which are replacing the old capital ship are not spectacular symbols of power and prestige. The craft are inconspicuous and their sophisticated capabilities are evident only to experts. Nor can the effectiveness of rival systems be compared by the layman. In the past naval power has been both spectacular and calculable, even if the course of hostilities subsequently showed the calculations to have been misleading. The British and the German navies before 1914, because their power was visibly crystallized in battleships, were major elements in international politics, and they did not have to fire a shot in order to be so. 'Command of the sea' was a mathematically calculable affair, and if Tirpitz had succeeded in out-building the British in dreadnoughts it would have been universally assumed that this command had passed to imperial Germany, with profound consequences for international relations.

It is hard to see that this could be so in the case of Admiral Gorshkov. The Soviet Union can, and perhaps has, built up a fleet of sufficient strength to deny to the United States any claim to command the seas, but unless she achieves a truly crushing superiority at all levels she will not be able credibly to claim that she commands it herself. The consequences of a conflict between the two navies would be so unpredictable that no naval supremacy could be established sufficiently unchallengeable to be translated into political dominance. The sea will in fact be 'uncommanded' – which, as that most intelligent of naval strategists Sir Julian Corbett pointed out in *Some Principles of Maritime Strategy*, is its natural condition.[2] 'Command of the sea' in peacetime lies, like beauty, in the eye of the beholder, and in future it will not be easy to behold.

It has been further suggested that these technological developments, by calling the whole concept of naval superiority into question, will greatly increase the power of small states; that the missile, especially the precision-guided missile, will be 'the great equalizer' and therefore work to the benefit of the Third World. This is a claim that must be treated with caution. Firearms, like any other weapon, are of use only to those who can afford to buy them and are trained to use them. One needs to know not only what new weapons the technologists have in store for us, but how much they are going to cost. We are witnessing today the navies of the wealthy European powers shrinking dangerously as technological change prices them almost out of the market. The cost factor will rigorously limit the number of Third World states which can avail themselves of the fruits of the new technology.

A further limitation will be training. By this I do not mean simply training in the use of the weapons themselves. We all know that the more sophisticated any mechanical system is, the easier it is to manipulate – though not necessarily to repair. But one can no more create a navy by teaching men to fire precision-guided missiles than one can create an army by teaching men to fire machine guns. Navies consist of a great deal more than hardware. Ships and their armament have to be serviced, deployed and, if need be, fought by highly trained, highly skilled, and highly disciplined officers and men, and these do not come in the normal flow of the arms traffic. Oil-rich countries may buy the vessels and the weapons and have men trained in their use, but the building up of an efficient, reliable, operational navy, especially an ocean-going navy, is a very long, hard slog indeed.

Small states may equip themselves with a 'bee-sting' capacity to deter direct naval attack, and build up forces competent to patrol their territorial waters up to the 12-mile limit. But for a long time to come it is likely to be only the most wealthy and sophisticated states that can exercise power at sea. In this as in so much else the gap between rich and poor will become greater rather than smaller.

I conclude by restating my original thesis. Order at sea is part of an international system of trade and communication which has shown remarkable toughness and resilience in the past and in whose stability every state in the world, with the possible exception of the People's Republic of China, has a great and growing interest. If that order collapses it will be as the result of economic, social and political developments by land. Leaders may arise in the Soviet Union with a greater attachment to doctrinal purity than to economic development, and so more concerned with overthrowing capitalism than with exploiting it. The Western powers, if they fail to solve their economic problems, may become more predatory in their mutual relations and less accommodating to the needs of the Third World. The less-developed countries themselves may become desperate or impatient and fall into the hands of adventuristic and irresponsible leaders. But all these eventualities depend upon developments which are of their nature unpredictable and lie beyond the scope of this conference to discuss.

Notes

1 'Sea Power and Political Influence', in *Power at Sea: Part I: The New Environment*, Adelphi Paper 122 (London: IISS, 1976).

2 Sir Julian Corbett, *Some Principles of Maritime Strategy* (London: Longmans, 1911; reprinted London: Conway Maritime Press, 1972.)

CHAPTER SIXTEEN

Letter to the editor

Survival 20-2, 1978

In the course of his otherwise kind review in the January issue of *Survival* of our edition of Clausewitz's *On War*, Donald Brennan takes me to task for suggesting that in the aftermath of the Korean War 'it became almost impossible to visualize any political objective for which the use of such (nuclear) weapons would be appropriate'.

Mr Brennan acknowledges that I am entitled to my opinion, but in view of the part played by nuclear deterrence in protecting the freedom of my country he finds this an 'extraordinary statement'. Mr Brennan is not an historian, but he was around at the time, and if he cannot recall the anguished debates to which this issue gave rise in the 1950s he must be remarkably forgetful. It was a controversy which engaged the best minds in my country and his own. More specifically, it was precisely this question that led a group of concerned Christians and political and military analysts to convoke the Brighton Conference out of which the IISS later developed.

If most of us have since come to our own conclusions on this matter and learned to 'live with the bomb', it has been very largely as a result of the serious and informed international debate sponsored by the IISS itself. The refinement both of the crude political concepts and of the crude weapons systems of the 1950s have made it a great deal easier to do so. But whether a further factor has not been a gradual blunting of our moral sensibilities is something that a younger generation is entitled to ask. I am afraid that Mr Brennan's reaction to my rather moderate statement may raise this question in many very minds.

CHAPTER SEVENTEEN

Book Review: Offense and defense in the international system

Offense and defense in the international system, by George H. Quester
(New York: John Wiley & Sons, 1977)

Survival 20-3, 1978

Professor Quester starts with the hypothesis that some
weapons systems are more conducive to international stability
than others, and surveys the history of warfare in the West to
see whether any general conclusions can be drawn from this
which could provide a basis for arms control in the contemporary world. It is an ambitious project; the more so since his book
is little more than two hundred pages in length, and he has to
depend for his knowledge about the history of warfare before
the nineteenth century on half-a-dozen secondary works, all in
English and some of them lamentably out of date. If one were to
attempt a scholarly criticism of his earlier chapters it would be
difficult to know where to begin. He makes some good points:
the development of castles in the early Middle Ages and the
consequent strengthening of the defensive certainly made it
harder for princes to assert their authority over unruly vassals.
But to go on to suggest that mounted knights were in any
sense a 'defensive' system and that the development of archers
strengthened the 'offensive' is rather casuistical; while the view
that archers were part of a 'national' force in a way that men-
at-arms were not (when both were part of a fully stipendiary

force in the service of the English Crown from the latter part of the thirteenth century) is wildly anachronistic. Sensible things are said about the development of cannon, but nothing about disciplined fire-power on the battlefield. The reader would, in short, be well advised to skip the first part of the book and concentrate on the second, where Professor Quester is a great deal more at home.

It is in fact difficult to identify before 1870 any weapons-system or technological development which was inherently destabilizing. Siege guns at the end of the fifteenth century briefly gave an advantage to the offensive until siegecraft restored the balance, but otherwise the destabilizing factors were political, psychological and economic: the ambitions of princes, the rivalries of merchants, the capacity to mobilize fiscal resources, and, at the end of the eighteenth century, the unleashing of popular passions. Napoleon conquered Europe with weapons little different from those available to Marlborough and Frederick the Great. A study of weapons systems before the industrial age tells us little of significance about the development of warfare: a study of the fiscal mechanisms which enabled governments to maintain armed forces in the field tells us much, much more.

When he comes to the twentieth century, Professor Quester has many interesting things to say. He stresses quite properly the incentive to pre-emption which the military systems of the pre-1914 era gave to their governments, and the way in which this undermined traditional 'balance of power' policies. He also points out most interestingly how the contrary emphasis on the power of the *defensive* between the wars made possible Hitler's aggression in Eastern Europe, by creating the assumption that Germany could not be effectively attacked in the West. Fixed defences indeed, always facilitate the offensive by making possible the concentration of forces for the offensive.

Professor Quester reminds us of the hopeless attempts made at disarmament conferences to define 'offensive' weapons, and brings us down to our own paradoxical times, when the most unambiguously offensive weapons of all, intercontinental ballistic missiles (ICBM), directed against the most vulnerable and inoffensive targets of all, cities, are considered to be stabilizing, while any developments which improve the defences of those cities or increase the vulnerability of those missiles are seen as threatening the security of the international system.

Professor Quester shyly confesses that he shares the prevailing prejudice in favour of defence against offence. But he points out not only that there are many occasions when the enhancement of a defensive capability can be destabilizing, but that, taken to extremes, defences can make it impossible to create any effective political system at all. Some offensive capability, if only in the hands of a police force, is needed in any social organism, which is one of the difficulties confronting proponents of General and Complete Disarmament. In sum, Professor Quester does no more than remind us how difficult it all is. Even if he had written a longer and more learned study it is doubtful whether he would have been able to say anything very different.

MICHAEL HOWARD
All Souls College, Oxford

CHAPTER EIGHTEEN

Obituary: Sir John Slessor, Marshal of the Royal Air Force

Survival 21-6, 1979

Jack Slessor was a founder member of the Council of the original Institute for Strategic Studies and one of the first Vice-Presidents of the IISS. His outstanding career in the Royal Air Force and the honours bestowed on him as an officer who reached the summit of his profession have tended to obscure his role as one of the most influential strategic thinkers of our times. For it was he who in 1952, as Chairman of the British Chiefs of Staff Committee, devised the formula for nuclear deterrence – the prevention of war by the threat of unacceptable and unavoidable retaliation – that was to be adopted by the British Government as the foundation for its defence policy, taken up by the US Joint Chiefs of Staff the following year, and promulgated by John Foster Dulles in 1954 as 'the New Look'. From this acorn that Slessor planted has developed the whole vast jungle of strategic nuclear theorizing that envelops us all today.

The concept of deterrence through Air Power was not of course new. It had been the orthodox doctrine of the Royal Air Force between the wars and indeed, briefly, the policy of the British Government when it began to rearm in 1934. But Slessor had not then been one of its most enthusiastic supporters. A deeply pragmatic man, he knew better than most the practical problems involved. Born in 1897, he went straight from school into the Royal Flying Corps in 1915, for the reason, which so well reflected his personal courage, that an attack of infantile paralysis in childhood had lamed him for life and so made it impossible for him to join the Army. He thus became one of that unique generation who, as young men, virtually invented the techniques of air warfare that they were to apply a generation later in the Second World War.

Between the wars Slessor spent four years at the Army Staff College at Camberley. So, at a time when most of his contemporaries were obsessed with the role of the RAF as an independent force, Slessor was thinking through the problems of co-operation with surface forces, and in 1936 he published one of the very few books on the subject: *Air Power and Armies*. This perhaps did something to set him apart from his colleagues, and although he was to command a Bomber Group in 1941–2, it was as C-in-C Coastal Command at the height of the Battle of the Atlantic in 1943 that he made his most notable contribution to the winning of the war – a post which in the struggle for priorities set him across the table from his colleagues in Bomber Command. But no acrimony ever developed. Indeed, much of his most notable work during the war was done in senior staff positions, smoothing out differences between the Services and between the Allies. His shrewdness and breadth of vision was to become as famous in Washington as it was in Whitehall.

For the last two years of the war Slessor was C-in-C of the RAF in the Mediterranean and Middle East; and in this capacity his experience in trying to ferry support to the Polish resistance during the Warsaw rising of August 1944, which was wrecked on the non-co-operation of the Soviet authorities, gave him a view of Soviet character and intentions that he was never to change. In 1950, at the time of the Korean War, he became

Chief of the Air Staff and found himself faced with the same depressing task that had confronted him as a staff officer in the Air Ministry in the 1930s – making military bricks without financial straw. The development of Britain's nuclear weapons and of the V-Bomber force to deliver them pointed, however, to a solution that had not been available before the war; and it was this that he persuaded his colleagues on the Chiefs of Staff Committee and later his Government to accept.

Slessor retired in 1954 and turned to writing and lecturing. His two books *Strategy for the West* (1954) and *The Great Deterrent* (1959) were vigorous if simplistic statements of the original doctrine of 'Massive Retaliation'. The controversy they helped to provoke brought him into contact with such critics of the theory as Rear-Admiral Sir Anthony Buzzard and Professor P. M. S. Blackett; and it was the discussions between these and other authorities that led to the foundation of the Institute in 1958.

Slessor's support for the Institute, and the weight his name carried in both Washington and London, was very largely responsible for its early success, and for some five years he played a leading part in its affairs, displaying in all its discussions not only all the expertise and political acumen to be expected from an authority of his experience, but an intellectual humility, an open-mindedness and a courteous readiness to listen to younger and far less experienced thinkers that was in itself an education in constructive thinking. Only his increasing lameness forced him to abandon his visits to London and to lose regular touch with the Institute's activities. We were intellectually impoverished by his absence; and his death marks the end of an epoch in our affairs.

MICHAEL HOWARD
All Souls College, Oxford

CHAPTER NINETEEN

Deterrence, consensus and reassurance in the defence of Europe

From Adelphi Paper 184, 1983

To ask a historian to look into and prescribe for the future is to invite a presentation consisting of as much past history as the author thinks he can get away with and as little prophecy and prescription as he thinks his audience will accept. Historians have seen too many confident prophets fall flat on their faces to lay themselves open to more humiliation than they can help. We know that all we can do is to help diagnose the problem or, better, expose false diagnoses. We also believe that in doing this it is helpful to consider how a situation has developed. I make no apology therefore for spending a few moments in casting a backward look over the origins and development of the Western Alliance to see how we have got to where we are now. There is little point in considering where we should be going if we do not first decide where we are starting from.

Let us go back thirty-five years, a third of a century, to the immediate aftermath of the Second World War. After the 'Battle of the Books' between the revisionist and counter-revisionist schools, a picture has now emerged over which most historians now agree. It is one of wartime understandings between the Soviet Union and her Western Allies – understandings based largely on Western illusions or at best the most fragile of hopes – breaking down within a few months of the end of hostilities. The Soviet Union moved in to consolidate, as part of her Empire, the territories already occupied by her armed forces – economically, politically and militarily. Simultaneously the United States was liquidating her wartime commitments to her European allies as quickly as – some might say more quickly than – she decently could. As a result, Western Europe in 1946–7 trembled on the verge of economic collapse, a collapse which its Moscow-orientated Communist parties were fully prepared to exploit. In Germany, and especially in Berlin, democratic political parties fought what seemed to be a losing battle against strong, well-organized and confident Communist opponents who, for the past fifteen years, had been preparing for just such an opportunity. There was a widespread fear, not so much of Soviet military attack on Western Europe, but of a disintegration of the whole political and economic structure that would make any such attack unnecessary.

It was to prevent such a disintegration that the United States initiated, in 1947, the European Recovery Programme. This programme may have had an unforeseen escalatory effect in that it was perceived by the Soviet Union as a threat to their own control of Eastern Europe, and so precipitated those actions in Prague and Berlin in 1948 that were read by many in the West as clear evidence of Soviet aggressive intentions. If the Russians were thwarted in their use of political means for attaining their objectives (so the argument went) might they not use military ones – unless they were deterred from doing so by the clear perception that any such move would bring them up against the enormous latent power of the United States?

Strategic reassurance

This was the thinking that led to the creation of the North Atlantic Treaty Organization in 1949. In Western Europe serious expectation of Soviet armed attack was still not high. It was to increase dramatically for a few months at the time of the Korean War, but even then the Europeans were less conscious of any imminent 'Soviet Threat' than they were of their own weakness, disunity and inability to cope with such a threat if one emerged. The American military presence was wanted in Western Europe, not just in the negative role of a *deterrent* to Soviet aggression, but in the positive role of a *reassurance* to West Europe, the kind of reassurance a child needs from its parents or an invalid from his doctors against dangers which, however remote, cannot be entirely discounted. This concept of *reassurance* has not, so far as I know, hitherto been a term of art in strategic analysis, but it should be, and so far as I am concerned it is now.

Whether the North Atlantic Treaty and the steps taken to implement it were really necessary to deter the Soviet Union from a military onslaught on Western Europe we cannot tell until the Soviet Union is as generous with access to her official documents as we are in the West. It is, however, improbable, given both her historical record and her political philosophy, that she would have seriously contemplated such an action unless and until a recognizable 'revolutionary situation' had developed in the West in which they could plausibly intervene to give fraternal support to the toiling masses and to a powerful indigenous Communist Party that would act as their agent in controlling the region after its conquest. These requirements seemed, in the 1940s, to be developing quite nicely. Within a decade they had disappeared. Whatever the effectiveness of *deterrence, reassurance* had worked. The economy of Western Europe recovered, and with it the political self-confidence of the West Europeans. The Communist Parties withdrew from the centre of the political stage to the periphery, and increasingly distanced themselves from Moscow. Serious fears of Soviet attack dwindled and, after Stalin's death, they almost disappeared from the public consciousness. The outbreaks in Eastern Europe from 1953 onwards showed that it was the Soviet Union that was now on the political defensive. Its treatment of the Hungarian rising in 1956 led to massive defections from, and splits within, the Communist Parties in the West. In West Germany the economic miracle sucked out of the Eastern Zone by the hundreds of thousands precisely those well-qualified young people that the DDR needed to reconstruct her own economy. By the end of the 1950s Western Europe was an economic power-house that would have dominated Eastern Europe if the Soviet Union had let it. A decade later it was beginning to rival its own protector.

During this period the success of *reassurance* was, in some respects, an obstacle to *deterrence.* The peoples of Western Europe were so effectively reassured that they were prepared to run those military risks that have given their military leaders nightmares for the past thirty years. In 1950 there may have been serious fears of Soviet attack. Three years later, when the European statesmen came to consider the price which their military advisers had calculated, at the Lisbon Meeting in 1952, that they would have to pay for a credible deterrent military posture, such fears had almost disappeared. The re-establishment of economic stability was considered to demand overriding priority and the 'Lisbon Force Goals' went out of the window. In the judgment of the political leaders of Western Europe the danger of Soviet military attack did not appear great enough to warrant the costs involved in building up the kind of defensive forces that, on a purely military calculus, would be needed to deter it.

The nuclear alternative: defence on the cheap

It was then that thermo-nuclear weapons came to the rescue of soldiers and politicians alike, providing a deterrent that appeared militarily credible at a socially acceptable cost. The long-term implications of depending on weapons of mass destruction for national security worried only a politically insignificant minority. Governments, and the majorities on which they relied, found in nuclear weapons so convenient a solution to their budgetary problems that they were adopted almost without question. 'Conventional forces', with all their heavy social costs, could be reduced to the status of trip-wires, or at most, of shields to repel an enemy assault for the brief time needed for the Strategic Air Command to strike decisively at targets within the Soviet Union. The critiques both of the moralists and of the military specialists made no impact on those real centres of power in Western governments, the Treasuries, centres which owe their power to their capacity to reflect and enforce broadly accepted social priorities. Whatever their defence specialists might tell them about the balance of military forces, the peoples of Western Europe, so long as they remained prosperous, saw little danger of Soviet attack and wanted defence on the cheap. They remained *reassured*, though whether this reassurance came from shrewdness or from self-delusion, from confidence in American nuclear supremacy or basic disbelief in the reality of any Soviet threat, it would probably be impossible to say. In any case throughout the 1950s and the 1960s deterrence and reassurance both worked. The Europeans did get defence on the cheap, as they were getting energy on the cheap, and, thanks to the benevolent Keynesianism of the ruling economic pundits, everything else on the cheap. As one European leader remarked of his own nation, they had never had it so good.

Pleasant as this condition was so long as it lasted, it had two characteristics which in historical perspective emerge very clearly. One was that the credibility of the *deterrent* posture depended on a continuing American nuclear ascendancy over the Soviet Union, something about which I shall have more to say in a moment. The second, and perhaps more significant, was that the peoples of Western Europe effectively abandoned responsibility for their own defence. Their own armed forces, forces which have always had the social role of embodying national self-consciousness and will to independent existence, became almost peripheral, part of a mechanism of nuclear deterrence the ultimate control of which lay elsewhere. The reluctance of the British and French Governments to accept this situation and their development of strategic nuclear capabilities of their own has to be understood in these psychological terms, rather than those of the somewhat tortuous rationales which French and British officials now advance to justify their existence.

And even if these nuclear strike forces do, however marginally, enhance national independence, they are not 'popular' forces. That is, they are not forces with whose fortunes the nation can identify itself, as the British people identified themselves with the fortunes of their forces in the recent Falkland Islands campaign. To show the significance of this fact, permit me a brief excursion into history. Popular involvement in war, as all readers of Clausewitz will know, is a matter of comparatively recent origin. In the eighteenth century, wars in Europe were fought by specialists responsive only to the requirements of absolute governments, and the less the population was involved in them the better. The role of the good citizen was to pay the taxes needed for the upkeep of these specialists, to acquiesce philosophically in any incidental hardships that their operations might cause him, and to keep his mouth shut. It was the French Revolution that (after the American Revolution) made popular involvement an intrinsic factor in war, a factor that was to become of growing importance until, in the First World War, it overshadowed everything else. In that conflict popular passion rather than military skill, much less political wisdom, determined the course of the war and ultimately its outcome. In the Second World War popular participation was still an essential element, although the contribution of scientific and technical specialists was increasingly decisive. But in the nuclear age those specialists have again reduced peoples to the passive roles they played, or were supposed to play, in the eighteenth century. It is assumed that war, if it comes, will be fought for them by experts, over (if they are lucky) their heads.

The experts and the public

The extent to which this has occurred can be seen by considering the debates over NATO strategy that have taken place, whether in official circles or in centres for strategic studies during the past twenty years. Increasingly the defence of Western Europe has been considered simply as a problem of 'extended deterrence' involving calculations of possibilities and probabilities as abstract as those of a chess game; as a problem to be solved by various combinations and deployments of delivery systems, strategic, intermediate or tactical, land-based, sea-based or air-based, but all under American control. The expertise needed to make these calculations is shared only by small groups of specialists and officials in European defence ministries, who have seldom seen it as their duty to expound these calculations to a wider public. The efforts of such bodies as the International Institute for Strategic Studies and its associates elsewhere in Europe to educate public opinion in these matters has had at best limited success. They are too abstract, too arcane. Whatever the merits of the argument, for example, that the Soviet deployment of SS-20 missiles had to be countered by the emplacement of cruise missiles and *Pershing* IIs, it did not arise out of any profound and widely held anxiety among the peoples of Western Europe. It was a debate between specialists – and specialists who did not have the political antennae to foresee that such emplacement might make people feel more vulnerable rather than less. Such specialists are like theologians. When they lose touch with the springs of popular belief, when their analysis becomes too complex and remote, their authority becomes attenuated. New teachers will arise, Martin Luthers, John Wesleys, pastors whose beliefs may be simplistic to the point of lunacy, but whose message is responsive to popular needs and who can speak in a language that everyone can understand.

This is not to say that the specialists are to blame for this failure in communication. In defence questions as in any other area of government – economic policy, for example, or finance – the layman does not expect to have to master the technical details. He employs the expert to handle them for him. In defence as in these other fields there is always likely to be a difference between expert and lay perceptions, and it is the job of political leadership to reconcile them. In the field of defence this difference appears nowhere more clearly than in the distinction I have made between *reassurance* and *deterrence*. For the expert the two are indistinguishable. He will not believe his country to be safe unless he is satisfied that provision has been made to counter every option open to every likely adversary. The layman may be less demanding, but sometimes he is more. In certain moods, for example, the Congress of the United States has refused to be reassured by the deterrent posture that its military specialists have pronounced to be adequate. In Europe, on the other hand, the peoples of the Western democracies have accepted as amply reassuring a deterrent posture that their experts have repeatedly told them is dangerously inadequate, and if the events of the past thirty years are anything to go by, popular instinct has proved more reliable than expert fears. In spite of the repeated warnings of its military specialists, no threat has materialized. Instead, the prosperity of the West has reached unheard of heights. It is the Communist societies, those which thirty years ago seemed so psychologically as well as militarily menacing, that now appear to be on the verge of economic and political disintegration.

Changes in the international structure

Since the system that we have adopted has proved so successful for so long, is there really anything for us to worry about? Is there any need to reassess the requirements for defence, deterrence or reassurance for the 1980s and 1990s. I must admit once more to a historian's bias, which predisposes me to assume the obsolescence of any international structure with the passage of time. The Vienna Settlement of 1814–15, for example, lasted for about forty years. So did the Bismarckian Settlement of the 1870s. The structure is bound to be transformed by the dynamics of social change, by the altered perspectives and beliefs of a new generation sceptical, and usually rightly so, about the settled assumptions of its predecessors. We must ask not only whether the existing solutions are still valid for the problems that evoked them, but whether the problems themselves remain unchanged, and whether attitudes stereotyped in the late 1940s will still be relevant half a century later.

There can be little doubt that since 1949 changes have occurred, both objective and subjective, on a scale comparable to those between 1815 and 1854, or between 1870 and 1914: changes in the relationship between Western Europe and the United States; and changes in the military balance between the United States and the Soviet Union. These have been on a scale quite sufficient to compel a reappraisal of requirements for deterrence and reassurance established a generation ago.

The various causes and symptoms of transatlantic tension have been discussed so generally and so repeatedly that I propose to focus only on that most relevant to our immediate problem, that is the degree of anti-American sentiment now so evident in so many countries of Western Europe, to say nothing of the understandable resentment this has created in the United States. Opinion polls have revealed this anti-Americanism to be far less widespread than its more dramatic manifestations may sometimes suggest but, whatever its strength and incidence, it is disturbing enough to demand an explanation and to be taken seriously into account. It indicates that, for an appreciable number of Europeans, what was once seen as the prime requirement for *deterrence*, that is the commitment of American power to the defence of Western Europe, no longer provides the political *reassurance* that once it did; in some respects indeed it provides the exact opposite. So far from the Americans being in Europe to help the West Europeans defend themselves, they are seen in some quarters as being here in order to prosecute *their* war, a war in which the Europeans have no interest and from which they will be the first to suffer.

How has such a widespread and grotesque misunderstanding come about? Obviously there is a whole complex of reasons, in which simple cultural friction plays its part. But it is at least in part the outcome of the process I have described, by which the defence of Europe has become perceived not as the responsibility of the Europeans themselves but increasingly in terms of a system of 'extended nuclear deterrence' manipulated from the United States in accordance with strategic concepts with which few Europeans are familiar. If I may return to my historical discourse, in the eighteenth century the European bourgeoisie was well content to leave the conduct of war to its specialists and enjoy the improved quality of life made possible by that division of labour. But it was precisely this divorce of the bourgeoisie and their intelligentsia from the whole business of national defence that gave rise to the first 'Peace Movements', comprising intellectuals who maintained that, because wars were conducted by monarchical states with aristocratic-led professional soldiers, it was this war-making mechanism that actually *produced* wars, and that all that was needed to abolish war would be to abolish monarchs, aristocrats and the military profession. After that it could be assumed that the peoples of Europe would live together in peace and harmony. The wars of the French Revolution were to disillusion them, as the First World War was to disillusion another generation of peace-bred intellectuals and the Second World War yet a third. But it takes only one generation of successful peacekeeping to engender the belief, among those not concerned with its mechanisms, that peace is a natural condition threatened only by those professionally involved in preparations for war. The military become the natural target for the idealistic young. And how much more will this be the case if those military are predominantly foreign? If the decision for peace or war appears to lie with a group of remote and uncontrollable decision-makers whose values and interests do not necessarily coincide with one's own? And if war is going to involve slaughter on so unimaginable a scale? Is it not these foreigners who are actually provoking the war? Are not the bases they have established in our territories a standing provocation to attack, eroding rather than enhancing our security? So the growth of pacifism, always endemic in a society that delegates defence questions to specialists, has in contemporary Europe become associated with anti-Americanism, and derives from that a populist veneer that otherwise it might lack.

It is here that the change in the military balance comes in. I would not like to judge how far the effectiveness of American *reassurance* in the 1950s and 1960s was due to any general perception in Western Europe of American nuclear predominance. Certainly neither European nor American defence experts habitually cited this as evidence for the credibility of nuclear deterrence. One can only say that expectations of the damage Western Europe might suffer as a result of Soviet response to that American 'first use' on which NATO strategy explicitly depended led to no widespread questioning among Europeans of the validity of that strategy. It was the Americans, under Mr McNamara, who were unhappy about it, but they could find few people in Europe, outside our tiny defence community, to share their doubts. The fact that the 'Peace Movement' has become active in Western Europe at the precise moment that the United States has publicly admitted Soviet nuclear parity may or may not be coincidental. It does mean however that the 'Peace Movement' can now support its arguments with some fairly tough strategic analysis, and find more sympathy within the defence community than would have been the case twenty years ago. It is no longer only a minority of anti-militarist intelligentsia who question the validity and credibility of a deterrent posture which would, if activated, destroy everything it is concerned to defend.

The result of these developments has been a serious disjunction between *deterrence* and *reassurance*. The object of *deterrence* is to persuade an adversary that the costs to him of seeking a military solution to his political problems will far outweigh the benefits. The object of *reassurance* is to persuade one's own people, and those of one's allies, that the benefits of military action, or preparation for it, will outweigh the costs. It is true that the Europeans were reassured in the 1950s not by any careful calculation of what they would lose or gain by war, but by their perception of the reverse – of how much the USSR would have to lose and how little to gain. She could threaten, or rather her allies could threaten, such cataclysmic damage to the enemy, at such low *immediate* social cost to herself, that the risk of any comparable damage to herself was seen as remote enough to be tolerable.

This is the situation that has been changed by nuclear parity, and it is a change of which all Europeans and an increasing number of Americans have now become conscious. Defence specialists may be puzzled and scornful that people who have been under threat of nuclear attack for at least twenty years should only now be beginning to take the problem seriously, but that they have now begun to do so is a new political fact that governments will have to take into account. It is also apparent, at least in Europe, that *reassurance* cannot be re-established by any improvement in the mechanism of *deterrence*, certainly not of nuclear deterrence. Perhaps the people of Western Europe ought to feel safer when the installation of *Pershing* II and cruise missiles has made clear our capacity to counter an SS-20 first strike, but I doubt whether they really will. Perhaps we should all feel safer if the United States did develop the capacity to carry on, and 'prevail' in, a prolonged nuclear exchange with the Soviet Union but in fact public opinion in Europe is terrified by the prospect – and so is much of it in the United States. In the calculus of nuclear deterrence both developments may appear appropriate, even essential, but such a calculus does not translate easily into the language of political reassurance and certainly not in a Europe where any nuclear exchange, on however limited a scale, spells almost inconceivable disaster. Limited nuclear options do not look very attractive if we are likely to be one of them ourselves.

The fear of nuclear war

Any consideration of domestic consensus on defence questions must therefore begin with the realization that in Europe the Soviet Union is very widely seen as less of a danger than is the prospect of nuclear war. I state this dogmatically and can support the statement with no evidence from opinion polls. It is an impression gained from a wide study of the press, the media, and discussion with friends and colleagues outside the defence community. It is also important to realize that the nuclear war anticipated is not seen as one arising out of a Soviet attack on Western Europe, but rather from some self-sustaining process of escalation, perhaps originating in an extra-European conflict, but essentially caused by the whole apparatus of nuclear weapons in some way 'getting out of control'. Nuclear war is seen as a *Ding an Sich* (thing of itself), unrelated to the existing political situation or to any security requirements likely to arise out of it. It is therefore against the prospect of nuclear war itself, rather than that of Soviet attack, that Europeans now require reassurance, and any measures taken to deal with the latter that make the former seem more likely will continue to be deeply disruptive. The explanation that any measures effective in deterring Soviet attack make nuclear war *less* likely is no longer, for many Europeans, altogether persuasive. As fears of nuclear war become detached from fears of Soviet attack, so reassurance becomes divorced from deterrence. And it must be admitted that those calculations of nuclear strategy so distressingly prevalent in the United States, which take place in a kind of empyrean realm remote from the political realities of Europe or anywhere else, have powerfully contributed to this divorce.

Reconciling deterrence and reassurance

How are we to deal with this problem? How are deterrence and reassurance to be once more reconciled? This is the task that will confront statesmen and strategists for the rest of this century.

The task is complicated by differing perspectives on either side of the Atlantic as to what it is that we have to deter. The difference between European and American readings of Soviet power and intentions, to which we could and perhaps should devote an entire conference, have here to be accepted as given. As European fears of Soviet aggression have waned over the past thirty years, so American fears have grown. We have too the curious phenomenon that the countries most directly threatened by Soviet military power – West Germany and France – are those most confident in their ability to handle the Soviet Union through the normal machinery of diplomatic and political intercourse, while for the most remote, the most powerful and the least threatened of the allies – the United States – the Soviet Union still bulks as a figure of almost cosmic evil with whom no real dialogue is possible. Whether the European attitude is the result of greater wisdom or merely of wishful thinking is a matter that we could debate endlessly but I believe that a significant element in this difference of view lies in the degree to which the Europeans have abandoned the primary responsibility for their defence to the United States. Europeans have come to take the deterrence provided by others for granted and now assume that the dangers against which they once demanded reassurance only now exist in the fevered imagination of their protectors. A certain American tendency to hyperbole, an attachment to worst-case analysis and some unfortunate attempts to make our flesh creep with official publications in gorgeous technicolour whose statistics have been questioned even by European defence specialists, have not helped improve matters. Such propagandistic efforts are widely discounted, and even when they are believed they are likely to engender not so much resolution as despair.

Our first task must therefore be to get Soviet power and intentions into perspective. The exaggerated melodrama implied in the term 'The Soviet Threat' seems and has always seemed to me unnecessary and counter-productive. There is a major problem of ideological hostility, and a major problem (though one not to be exaggerated) of military imbalance between a power the size of the Soviet Union and the smaller, even if richer and more dynamic, states of Western Europe. One does not have to attribute to the Soviet Union either predatory intentions or ambitions for global conquest to persuade all but a stubborn minority that the states of Western Europe have a problem of military security that must be solved if normal intercourse with the Soviet Union is to be sustained on a basis of equality. The Soviet Union has shown herself to be no more reluctant to use military means to solve political problems, when she can get away with it, than anyone else. It is not difficult to reach consensus within most groups of West Europeans that West Europe needs defences against the Soviet Union. Where consensus breaks down is over the question whether Europe can possibly be defended by nuclear war.

The second task therefore is to show that Europe *can* be defended, and that the costs of doing so would not outweigh the benefits. These costs must be seen as twofold: the prospective costs of nuclear war, with which public opinion is chiefly concerned; and the immediate costs of an economic kind, which are what worry governments. It is easy enough to say that no price is too high for the preservation of our independence, but it does not quite work out like that. Governments are concerned with independence, but they are also concerned with social stability. Even in the darkest days of the Cold War 'the soviet threat' was seen as ancillary to, and only given credibility by, the danger of social disintegation in the West. It is still a reasonable assumption that a stable and prosperous Western Europe will not present an attractive target to Soviet ambitions. Defence expenditure has therefore to be fitted in to a general framework of economic policy in which the maintenance of an industrious economy and a high level of social welfare (so far as these can be reconciled) must enjoy an overriding priority. This assumption has not altered over the past thirty years, nor is it likely to change much over the next thirty.

During the past thirty years this problem of costs was, as we have seen, taken care of by nuclear deterrence. The immediate costs were kept acceptably low, the risk of incurring the ulti-mate costs seemed acceptably slight. Now, although there is a far greater reluctance to incur those long-term risks, there is no greater readiness to accept any increase in immediate costs, especially during a period of recession when the danger of social instability seems greater than at any time since the 1940s. Again, it is easy to say that no price should be too high for the avoidance of nuclear war but, for governments concerned with their everyday tasks, nuclear war still remains a remote if terrifying hypotheses, while mass unemployment, commer-cial bankruptcies and industrial discontent are an imminent reality. A society where domestic consensus has collapsed is in no position to fight a war, nuclear or otherwise.

So where does this leave us? First, the requirement for effective deterrence remains, if only because the Soviet Union cannot be expected to observe a higher standard of conduct towards weaker neighbours than other states, whatever their political complexion, have shown in the past. Second, deter-rence can no longer depend on the threat of a nuclear war, the costs of which would be grotesquely out of proportion to any conceivable benefits to be derived from engaging in it. Third, proposals to make nuclear war 'fightable', let alone 'winna-ble' by attempting to limit its targets and control its course, however much sense this may make in the military grammar of *deterrence*, are not persuasive in the political language of *reassurance*. And finally the problem cannot be solved by any massive transferral of resources to conventional capabilities. The immediate social costs of doing so, whether one likes it or not, are unacceptably high.

Reducing dependence on US deterrence

Whatever the solution may be, I do not believe that it can be found at the macro-level of nuclear deterrence. There is a point beyond which the elaboration of nuclear arsenals ceases to bear any evident relation to the real problems faced by political communities and, so far as Europe is concerned, we passed that point long ago. It must be sought at the micro-level of the peoples, the societies that have to be defended, and for whose political cohesion, moral resolution and military preparedness nuclear weapons can no longer provide a credible substitute. There has been for many years what I can only describe as a morally debilitating tendency among European defence specialists to argue that, if the reassurance provided by the American nuclear guarantee were to be in any way diminished, European morale would collapse. I do not believe this to be true and, in so far as it is true, it is as a self-fulfilling prophecy, and one that American defence analysts have taken altogether too seriously. The reassurance on which most Europeans rely is the presence among them of American troops, a presence that makes the defence of West European territory appear a feasible proposition and has encouraged us to make greater provision for our own defence. What is needed today is a reversal of that process whereby European Governments have sought greater security by demanding an ever greater intensification of the American nuclear commitment, demands that are as divisive within their own countries as they are irritating for the people of the United States. Instead we should be doing all that we can to reduce our dependence on American nuclear weapons by enhancing, so far as it is militarily, socially and economically possible, our capacity to defend ourselves.

By 'defend ourselves' I mean defend ourselves in the conventional sense with conventional weapons. I know that this view will not be universally popular. It is often argued that no such defence is possible unless we are prepared to turn West Europe into an armed camp, but that proposition would be true only if we intended to fight a total war aiming at the destruction of the

Soviet armed forces and the dictation of peace in Moscow. It is also argued that, whatever effort we made, the Soviet armed forces would ultimately overwhelm us. Of course they could, if they were prepared to pay a very high price, which is why I for one would be unwilling explicitly to renounce under any circumstances the use of nuclear weapons. It has been argued that, for those exposed to it, conventional war is no less terrible than nuclear war, and indeed events in the Lebanon have shown us just how terrible it can be – especially for those who have no means of defending themselves. But terrible as conventional war would be in Europe, nuclear war would be unimaginably, unendurably worse. Modern societies recover from conventional war within a generation. Whether humanity would ever recover from nuclear war is a matter for legitimate doubt.

Let us remember what we are trying to do. It is to deter the Soviet Union from using military force to solve its political differences with the West and to deter them in a way that will be credible to their leaders and acceptable – *reassuring* – to our own peoples. It is to make clear to the Soviet Union that in any attack on the West the costs will hugely outweigh the benefits, and to our own people that the benefits of such a defence will outweigh the costs. We have to make it clear to our potential adversaries that there can be no easy military solution to their political problems, no 'quick fix'. And this is best done by showing that any attack would be met by lethally efficient armed forces, backed up and where necessary, assisted by a resolute and prepared population, with the distinct possibility that the conflict might escalate to nuclear war and the certainty that, *even if it did not*, their armed forces would suffer casualties out of all proportion to any likely gains. The object of such defence would not be just the denial of territory. It would be the infliction of damage on the attacking forces on a scale incommensurate with any political objective they could conceivably gain by their attack. The image that the West Europeans need to present is that of a hedgehog – painful to devour and impossible to digest.

This is no doubt an ideal model but I defy anyone to think of a better. The probable alternative is one of inadequate, ill-equipped and undertrained forces, fighting on behalf of a divided or an indifferent population and dependent on an American President being prepared to sanction a nuclear release that would certainly destroy all they were fighting to defend and that might very well unleash a global holocaust into the bargain. That is the prospect that worries so many of us today, and the 'Peace Movement' is only articulating, in extreme form, many widespread and legitimate doubts. To escape from this situation and move towards the goal I have suggested would mean a change of emphasis from nuclear deterrence to conventional, or even unconventional defence. It would mean a shifting of primary responsibility to the Europeans for the defence of our own continent. It should also involve a greater degree of popular participation in defensive preparations, participation the more likely to be forthcoming if it is clear that such preparations were predominantly if not wholly non-nuclear. An invitation to participate in such preparations would indeed be the acid test for the 'Peace Movement', sorting out those who were interested only in making moral gestures and those whose sympathies lie on the other side of the Iron Curtain from the great majority of thoughtful citizens seriously concerned with questions of defence.

Progress along these lines, however modest would do much to resolve the difficulties within the Alliance and create what Professor Lawrence Freedman has called 'a more mature relationship'. It would create a defence posture acceptable to our own peoples as well as credible to our potential adversaries. It

would not solve the problem of deterring a first nuclear strike by
the opposition. For that, as for much else, the Europeans must
continue to depend on the United States, and few Americans
would wish it otherwise. But this reliance must be placed in
perspective. A Soviet nuclear attack on Western Europe, or the
plausible threat of one, is perhaps not utterly inconceivable. It
is certainly an option that we need to deter. But it does not
rank high on the list of political probabilities, and the measures
taken to counter it should not be regarded or depicted as being
basic to the defence of Western Europe. The necessity for such
counter-measures should be fully and publicly explained, but
they should be put in the context of the fundamental task which
only non-nuclear forces can effectively carry out, the defence of
territory. Nuclear deterrence needs to be subordinated to this
primary task of territorial defence, and not vice versa.

It is the reassertion of this order of priorities, this reunit-
ing of deterrence and reassurance, that seems to me basic for
the creation of consensus within the Alliance over the requirements for the defence of the West in the 1980s, or indeed
for however long it may take to establish such intimate and
friendly relations with the Soviet Union that defence becomes
a pure formality. And in order to maintain consensus, the
achievement of this relationship must be seen to be our
long-term goal. I hope it goes without saying that any developments along the lines I have proposed should go hand in
hand with arms-control initiatives, both to eliminate unnecessary causes of tension and to keep the costs of defence on
both sides down to socially acceptable levels. But we should
not allow ourselves to expect any miraculous breakthroughs
as a result of such initiatives, or be unduly depressed or bitter
if they fail. 'The Dual Track' is essential to effective reassurance: peoples expect their governments to provide them with
adequate protection, but they also expect them to seek peace

and, if they are not seen to be doing so, consensus over defence will crumble away.

Above all we must stop being frightened, and trying to frighten each other, with spectres either of Soviet 'windows of opportunity' or of the prospect of inevitable, self-generating nuclear war. Defence will continue to be a necessity in a world of sovereign states. Nuclear war is a terrible possibility that nothing can now eradicate, but of whose horrors we must never lose sight. To deal with the dilemma arising from these twin evils we need clear heads, moral courage, human compassion, and above all a sense of proportion. The main condition for consensus in the 1980s is in fact that we should all grow up. This, unfortunately, may be the most difficult requirement of all.

CHAPTER TWENTY

Obituary: Raymond Aron, 1905–1983

Survival 26-1, 1984

Professor Raymond Aron, President of the International Institute for Strategic Studies since 1978, died on 17 October 1983, at the age of 78.

Although he was an academic by profession and never held any post of political responsibility, it would be misleading to classify Raymond Aron simply as 'an intellectual'. Like most of his generation, he learned from the hard experiences of the 1930s the need for intellectuals to become *engagés* in politics, to abandon the frivolous detachment and the equally frivolous flirtation which had made possible the rise of Fascism. But his *engagement* went far beyond that of his friend and rival Jean Paul Sartre and Sartre's imitators in London and New York who had little idea where their philosophies might lead and who cared still less. Aron was a true disciple of Clausewitz, the philosopher about whom he wrote his last great book. For him what mattered was *the object*: not the logical coherence or intrinsic harmony of ideas in themselves, but what happened in the real world when people started applying them. The test of their validity was whether they worked: whether the political structures which embodied them were truly conducive to justice internally and peace internationally – not in some remote messianic future, but here and now. For Aron, therefore, *actualités* were just as important as ideas, and his contributions to *Le Figaro* no less significant than his lectures at the Sorbonne.

It was this pragmatism that made Aron so sympathetic to the ideas and ideals of the Anglo-Saxons and distanced him from so many of his French contemporaries – not least from Charles de Gaulle. But he may have learned something from his experiences among Anglo-Saxons during the Second World War. His initial studies lay in exactly the opposite direction, among the German idealist philosophers of the nineteenth century. It was easy enough for someone, especially a Jew, who witnessed the Nazi revolution to discern, from their obscene outcome, the fallacies in the reasoning of the neo-Hegelian worshippers of state power. It required an altogether cooler head to resist the Gadarene stampede into the apparently opposite, factually almost identical camp of Marxism, and steely courage to spend the rest of his life, among the jeers of students and colleagues on the Left Bank, exposing with patience, good humour and unanswerable logic the fallacies of that always fashionable cause. His *L'Opinion des intellectuels* (1954) will remain, like Karl Popper's *Open Society and its Enemies*, an enduring monument of bleak common sense after the romantic neo-Marxist extravagances of the 1960s and 1970s have been exploded and forgotten.

The Second World War swept Aron into political and journalistic activity. He spent the bulk of it with de Gaulle in London, editing *La France Libre* and perhaps learning that tolerance, if not admiration, for British *moeurs* which made him so easy and acceptable a visitor after the war throughout the English-speaking world. Certainly it gave him experience of a political system that was not polarized, like the French, between Fascism and Communism, but expressed those qualities of moderation and balance which were so signally to characterize his own writings once he returned to France.

The scope and volume of these writings were to be formidable. For nearly forty years he contributed his weekly article to *Le Figaro*. He lectured prolifically, first at the *Institut d'études politiques*, later (from 1956–72) at the Sorbonne, finally at the *École pratique des hautes études*. Many of his works were spin-offs of his courses; one in particular, *Main Currents in Sociological Thought* (1965) remains a textbook much in demand by students on both sides of the Atlantic for the lucidity with which it unravels the somewhat inspissated texts of the sociological pioneers. But his own original contribution was made in the field, not of sociology, but of international politics. His huge *Paix et Guerre entre les Nations* (1962) surveyed the whole field of international relations in the nuclear age with unprecedented scope and thoroughness. As a framework for analysis it remains unsurpassed.

But Aron was not concerned with analysis alone. His ultimate concern was action, and his conclusions were addressed as much to statesmen as to his academic colleagues. His wisdom contained no paradoxes or surprises: for him the ultimate virtue of the statesman lay in *prudence*; the sagacious exercise of responsibilities which in the nuclear age were almost unendurably heavy.

Without being in the least Machiavellian, his writings, like those of Machiavelli, were designed for the practitioners of statecraft; he was concerned neither to dazzle with intellectual skill nor to achieve striking conceptual breakthroughs. Much of his best work lay in the careful discussion of the ideas of other people. He was above all *sensible*, in the best eighteenth century meaning of the term. Dr Johnson and Voltaire would have enjoyed his company; Rousseau would not. His ideas and his politics were instinct with those standards of sanity, tolerance and moderation which lie at the heart of Western civilization; standards always as vulnerable to collapse from within as to destruction by external barbarians. There are all too few such leaders, whether political or intellectual, left to us in the world today.

MICHAEL HOWARD

CHAPTER TWENTY-ONE

In memoriam: Hedley Bull, 1932–1985

Survival 27-5, 1985

Hedley Bull joined the Institute in 1960, when he was on the staff of the London School of Economics. At the time Alastair Buchan was organizing the Second Annual Conference on the topic 'The Control of the Arms Race', and he needed a rapporteur. In those days the rapporteur was very much a key figure. After briefing by a small study group, the rapporteur wrote a series of papers which provided the basic material for Conference discussions and in due course became chapters in a published book. Hedley's papers were such masterpieces of lucidity and compression that they left little more to be said. He brought to his work the rigour of a trained philosopher, cutting with the cold precision of a Descartes through the technical complexities and conceptual confusion which had hitherto characterized almost all discussion on the subject. Largely as a result of Hedley's formulations the Conference marked something of a turning point in Western thinking about arms control; and the resulting book, *The Control of the Arms Race* (1961), still ranks with Thomas Schelling's *Strategy of Conflict* as one of the great seminal works in the field of strategic studies.

Almost overnight Hedley thus became an international figure. A few years later he was to establish a comparable reputation in the broader field of international relations theory with a devastating onslaught on the American behaviouralist school in an article in *World Politics* (April 1966). Like *The Control of the Arms Race*, this and subsequent writings displayed the full quality of Hedley's thought: common-sense hard as a diamond, sharpened to stiletto point, and directed with unerring aim against imprecision, verbosity and cant. It was a quality which he displayed quite dazzlingly in his interventions at the Institute's conferences where he became a regular attender, and where he cut people down to size with the speed of a Chicago meat-packer and the elegance of a matador. An Australian – and a New South Welshman – to the marrow of his bones, he had no time for British pomposity and mistrusted American pretensions even more. But he made his thrusts with such elegance and humour, was a thinker of such formidable quality and, above all, was such a delightful man that British and American universities fell over one another in competing for his favours.

As was proper, however, he returned to his own country to take up the Chair of International Relations at the Australian National University in 1967. This did not mean that the Institute lost his services. Almost simultaneously the Council was enlarged to include Australian and Japanese members, and Hedley was elected as the first Council Member from Australia. The Antipodean perspective which he was now able to bring to the Institute's programmes helped to wean them away from the fixation over the East–West confrontation which had understandably dominated the first decade of the Institute's activities. A year in India made Hedley especially sensitive to the emerging problem of the North–South relationship, and an element of controlled passion began to appear in his writings. More and more did he find himself out of sympathy with American strategic analysts who reduced the complexities and tragedies of the world to calculations of the nuclear balance, and he intensified his search for an analysis of international relations which would fully comprehend the full diversity of international society. It came with *The Anarchical Society* (1977); a more difficult, but fuller and richer book than *The Control of the Arms Race*, and likely to rank with Raymond Aron's *War and Peace Among Nations* as one of the foremost works in its field to appear in the second half of the present century.

In 1976 Hedley Bull came to Oxford as a Visiting Fellow of All Souls College, and was with us when Alastair Buchan, then the Montagu Burton Professor of International Relations, so suddenly and tragically died. Hedley was so evidently the obvious candidate to succeed Alastair that he reluctantly abandoned his work at Canberra and returned to Oxford the following year. The administrative burdens laid on Oxford professors by a university which gives them responsibility without either power or money, combined with an unstinting devotion to the scores of research students who were to flock to him from all over the world, were to inhibit any further major original work, but Hedley's skill as an editor and organizer still had full scope. It is perhaps seen at its best in the collection of essays which he edited with Adam Watson, *The Expansion of International Society* (1984): a remarkable and as yet undervalued book, every chapter of which bears the stamp of Hedley's influence.

Hedley did not allow the chores of Oxford to lessen his devotion to the Institute, to whose Council he had been re-elected in 1981. He regularly attended its meetings, and those of the Executive Committee, until March 1985, when he came to London for the last time to hear Paul Nitze give the Alastair Buchan Memorial Lecture. By now he was all too evidently a dying man. He had been struck down with cancer of the spine in the summer of 1984, and by the spring of 1985 it was clear that the case was terminal. It was typical of Hedley that he continued to see his students until within two days of his death on 18 May 1985. They, perhaps even more than his writings, were to be his true legacy to mankind.

MICHAEL HOWARD

CHAPTER TWENTY-TWO

IISS – the first thirty years: a general overview

Adelphi Paper 235, 1989

Thirty years have passed since the first annual conference of the ISS (as it then was) assembled in Oxford in 1959 to consider the problems of 'Independence within NATO'. But the Institute had in fact been conceived at an earlier conference which had met in this town of Brighton two years earlier in January 1957; and the convening of that conference was the outcome of discussions which had been going on for most of 1956. It is worth considering for a moment what those discussions were about, and what the original founders of the Institute had in mind, before we go on to ask how successful we have been in carrying out their intentions.

The true founding fathers of the Institute, I suppose, were the men who invented nuclear, and in particular thermonuclear, weapons. It was the development of these weapons in the 1950s, and especially the declared intention of the government of the United States in 1954 to place primary reliance upon them to deter aggression, that elevated the whole question of the conduct of war from the level of a professional speciality for the military to an issue carrying the profoundest and most horrifying implications for the destiny of mankind.

For some the answer seemed easy: simply abolish nuclear weapons, either unilaterally or by agreement. That was and remains the message of the Campaign for Nuclear Disarmament, whose establishment was almost simultaneous with that of the ISS. But for those who were less sanguine about the transformation of the international political system which this would involve, neither that nor the apparently equally simple formula of 'massive retaliation' provided a feasible way forward. International conflict, in particular confrontation with the Soviet Union, was likely to continue, with or without nuclear weapons, for a very long time to come. Given such continuing tensions, war remained an immanent possibility: indeed a power which could not invoke it as a possibility was by definition defenceless. But how could a war be fought between nuclear powers without involving a degree of mutual and collateral destruction far transcending any conceivable political issues at stake? And if it could not be fought, how could it be credibly threatened? And if it could not be credibly threatened, how could deterrence work?

These questions were being insistently asked by laymen – journalists, politicians, academics, political commentators – throughout the later 1950s. The inability of officials to give any satisfactory answers, even to themselves, no doubt strengthened their reluctance to discuss such questions with irresponsible amateurs. In the United States there were indeed *foci* of informed discussion, especially at RAND Corporation and on the Charles River, but in Europe there was nothing, and no willingness by governments to promote anything. In London, however, the Royal Institute for International Affairs – Chatham House – did provide facilities, in early 1956, for a small study group to examine the ideas which one of its members, Rear-Admiral Sir Anthony Buzzard, was developing about the feasibility of using nuclear weapons on a limited scale, to provide what he called 'graduated deterrence'; a concept which later became known as 'Flexible Response'. The other members of the study group were Richard Goold-Adams, a leading figure at Chatham House and a former member of the editorial staff of *The Economist*; Professor P.M.S. Blackett, a distinguished physicist whose work in nuclear physics had won him a Nobel Prize and who had pioneered the science of operational analysis in World War II, and Denis Healey, then spokesman for the Labour Party on defence questions, and later a formidable Secretary of State for Defence.

The group produced a pamphlet, *On Limiting Nuclear War*, which still bears re-reading. Meanwhile Tony Buzzard, who was a keen churchman, had brought his ideas to the attention of the bishop of his diocese, Dr Bell, Bishop of Chichester; a man who had had the courage to question the morality of area bombing at the height of World War II and who was deeply concerned over the ethics of nuclear war. Bell invited Buzzard to discuss his ideas with the Chairman of the Commission of the Churches on International Affairs (CCIA), Sir Kenneth Grubb, with a view to organizing a small conference to consider them and perhaps give them wider publicity. Grubb agreed to organize and chair such a conference, using the facilities of the London office of the Commission, and put its new Secretary, the Reverend Alan Booth, in charge of arrangements. The invitees, about seventy of them, were chosen very much at random from the services, politics, the universities and the press. We received invitations out of the blue and turned up at the Bedford Hotel on the evening of 18 January 1957, largely out of curiosity. Little did we realize what we were starting.

The discussions at the conference were not in themselves memorable – at least, I cannot remember them. The personal links established among its members, across professional and national boundaries (there was a healthy sprinkling of

Americans) were. The suggestion therefore that some structure should be established to keep us in touch with each other and if possible arrange another meeting of the same kind was passed by acclamation on that grey Sunday afternoon, and a collection was taken to fund it. So the Brighton Conference Association came into being. Kenneth Grubb was its President, Alan Booth its secretary, and its committee consisted of the original Chatham House study group, with the exception of Blackett, who was too busy to take part, and the addition of me.

The aims of the BCA were initially defined as being 'to promote further interest, to discuss and to study the limitation of war in the nuclear age'. For a few months we did no more than collect and circulate articles and materials bearing on this topic. This meant finding out what was going on in the United States, which was, of course, a great deal; and, if we did nothing else, we made the names of Wohlstetter and Brodie, Schelling and Nitze, Kissinger and Kahn familiar on this side of the Atlantic. But we felt that simply to provide an information service was not enough. There should be a centre, preferably international in scope, where these questions could be studied in depth; and there seemed everything to be said for establishing it in London. Denis Healey was able to interest Shephard Stone of The Ford Foundation, and after prolonged discussions The Ford Foundation approved a grant, in November 1958, of $150,000 spread over three years. Meanwhile we had recruited Alastair Buchan, then defence correspondent of *The Observer*, as Director designate, and the Institute for Strategic Studies was formally incorporated under British company law on 20 November 1958.

Once Alastair was involved, the Institute became his enterprise, and the rest of us faded gracefully into the background. He was an inspired choice, and we still quarrel genially over who was responsible for recruiting him. Apart from his intelligence and his driving energy, Alastair was a true Atlantic man, equally at home in London, Ottawa and Washington and on first-name terms with anyone of any importance in all three capitals. He stood no nonsense from any of the founding fathers. It was he who insisted on the title, the Institute for Strategic Studies; that was the one thing over which he and I ever seriously disagreed. I wanted to call it the Institute for the Study of International Security. After all, strategy, the art of conducting war, was the last thing we wanted to study: we were in the business of preventing it, as the title of our new journal *Survival* (which *was* Alastair's choice) made clear. But Alastair was a shrewd journalist, not an academic pedant. He knew what would sell and what would not. So the ISS it was, and the IISS it ultimately became. It worked, so he must have been right.

More important, Alastair was not prepared to confine the activities of the Institute to what he sardonically described as 'Buzzardry' – the limitation of nuclear war – much less the conduct of limited nuclear war. The Institute, he insisted, should cover the whole question of the relationship between defence and foreign policy; of the utility of force in the nuclear age. This not only meant disappointing Tony Buzzard, who more than any other single man deserves credit for the inception of the Institute. It meant downplaying those moral issues which had initially attracted the attention of Bishop Bell and the CCIA and persuaded their officers to play so major a role in its foundation. Those officers long remained leading members of the Institute – Kenneth Grubb as Chairman of the Council, Alan Booth as one of the Council's founder members. But they accepted that, central as those moral issues undoubtedly were, there was a limit to the time that could be spent profitably discussing them. To create an environment in which people could think clearly and dispassionately about defence questions, on the basis of the best possible information and with their attitudes as little distorted as possible by national prej-udice – this was the most valuable contribution the Institute could make to the clarification of the moral issues. Whether or not it sponsored moral debate, the Institute could at least ensure that any such debate was well-informed.

So the terms of reference of the Institute were defined at its foundation as being 'to study the effect of developments, both in weapons and in international relations, upon strategy and upon Western defence and disarmament policies; [and] in co-operation with similar bodies in the United States and elsewhere to study means by which those policies might be strengthened'. It would provide a focus for discussion and a reference centre 'which will make it possible for all who are interested to keep abreast of the broad trends of opinion and of national policies, not only in the West but in the Soviet bloc and in the uncommitted countries as well'. While it was hoped to create 'cordial and confidential relations' with government officials, the Institute '[would] not seek access to classified information but [would] work on the corpus of publicly known facts about weapons, about official policies, and their effects on strategy'. 'Finally,' the directive concluded, 'although it is hoped that its independent studies will have an influence on informed public opinion and the trends of official policy, it will not function as a pressure group or the advocate of any dogmatic school of thought'.

Opinions may differ as to how successfully our performance has matched our promise. I think we have done rather well. In the anxious years that followed the launching of *Sputnik* and the discovery of a so-called 'missile gap' – one of those not infrequent periods when Americans swung from the heights of self-confident euphoria to a dismal conviction that they were doomed, and publishers' lists were full of such titles as 'Can America Survive?' – the immediate need was for reliable information about the true facts of the military balance; and the work on which, more than any other, the reputation of the Institute has been built first appeared in 1959. Alastair and his successors were later to lament that they had got themselves stuck with the title *The Military Balance,* providing as it does so stark and conceptually misleading an idea of the complex nature of military power; but stuck they are, and 'MilBal' has become the Institute's flagship. But it was a ship that could never have been launched or kept afloat without the co-operation of officials, and the skill and patience with which Alastair established the credibility of the Institute with the really significant figures in Washington and Whitehall.

But it was not only Washington and Whitehall that mattered. Atlantic Man though he was, Alastair realized from the beginning the need to gain credibility in continental Europe. The moment was not auspicious: neither de Gaulle's France nor Adenauer's Germany looked kindly on a British-based Institute claiming to speak on their behalf, and even the most friendly elements in those countries were hesitant about co-operating in a venture which had so evidently a British provenance and infrastructure. Alastair brought them along with a mixture of tact and firmness which it was a joy to watch. An International Advisory Council with largely honorific duties was gradually involved in policy formulation, until in 1964 the Institute itself was internationalized, with Council members drawn from all NATO countries, and the agreeable practice was established of holding the annual conference in each of them in turn. We elected an Indian Vice-President in 1964, and four years later we extended our range to the Pacific, with council members from Australia and Japan. Now the Council is drawn from 17 countries, and Institute membership from 76.

But it was, understandably, Atlantic affairs that the Institute discussed at its first annual conference at Worcester College

Oxford thirty years ago. Charming as they appear to the casual visitor, Oxford colleges are still far from luxurious. In those days their accommodation had changed little since sanitary arrangements (of a kind) had first been installed some time in the 1870s. Jet-lagged Americans, once they realized that they were seriously expected to sleep in the place, stampeded to get rooms in the nearby Randolph Hotel; only to find that their better-informed British colleagues had prudently booked them all. In spite of this inauspicious beginning we had what was possibly the first, but was certainly not the last, wide-ranging transatlantic dialogue outside official channels about what we have learned to call 'extended deterrence'. Its scope and conclusions are set out in Alastair's own book *NATO in the 1960s*.[1]

Today, frankly, the book makes depressing reading. Nothing seems to have changed. Then, as now, the credibility of the United States using its nuclear weapons against the Soviet homeland in the event of a Soviet attack on Western Europe had been eroded, if not destroyed, by Soviet intercontinental capability. Further,

> The United States has been running an adverse balance in the last two years, primarily with Western Europe. … American expenditure on troops and defence installations around the world costs over \$3,000 million in foreign exchange, of which \$1,000 million is spent in Europe. President Eisenhower has already said ... that the United States can no longer be looked upon as 'an Atlas trying to carry the whole world', and though he appears to have been thinking in terms of greater European participation in aid for the undeveloped countries, it is also certain that the United States will ask her European NATO partners to assume a greater share of the costs of European defence.

So two things were necessary. First, the Europeans must improve their contribution in conventional forces, both in absolute terms and by achieving a greater degree of interoperability. Second, a credible nuclear deterrent system must be based in Europe itself, created and controlled by the Europeans.

The first requirement pointed to a goal towards which the Europeans have been striving, with only a moderate degree of success, for the past thirty years. The second merely emphasized an apparently insoluble dilemma. Alastair's proposal, in those pre-*Polaris* days, was for a mobile force of intermediate-range missiles, based in Western Europe, jointly procured by the Europeans and jointly controlled by them. But though discussion about such a force continued for a further five or six years – it reappeared under the Kennedy Administration as a seaborne Multi-Lateral Force, or MLF – no one was able to say how such weapons, even if they could be jointly procured and administered, could be jointly controlled: who would press the button? And until that question was answered, the buck of nuclear deterrence remained firmly on the desk of the President of the United States. The Institute devoted a great deal of its time in the early 1960s – perhaps too much – to examining a problem which still remains unanswered. But, as so often happens in research, the process itself, sterile as it might appear in retrospect, had beneficial side-effects. The intra-European discussions which it engendered under the auspices of the Institute, the Gesellschaft fur Auswärtige Politik in Bonn and the Institut des Hautes Etudes Etrangères in Paris helped bring together if not create European specialists in these strategic questions; of whom Jacques Vernant and Andre Beaufre, Ted Sommer and Klaus Ritter, Curt Gasteyger and Urs Schwartz, Altiero Spinelli and Cesare Merlini, Nils Haagerup and Johan Holst are only the first names to come to mind; men who not only developed strategic studies within their own countries but constituted a supra-national network of friends and colleagues which has played no small part in the building of Europe and the formation of a European voice in the transatlantic strategic dialogue. That voice was to become still more powerful when Christoph Bertram was appointed Director of the Institute in 1974.

In any case, by the mid-1960s the central balance appeared to be sufficiently stable for the problem of extended deterrence to appear largely academic. The building of the Berlin Wall in 1961, and the resolution of the Cuban missile crisis the following year, had laid down the parameters of super-power relations which each seemed content to observe. Not even the Soviet invasion of Czechoslovakia in 1968 shook the stable basis of the international system. The Institute tested the possibilities of this stability by making tentative overtures to colleagues in Eastern Europe, especially Poland and Yugoslavia, and in 1966 it held a conference in Vienna, to which the Soviets were invited, to discuss the state of East–West relations. The contrast between the cautious pragmatism of the East Europeans and the blank, impermeable hostility of the Soviet delegates (as they may be correctly described) provided a salutary lesson in the harsh realities of world politics. To that extent the conference, disagreeable as it was, was a success. Three years later, in 1969, we tried again. It was Alastair's last conference, at Scheveningen, and the topic was US–Soviet relations. The presence, and contributions, of Georgi Arbatov made a very different impression from the ideological immobilism of his predecessors. It was clear that there were now people within the Soviet Union whom one could talk to – as Henry Kissinger, himself a not infrequent attender at IISS conferences, was to discover at a higher level. The technical problems of nuclear deterrence might seem as intractable as ever, but when Alastair bowed out, after ten years as Director, we seemed well on the way to political detente.

But the action on the world scene had already moved else-where, and the focus of the Institute's attention with it. We have sometimes been accused of being too Euro- or Atlanto-centric. But our third conference, in 1961, was on the topic of 'World Order and New States' and resulted in a sharply prescient book by Peter Calvocoressi. In 1964, on the eve of the Vietnam conflict, we considered 'Conflict and Co-existence in Asia' and the following year the problems of the Middle East, a topic to which we returned in 1974. In 1967 we sponsored conferences in India and Japan on the topic of non-proliferation, a year before the signature of the Non-Proliferation Treaty. And in 1972, with the Japanese now firmly on board, we held our first conference in North America, in Canada, on the topic of 'East Asia and the World System'.

The Institute's concern for extra-European questions was fuelled partly by a concern among its British members for their former imperial responsibilities, partly by American concern for 'out of area' questions, but more specifically by 'the Australian connection'. Hedley Bull, at that time a Lecturer at the London School of Economics, had been the *rapporteur* at our second conference, on the 'Control of the Arms Race', in 1960, and the book which resulted from it was probably the most influential study that we have ever published. Its cool common sense cleared away the cant that had hitherto attended the whole question of disarmament and forced us all to look at the topic in a radically different way. Thereafter, Hedley was, next to Alastair himself, the most powerful intellectual influ-ence within the Institute, from which he was never far removed for very long. His continual prodding forced us to realize that there was a great deal more to the international system than the confrontation of the super-powers and the security of Western Europe. With the appointment of Robert O'Neill as Director in 1982, of course, Europe shrank to its correct proportions as a minor peninsula on the unfashionable side of Asia. It remains to be seen whether the present Director can persuade us to see it as anything else.

What we never considered was, specifically, Vietnam, and we have been criticized for it. It is true that we abstained from doing so partly from reluctance to tackle so blatantly divisive an issue, but I doubt whether a conference on that conflict would have been very fruitful. We have been quite good at identifying and analysing up-coming problems, as we did in 1960, before the meeting of the 18-nation committee on General and Complete Disarmament, or at reviewing broad politico-strategic issues as we did for the Mediterranean in Barcelona last year. But I doubt whether we could have said anything very fruitful about a war which many of our members thought should not be being fought at all. It is, however, possible that we have considered third-world problems too narrowly in terms of the emergence of new states and inter-state relations, and of the threats which the resulting turbulence have offered to international stability. Our conference at Stresa in 1980 dealt specifically with 'Third World Conflict and International Order'. Perhaps we should have tried to tackle at a more profound level the gigantic problems of modernization and nationalism within those states, which have spread out like a seismic shock wave from a Europe where they caused two terrible conflicts in the first half of this century, and which may well take the best part of another century to work themselves out over the rest of the globe.

For that is the fundamental problem which the Institute really exists to study: how to maintain stability in a world which is in a condition of continuous flux, and where stability is seen by many – as it was in nineteenth-century Europe – as perpetuating a condition of injustice and oppression. It is indeed true that we are concerned with the preservation of a framework of international order from which some of us benefit a great deal more than others. In the past, every such framework has been challenged, sooner or later, by forces of discontent, and wars have been fought to test their continuing validity or to create a new one. Normally, as a historian, I would be warning an audience such as this to accept the inevitability of future wars, and I certainly warn you to expect the inevitability of future conflicts likely to erupt into wars. But in the past there were no nuclear weapons to make such confrontations potentially lethal for the whole of mankind. So our task remains unaltered since that first Brighton Conference thirty years ago: the study of the *containment* or *limitation* of conflict, however inevitable, just or necessary that conflict may appear to be. And however widely we may range in our survey of possible conflict areas, we have always to come back to examine the foundation on which the international order inexorably rests; the stability of the central balance, the credibility of extended deterrence, the limitation of regional conflicts, and the exercise, explicit or implicit, of arms control.

The variables which make it necessary for us to keep these constants under frequent review are two: technological and political. The scientists with their 'blue skies' research and the technologists with their Promethean ingenuity are continually presenting us with what are apparently new solutions, but which are in fact new problems. In the past thirty years they have produced new hard-based systems, *Minuteman* and *Polaris* and their successors, only to cancel out the contribution which these seemed likely to make to stability by developing MIRV and pin-point accuracy of delivery. Now they promise – or some of them promise – renewed stability with strategic defences – only at the cost of extending the arms competition into space. Simultaneously, conventional weapons have become increasingly unconventional in their power, range and accuracy, and their use has been transformed by a communications revolution – without, however, in any way eroding the central role which human morale and human judgment (and, alas, human error) will always play in the conduct of war. Once in each decade we have assembled to discuss where technology is taking us: at Elsinore in 1967, at Bruges in 1977, and at Avignon in 1984. The predictable conclusion to be drawn from all these conferences was that we had, like Alice in looking-glass land, to run faster and faster (and incidentally spend more and more money) to stay in the same place. Technology provides us with tools, not solutions; and the tools which it does provide, if clumsily handled, will only make our problems worse.

The political variables are more diverse and more significant. By far the most important in the long run is the rise to political self-consciousness of the vast masses of humanity beyond the historic area of Christendom, or 'the West'; a process as likely to dominate the twenty-first century as the growth of national self-consciousness did that of Europe in the nineteenth and early twentieth. But in the shorter run there are more immediate political changes. Nearly half a century has passed since the end of World War II, and an entire generation has come to maturity on both sides of the Iron Curtain whose attitudes have not been determined by personal experience of that conflict and its aftermath. Symbols such as 'Munich' or 'Pearl Harbor', and their Soviet equivalents, no longer have their old incantatory power. In Western Europe, stability has resulted in economic recovery, and economic recovery has produced a prosperous, pacific, debellated society decreasingly conscious of the need to sustain military burdens; a problem we considered at our conference in The Hague in 1982. In the United States, demographic and cultural changes have eroded that sense of commitment to the defence of the Western European democracies so effectively cultivated by American political leaders in the 1940s and 1950s. In the Soviet Union, the agonizing process of recovery, first from the Revolution and Civil War, then from World War II, has now been sufficiently complete to produce a leadership prepared to question the old orthodoxies and adventurously explore alternatives. Further afield, Islamic fundamentalism has emerged as an ideology as formidable and at least as influential as Marxism-Leninism. Japan has developed into an economic super-power; and China is in the throes of a long-term transformation whose consequences for the international system are incalculable. The world of 1945 must seem to the younger generation almost as distant as that of 1914 does to my own contemporaries.

It is within this context of ceaseless political change that we have to preserve stability and some kind of order, and it is the function of this Institute to monitor that change and constantly to re-examine military requirements and possibilities in the light of it. It is our business neither to be conservative nor radical; but we should be prepared to re-examine our own orthodoxies at least as ruthlessly as Gorbachev is examining his – without trying, however, to create a dream world which never can exist. Our problem is how, peacefully, to maintain our values and the political structures which preserve them in a rapidly changing world; how to remain firm without rigidity, to adjust without surrender, and to be realistic without confusing realism with worst-case analysis. The exercise is likely to keep us in business for a very long time to come.

Notes

[1] Alastair Buchan, *NATO in the 1960s* (London: Weidenfeld & Nicolson, 1960), p. 38

CHAPTER TWENTY-THREE

The remaking of Europe

Survival 32-2, 1990

The IISS was founded in 1958. A few months earlier, the launching of *Sputnik* had shown that the Soviet Union had achieved, or was capable of achieving, strategic parity with the United States. A new sombre prospect confronted the peoples of the West. It seemed that our very survival was now threatened, and would continue indefinitely to be threatened, by the existence of thermo-nuclear weapons on the one hand, and global confrontation with a declared and formidable adversary on the other.

In essentials this situation remained unchanged for 30 years, and the task of the IISS was to explore ways of living comfortably and safely within it. We became indeed so accustomed to the prison that history had built for us that, like recidivists or long-term hospital patients, we became almost incapable of visualizing any other kind of existence. No other world, it seemed, *could* exist. We had to make the best of this one.

Now the walls of our prison have suddenly collapsed and we emerge, bewildered, into a new and unfamiliar world. How can we adjust to it? What changes must we make in our settled habits? What are the options that lie before us, and what are the necessities? How much of our old lives must we leave behind, and what new skills do we have to learn?

I shall deal first with our relationship with the Soviet Union; then discuss Eastern, or as I prefer to call it Central Europe; then turn to Germany and Western Europe; and finally consider the relationship between the United States and the newly-emerging European commonwealth: the new shape, in fact, of the West.

The Soviet Union is of course the key to the whole process. If the changes which we have been witnessing over the past few years are not irreversible, if all depends upon the will or the survival of a single man, then nothing has changed and our hopes are illusions. The caution with which our governments have so far reacted to events in Russia is understandable: too much hangs on the correctness of their judgment. But most of the questions asked in the West, and many of the answers given seem to me to have missed the point. They have tended to focus upon the person of Mikhail Gorbachev: his intentions, his prospects of survival, whether we should help him and if so how.

It has been argued that we should withhold approval from his policies because his objective is still the preservation of Marxism-Leninism, albeit in a softer form. It has been urged that his failure is inevitable since communist *dirigisme* is incompatible with a market economy. Such arguments as these are interesting, but hardly basic to the issue, which is surely this. Changes are occurring, and have for long been going on, in Soviet *society* – developments of which Gorbachev is as much the symptom as he is the catalyst. A point has been reached where the incompatibility between the demands resulting from these developments and the structure of state power has become glaringly obvious to the Soviet leaders themselves. Gorbachev was put into power by his colleagues with a

mandate for radical change, and continues, in spite of all difficulties, to command their support.

Whether or not he survives in power, Gorbachev has already
achieved his historic task of setting on foot a transformation in
the structure of the Soviet state that is both open-ended and irreversible. *Glasnost* has revealed the Soviet people to themselves,
and they do not like what they see. *Perestroika* may not yet have
created viable new structures, but it has fatally weakened the
old. Naturally, multi-party democracy has not yet developed in
the Soviet Union: given the nature of Russian political culture
that is hardly to be expected. But there is emerging throughout
the Soviet Union an articulate civil society pressing upon and
transforming the instruments of the State – the bureaucracy, the
Party, the Army and the KGB; a public opinion operating not
only upon these bodies but within them. Their members will in
future be operating according to very different standards and
using very different methods from those applied in the past.

The most important consequence of Gorbachev's policies
has thus been to destroy the old docility that made totalitarianism possible. The Soviet peoples have shown themselves to be
intelligent and critical, with a lively sense of their own interests.
They are no longer an inert mass to be manipulated by a small
group of ideologues. They may indeed prove ungovernable; but
the suggestion made by some Western alarmists, that a future
government might distract them from their domestic problems
by militaristic foreign adventures, is highly implausible. For
one thing, too many coffins came back from Afghanistan.

Historians and economists will long debate the causes of
these changes, but they are likely to agree about one factor;
the supreme importance of the communications revolution.
Freedom of information is as necessary to political development as air is to sustain life. It has been the universal availability
of instant information through telecommunications, the media

and linked computers that has dissolved the congealed mass of ignorance and conservatism that made possible the maintenance of totalitarian control and has enabled the Soviet peoples to communicate freely, not only with the outside world but with one another.

If we in the West want to ensure that these changes remain irreversible, the surest way to do it is to ensure that the flow of information and of information technology does not diminish. To deny the Soviet Union this technology on the grounds that it has, or might have, military utility is as short-sighted as it is counter-productive. This is the surest way to preserve the social backwardness that made the Soviet Union such a danger for so long. Modernization in itself does not guarantee a peaceful society: Nazi Germany stands as a gruesome example to the contrary. But however sophisticated the weapons with which it is armed, a Soviet people with whom we can freely communicate, who understand what is happening in the outside world and can apply its lessons to their own society will be a far more reliable partner in the maintenance of world order, both inside and outside Europe, than one which believes and knows only what its government allows.

It is only with such a society, furthermore, that far-reaching arms-control agreements will be possible. As we all know, strategic arms control is driven by a logic of its own that bears little relation to political circumstances. It is a closed world inhabited by experts whose task it is, like that of insurance brokers and lawyers, to guard against every conceivable risk, however remote the possibilities may be. It is for political leaders, in the light of political circumstances, to decide what risks they are prepared to take. As the political climate changes, the calculations of strategic analysts, however logical, become increasingly remote from real probabilities. Eventually a point is reached when the calculus of military capabilities is overtaken by that of perceived intentions; intentions shaped not only by state interests but by political culture. If the Soviet state is no longer regarded as hostile and aggressive, if Soviet society is known to be one with which one can interact as freely as we do with one another, then the strong wine of nuclear calculations (to paraphrase Lord Salisbury) will need to be adulterated by the cold water of common sense, and the even colder water of economic necessity. Senator Sam Nunn spoke expertly of this in his Alastair Buchan Memorial Lecture last year, and I have nothing to add to his wisdom.

In Europe, however, rightly or wrongly, we are concerned less with Soviet nuclear capabilities than with their conventional forces, which are seen as far more precise indicators of political intentions. There have been until recently some half a million Soviet troops stationed beyond the western borders of the Soviet Union, and the speed with which they are withdrawn will provide the most reliable evidence of Soviet intentions to liberate their former European satellites. There can now be surely very little doubt about those intentions. Last year, one after another, the members of the Warsaw Pact declared their political and (more important) their ideological independence of the Soviet Union. Not only did the Soviet government acquiesce in this, but the Soviet peoples remained apparently indifferent. Under the new regime of *glasnost* President Gorbachev has been criticized on many counts but his bold decision to make the best of a bad job in Central Europe and rid himself of an immense political liability has not been challenged, to the best of my knowledge, by any of his domestic enemies. His military advisers, whatever their professional reservations, must know that returning Soviet armies would not find a single friend to help them, either to reconquer these countries or to rule them afterwards. The Soviets appear to have divested themselves of their Empire in the West as completely as the British divested themselves, 40 years ago, of their Empire in the East. Now the divided halves of the European family can once more come together and remain together. The remaking of Europe is at last possible, and that is the task to which all our minds must now be turned.

I want to make here a distinction (which I know is made in these countries themselves) between Central Europe and Eastern Europe. 'Central Europe' consists of those lands which once formed part of Western Christendom; the old lands of the Habsburg Empire, Austria, Hungary and Czechoslovakia, together with Poland and the eastern marches of Germany. The term 'Eastern Europe' should be reserved for those regions which developed under the aegis of the Orthodox Church: the Black Sea communities of Bulgaria and Romania which only emerged from Ottoman domination in the nineteenth century, and the 'European' parts of the Soviet Union. (Yugoslavia is an uneasy amalgamation straddling the two, its former Habsburg provinces of Croatia and Slovenia increasingly at odds with their southern neighbours, and it remains to be seen how long that amalgamation can survive.) It must be these old nations of Central Europe that we should welcome first and most warmly into our European commonwealth, and ultimately, I believe, into the European Community. It is these that we are best placed, in terms both of geography and of common culture, to help.

It is not mere historical nostalgia that makes me urge that the countries of Central Europe should be admitted as soon as it is feasible into the European Community. There are two other immediate reasons. One is that their own history has been characterized as much by antagonism as by co-operation; antagonism between Germans, Czechs and Poles, between Hungarians and Slovaks, Romanians and Croats. It was their growing and incompatible self-assertiveness that shattered the unity of the Habsburg Empire, something that many of them have regretted ever since. Common suffering has done much to bring them together, as it brought together the warring peoples of Western Europe 40 years ago. But they still communicate more easily with the West than they do with one another, and co-operation among them is likely to develop far more easily within the framework of the Community than on any purely regional basis.

The second reason is that they do share, I am afraid, a highly ambivalent attitude towards Germany, especially the prospect of a reunited Germany; however sincere the professions of reconciliation made by their political leaders may be. The generation whose understandable detestation of the Germans made them welcome the Russians as liberators has almost passed away, but their successors remain wary; nowhere more so than in Poland. None the less their need for German capital, technology and general expertise is such that the development of a German economic policy in Central Europe should be conducted in close association with their Western partners, within the framework of a European Community which has already so successfully mitigated historic antagonisms in Western Europe. Otherwise the peoples of those countries may come to feel that they have exchanged one kind of hegemony for another; a more beneficent and benevolent hegemony, certainly, but one they would none the less cordially resent.

Our first task must therefore be to reabsorb the peoples of Central Europe into our cultural and economic community where they properly belong: to reknit the ties between London, Paris, Rome, Munich, and Leipzig, Warsaw, Prague and Budapest. But if they are so reabsorbed, will they join our security community as well?

Ultimately, we hope, yes. A single security system embracing the whole of Europe, involving the dissolution or the amalgamation of the existing pacts, is certainly a reasonable long-term goal. This is the objective at which we should aim in the CSCE negotiations at Helsinki. But political circumstances dictate that we must take our time getting there. If such a system were to include Eastern Europe (that is, the Soviet Union) it would at present be unacceptable to many of its other members. If it did not, it would be seen by the Soviet Union as at least potentially hostile, especially if it was still linked with the United States. The Soviets are in a position to block the creation of any security system extending simply from 'Brest to Brest'. Even if they were not, we should have learned by this time the profound unwisdom of imposing an unwelcome settlement on nations in no position to resist them, but which they will challenge as soon as they have recovered their strength.

So a special military status for the nations of Central Europe seems, for the time being, unavoidable. This might well be a status comparable to that of Finland: politically independent and free of all foreign military forces, but accepting that the Soviet Union had a certain *droit de regard* which might or might not be exercized through the mechanism of the Warsaw Pact. Their independence might indeed be formally guaranteed by both sides. This status might ultimately be enjoyed also by the Baltic Republics if – as seems quite possible – they regain their freedom. Such a *cordon sanitaire* extending from Finland through the Baltic States, Poland, Czechoslovakia and Hungary to Austria and Yugoslavia should satisfy the security interests both of the Soviet Union and of the West. More important, it would almost certainly conform to the wishes of the peoples themselves – so long as they enjoyed in every other respect unimpeded membership in the commonwealth of Europe.

As for the military status of a reunified Germany, the wishes of the German people themselves will be paramount, whether we like it or not. We will await with interest the results of the internal debate that will now take place within the two

Germanies both before and after reunification. But their allies and their neighbours and their former adversaries have a deep and legitimate interest in the outcome of those debates and a right forcefully to express their views. They are likely, jointly or severally, to make two major stipulations. The first, on which the Soviet Union in particular is likely to insist, is that there should be, at least *ad interim*, a special military status for the territories which at present constitute the German Democratic Republic. Either there should remain on these territories Soviet garrisons, even if their presence is largely symbolic; or they should contain no foreign forces at all. The second stipulation, which has been firmly set out by the President of the United States, is that Germany should remain a member of the Western alliance. A neutral Germany would be dangerously destabilizing; not only for Europe, but also for the world.

On this last point the Western allies, the Poles and at present a majority of the inhabitants of the Federal Republic are at one: a reunited Germany should remain a member of the NATO Alliance. The Soviet Union so far maintains the official view that a reunified Germany should belong to neither alliance, but they must be at least as aware as anyone else of the problems that a powerful unaligned Germany would present for the stability of Europe. But the East Germans at present see things differently. Opinion polls there indicate a strong preference for neutrality, and in a reunited Germany they might find more allies than at present we expect. That is very likely to happen if one part of Germany has to sustain the burden of hosting considerable foreign armed forces while the other does not.

At this stage it would be well to remind ourselves of what the obligations of the North Atlantic Treaty consist. They are to 'maintain and develop . . . individual and collective capacity to resist armed attack' (Article 3); to 'consult together whenever ... the territorial integrity, political independence or security of any of the Parties is threatened' (Article 4); and to consider 'an armed attack against one . . . an attack against them all', and to take 'forthwith, individually and in concert with the other Parties, such action as it deems necessary, including the use of armed force, to restore and maintain the security of the North Atlantic area' (Article 5). That is what the Americans would call 'the bottom line'. All else is superstructure: the integrated military organization, the command system, the location of troops, the overall strategy – all this was negotiated separately and need not be considered in any way sacrosanct.

I can well understand the depression with which the civil and military officials of the Alliance must contemplate the prospect of *perestroika* within NATO – of demolishing and rebuilding a structure which they have created in the face of almost insuperable difficulties as a result of innumerable compromises, and which has hitherto served us all so well. But the fact must be faced, that a structure created to meet the needs of the 1950s is in danger of becoming, after 40 years, an archaic anachronism. A Soviet Union which has withdrawn its legions within its own borders and is in a condition of internal crisis likely to persist for many years to come; a Central Europe which has in every respect (except perhaps militarily) rejoined our own Western society; above all, a reunified Germany with a population of 80 million and an army numbering perhaps 600,000 strong: this is the situation for which we now have to plan. Will there in fact continue to be a need for Allied forces on the soil of Western Germany at all? If so, what purpose should they serve? How should they be deployed? What strategy should they adopt? There is today a need for thinking at least as bold and as innovative as that called for 40 years ago if NATO is not to be seen, both inside Germany and beyond its borders, as an antiquated dinosaur, an obstacle to rather than an instrument for the remaking of Europe.

The Alliance itself, as I suggested, should be sacrosanct, however radically we may revise the manner in which it operates; and especially sacrosanct should be the participation of the United States. There are three good reasons for this. First, the Soviet Union, whatever course its internal evolution may take, will remain a very strong military power with a formidable arsenal of nuclear weapons. And it will remain, I am afraid, at least for the time being, an alien power. However sincere Gorbachev's wish to be admitted into the common European home, the course charted by Lenin and Stalin has removed the Soviets so far from the structures and values of Western society that it may take a generation of sustained reciprocal effort before we can really treat them in the same fashion as we do one another. It is an effort that we should do our best to encourage and help. It might indeed become easier if the Soviet Union was to shed its Asian dependencies and – as did the British when we abandoned our Empire – return to its European roots. But in the meantime Soviet power – especially Soviet nuclear power – still needs to be balanced in Europe by that of the United States.

The second reason is generally admitted but seldom mentioned in polite society. There *is* a German Problem. It may be only a problem of perception, but it exists none the less. An alliance without the United States would be an alliance dominated by Germany. The peoples both of Central Europe and the Soviet Union, rightly or wrongly, would see this as a threat. Even the West European allies would be uneasy; not so much because of the record of Wilhelmine and Nazi Germany as because of more deep-rooted instincts about the need for a Balance of Power in Europe. So long as these feelings are strongly held, there will be an equally strong need for the United States to remain entangled in the Alliance, to balance German as well as Soviet power. We may regret these sentiments, but they do undeniably exist.

The third reason for continuing American participation is no less important. If the price of reconstructing Europe is to be the disintegration of the Atlantic Community, then we will have made a very bad bargain. The Atlantic Alliance was intended not as a temporary expedient but as a lasting supra-national community, not only protecting but enriching its members, widening their horizons with a sense of common destiny and common responsibility. We should be welcoming our Central European neighbours into that community, not putting the clock back to the introverted Europe of 1939. They themselves, indeed, see it that way. Many of them feel at least as much at home in Chicago, Toronto, or New York as in London, Amsterdam, or Paris, and I suspect that the Poles may prove to be the most enthusiastic Atlanticists of us all.

But the balance within the Alliance must now shift. Under the new circumstances the European members of the Atlantic Community can and must make proportionately a far larger contribution to their own security. The role of the United States should in future be supportive rather than dominant. NATO must not be seen in the future, as it has been too often seen in the past, as a mere extension of American power. A shift in the balance of command responsibilities might do much to defuse incipient neutralism in a reunified Germany, as well as reconciling the French to common structures and planning. A more flexible, less obtrusive and less costly deployment of American forces in Europe could provide sufficient 'linkage' while satisfying critics of the Alliance on both sides of the Atlantic. But this can only come about if we Europeans cease to look to Washington for direction and leadership and show ourselves capable of creating our own security community appropriate to the new conditions with which we are faced.

The study of how this can best be done should keep the IISS in business for at least another 30 years. Until now our concern has been how to preserve the world. Now it must be how to change it.

Sir Michael Howard is President of the IISS and Robert A. Lovett Professor of Military and Naval History, Yale University. This article is the prepared text for his Alastair Buchan Memorial Lecture, delivered on 12 March 1990.

CHAPTER TWENTY-FOUR

Brodie, Wohlstetter and American nuclear strategy

Survival 34-2, 1992

Bernard Brodie and the foundations of American nuclear strategy, by Barry H. Steiner (Lawrence, KS: University of Kansas Press, 1991); **On not confusing ourselves: essays on national security strategy in honour of Albert and Roberta Wohlstetter**, by Andrew W. Marshall, J.J. Martin and Henry S. Rowen (Boulder, CO: Westview Press, 1991)

The four decades between 1950 and 1990 are likely to be seen, in historical perspective, as possessing the same self-contained quality as those between 1870 and 1914. In 1949–50, the Soviet Union emerged, not just as a political and ideological rival to the West, but as a formidable nuclear adversary. In 1989–90, it ceased effectively to be either. In the meantime, some of the best minds in the Western world addressed themselves to the problem of maintaining an effective balance of power without having to fight a war that nuclear weapons would render inconceivably terrible to both sides. A huge literature developed, misleadingly labelled 'strategic studies': misleading, because the subject under discussion was not how to fight wars, the traditional concern of strategists, but how to prevent them. Most of the contributors had never heard a shot fired, or even a bomb dropped, in anger, which gave their writing a curiously arid quality; but then, their concern was not how to do it, but how to ensure that it was never done. Now their work is beginning to seem as remote as that of sixteenth-century theologians, their jargon as abstruse and irrelevant as the vocabulary of transubstantiation and consubstantiation.

When librarians consign their collections, first to the remotest stacks, then to the cellars, finally to the recycling process, what will be left?

Two names are likely to figure on any short list, those of Bernard Brodie and Albert Wohlstetter, not only because of what they wrote, but also because of what they stood for. Some have seen them as the Carl von Clausewitz and the Henri Jomini of their day, the one for the profundity of his insights, the other for the clarity of his analysis.[1] Another comparison, to continue the theological analogy, might be with Martin Luther and John Calvin; the first for his pioneering perception of a central and fundamental truth, the second for his implacable logic in following the trail of reasoning, however unpopular the conclusions to which it led. In any case, Brodie and Wohlstetter stand as pole and antipole in the strategic analysis produced since World War II, and it is highly appropriate, as the sun sets over the Cold War era, that two major works should appear commemorating them.

The books themselves are very different in style and intention. Barry Steiner has given us a massive critique of Brodie's thought; immensely thorough, but tough going. He provides 100 pages of footnotes to 250 pages of text, and because much substantial material is relegated to the footnotes, the work presents problems to all but the most dedicated reader. One wonders what Brodie himself, a master of succinct and lucid prose, would have thought of it. Nevertheless, it is likely to be indispensable, if only because no one else is likely to go through all the relevant documentary collections with comparable thoroughness. It is path-breaking because it deals for the first time with the classified work Brodie did for the US Air Force. As a scholarly monument to Brodie's work, fair-minded and thorough, it is unlikely to be surpassed. One could only wish that it made its subject a little more accessible.

Someone will do the same for the Wohlstetters one day, but as they are both still alive, well and immensely productive, that day is still long distant. This is a *festschrift* by their pupils and friends and is, quite properly, wholly laudatory. The contributions are inevitably uneven. Some are now of purely historic interest, having been rendered out of date by the events of the past two years. Others, such as the excellent essays by Fred Hoffmann and Jed Snyder, lay out programmes for strategic thinkers in the aftermath of the Cold War. The analytic study of the Soviet armed forces by William Odom deserves to be reprinted where historians as well as strategic analysts can get at it. The whole is tied together with chatty pieces about the Wohlstetters' penchant for good food and wine, which their friends will find endearing but could give a false impression to those unfamiliar with their more serious qualities. *Festschrifts* are designed primarily to give pleasure, and one hopes that Albert and Roberta will like this one. But is it too much to ask that some equally well-intentioned friends arrange to bring together all their widely scattered articles and publish them in a solid and lasting form – something that will stand beside Brodie's great trilogy, *Sea Power in the Machine Age, Strategy in the Missile Age* and *War and Politics* as the indispensable nucleus of a strategic studies library when all else has been swept away?

Brodie and Wohlstetter had little time for one another. Although trained as a political scientist, Brodie wrote primarily as a historian, interested less in analysis of static situations than in process and development, the significance of the contingent, the part played in history by accident and personality and by complexities of which only hindsight can make us aware. He discovered Clausewitz rather late in life, in the course of thinking about limitations on war and the primacy of policy over strategy, but it was the Clausewitzian concept of *friction* that fascinated him. Like Clausewitz, he insisted that war in reality was very different from war on paper; this was especially true of nuclear war. While initially welcoming the contribution that systems analysis could make to strategic thought and military planning, Brodie became increasingly sceptical about its utility, if only because systems analysts had, as he unkindly put it, 'no basis in their training or preoccupations for claiming special political insight of any kind'. Indeed, he remarked at a moment of particular frustration, that they seemed to have 'a trained incapacity for giving due weight to social and political imponderables'.[2]

If he had little time for systems analysts, Brodie had even less for the professional military – a failing that was, in his chosen profession, something of a disadvantage. Involved first as a young staff-officer in analysing naval operations in World War II and then as an independent consultant to the chief of the Air Staff in 1950, he complained bitterly about what he saw as the ossified nature of the military mind, the absence of flexibility and critical analysis in their thinking. Steiner quite reasonably suggests that much of the trouble lay with Brodie himself. He was a young man with a high opinion of his own abilities, who tended to reach conclusions rapidly on the basis of solitary contemplation and who lacked the patience and tact to argue through his conclusions in a group environment. In this, he had much in common with his British mentor, B.H. Liddell Hart, who was also a loner; crafting his concepts in the solitude of his study, enunciated them as dogmas, impatient of the bureaucratic process of translating ideas into programmes and resentful of his consequent lack of effective power.

Wohlstetter is the opposite. He is a mathematical logician by training, concerned less with deriving principles, analogies and unquantifiable 'wisdom' from the past than with solving the immediate problems of the present. He dismissed Brodie as a *belle lettriste*, whose ruminative essays had little practical to offer in solving the urgent questions of force deployment and weapons development with which the US armed forces were confronted. Where Brodie was deductive, Wohlstetter is inductive. Whereas Brodie deduced the requirement for invulnerable retaliatory forces from his overall concepts of deterrence, Wohlstetter started by asking what had to be done to make them invulnerable. Whereas Brodie derived from his historical studies the concept of 'limited war', Wohlstetter worked out the techniques of command and control necessary to keep it limited. Above all, whereas Brodie was contemplative and rather solitary by nature, Wohlstetter is an affable extro-vert, excelling in teamwork and group discussions, persuasive both with politicans and the military, above all acceptable to them because he offered practical solutions to their immediate problems.

Fundamentally, however, Brodie and Wohlstetter had much in common. Both began as young civilians trying to teach the US Air Force its job. In 1950–51, General Hoyt Vandenberg called on Brodie to advise on targeting policy against the Soviet Union. The Strategic Air Command (SAC) wanted to plan an all-out attack against Soviet industrial capability, focusing on the Soviet Union's electrical network. Brodie argued that with the limited number of atomic bombs available, this would have little effect on the capacity of Soviet armies to overrun Europe and that the SAC would do better to attack a small number of cities in the expectation that the shock to Soviet morale, with the threat of further punishment in reserve, would force a reversal of policy – a programme, in fact, of 'intra-war deter-rence'. Brodie failed to persuade his clients. Within a few years the development of thermonuclear weapons and Soviet retal-iatory capabilities rendered both strategies out of date. It was then that Wohlstetter, invited to advise on the siting of SAC bases at home and overseas, pointed out their vulnerability to a pre-emptive attack and initiated the search for a secure second-strike capability that was to dominate strategic thinking for the next 30 years.

Brodie was no less insistent on the need for secure retaliatory forces, which he described as 'unquestionably the greatest single military requirement for security in the atomic age, whether in war or peace'.[3] With the advent of a Soviet retaliatory capability, he abandoned his earlier proposals for targeting cities, relying primarily on tacit agreements and diplomacy to avoid this on both sides. Wohlstetter shared this objective, but focused on the technical mechanisms – improvements in missile accuracy and command-and-control facilities – whereby this could be done. Both agreed that a nuclear war could never be won and should never be fought. Brodie made his famous Lutheran declaration of principle as early as 1946: 'Thus far the chief purposes of our military establishment has been to win wars. From now on its chief purpose must be to avert them'.[4] It was slightly premature: four years later, he was advising the military establishment how to win a war. But by the mid-1950s, his declaration of faith was common ground among virtually all strategic thinkers, who differed only as to how it should best be implemented.

It was at this stage that the gap began to appear between 'existential' deterrence, as formulated in the United States by Brodie, and what might be termed 'credible deterrence', a school virtually founded by Wohlstetter. For Brodie, as for most European thinkers, the mere possibility of nuclear retaliation, irrespective of target, was deterrence enough: the explosion of a hydrogen bomb over a single city would be a catastrophe beyond imagination, and no sane statesman would contemplate running any risk of it happening. Brodie rejected Wohlstetter's contention that the mere feasibility of a Soviet pre-emptive strike made the balance of terror 'delicate'.

Such a belief, he maintained, 'took no account whatever of the inhibitory political and psychological imponderables that might and in fact *must* affect the conditions implied by that word "delicate". . . . Many things are feasible that we have quite good reason to believe will not happen'.[5]

In fact, strategic thinking, Brodie believed by 1955, 'had reached a dead end' because nuclear war could no longer serve its Clausewitzian purpose as an instrument of policy.[6] Some manipulation of nuclear risk would still be necessary, he agreed, to deter a Soviet attack on Western Europe, where he saw tactical nuclear weapons as having continued utility. Beyond that, he dissociated himself from the kind of detailed analysis that occupied his colleagues at The Rand Corporation, where his comments were increasingly sardonic and destructive. 'A plan and a policy which offers a good promise of deterring war', he wrote, 'is by orders of magnitude better in every way than one which depreciates the objective of deterrence in order to improve somewhat the chances of winning'.[7]

But such a criticism was to misunderstand, if not to misrepresent, what Wohlstetter and his colleagues were trying to do. Rightly or wrongly, they denied that 'existential deterrence' was enough. The Soviet Union, they maintained, would not be deterred by implausible threats; and threats to attack its cities, when it had the capacity to retaliate in kind against the West, were entirely implausible. (Brodie, incidentally, remained vague about what targets should be attacked if his own rules for the limitation of nuclear war prohibited attacks on cities.) Wohlstetter believed that it was necessary to present the adversary with a strategy that was not only feasible but *credible*: to maintain invulnerable retaliatory forces targeted in such a way that intra-war deterrence could be preserved by ensuring that whatever the Soviets did would be seen to result in greater suffering for themselves than they would be able to inflict on the United States and its allies. This was not, as Brodie depicted it and as some strategists have demanded of it, a 'war-fighting' strategy, much less a 'strategy for victory'. It was, rather, a sustained effort to map out the nightmarish territory that lay between the failure of deterrence and the escalation to extremes that Clausewitz had described and Brodie so much feared.

The 'Wohlstetter school' could be, and was, criticized on four counts. The first, as noted earlier, was the inadequacy of the kind of systems analysis used and the limitations of the people who practised it. Their calculations left too much out of account: there were too many imponderables that would distort their calculations once war began, too many opportunities for misperception and error, too much likelihood that decisions would be guided by human passion rather than calculation. Critics could point to the Schlieffen Plan, or to the calculations of the German Naval Staff that led to the introduction of unrestricted submarine warfare in 1917, as examples of meticulous analysis leading to unforeseen and ultimately disastrous results. Careful Jominian reasoning, argued Brodie and his followers, would be torn to shreds by Clausewitzian friction the moment the first missile landed.

It was a valid critique, but not a very helpful one. That may well be so, the military must reply, but what *should* we do? For what should we plan? At what targets should we aim? What should be our force structure? We are not asking for certainties, but for guidance, and if we are not getting it from systems analysts, where are we to look?

Interestingly enough, an answer emerges within the body of the Wohlstetter *festschrift* in the contributions on 'net assessment'. It is not clear what part the Wohlstetters themselves played in the development of net assessment, an activity generally associated with Andrew Marshall, but it is now an extremely fashionable concept, even if its proponents are modest about defining in what it actually consists. Stephen Peter Rosen indeed suggests that 'good net assessment requires a self-conscious rejection of a fixed definition of net assessment'.[8] Fundamentally, it is an attempt to comprehend all the uncertainties that systems analysis leaves out, and arrive at a *Gesammtkonzept* that will be a more reliable if less precise guide to policy formulation; a concept that includes all factors relevant to one's own performance, to that of the adversary, to the environment within which the conflict takes place and to the manner in which these factors will interact. It deals not with a static confrontation, but with a dynamic interaction over a prolonged period of time. It is 'a search for broad insights . . . eclectic in its use of analytic tools and methodologies', to borrow the words of George Pickett, James Roche and Barry Watts, whose article on net assessment is one of the most substantial contributions to the Wohlstetter *festschrift*.[9] The simple military query 'How many?' is amplified in net assessment by the retort, as typical of Brodie as of Wohlstetter, 'So what?' And to this much more difficult question the insights of the historian, as Andrew Marshall insists in his own chapter, can contribute at least as much as the techniques of the systems analyst.

The second weakness of the Wohlstetter school, at least in its earlier manifestations, was a tendency to 'demonize' the Soviet Union, both in terms of intentions and capabilities. 'Worst case' projections of both became the base-line for all military planning; a sagacious form of insurance at the level of strategy, but a less reliable guide in the more complex realms of real political intercourse. 'If you believe the soldiers', said Queen Victoria's Prime Minister Lord Salisbury, about very comparable projections of 'the Russian threat' at the turn of the century, 'nothing is safe. You must dilute their strong wine with the water of common sense'.

This was the aspect of Wohlstetter's analysis of the 'delicate balance' that so disquieted Brodie, and indeed many others. It assumed a Soviet leadership so ruthlessly bent on aggression, and so indifferent to the sufferings of its own peoples, that it would, if it saw a 'window of opportunity', make a pre-emptive strike against US nuclear forces on the assumption that their own people would suffer 'only' some 20 million casualties in return; a figure deemed acceptable because the Soviet people had endured this during World War II and still fought on to victory. Brodie was not the only critic to point out that casualties on this scale had not, in the past, encouraged anyone to risk them again, and that such adventurism was notably out of line with a record of caution in the conduct of foreign policy that had characterized the regime even of Stalin, let alone his successors. There might indeed be a finite risk that the Soviet leadership would behave so totally out of character, but what were the opportunity costs of guarding against it?

This controversy was to divide the United States' strategic and indeed political community for three decades, rising to successive peaks with the anti-ballistic missile (ABM) controversy of the mid-1970s and the Strategic Defense Initiative (SDI) controversy of the mid-1980s. Like all such confrontations, it was a clash not so much of arguments as of personalities and political cultures. Wohlstetter threw himself into it with a passion that was strangely at odds with his normal affability. If he sought consensus within his own community, he was quite ferociously confrontational with those who lay outside it, and he went to extreme lengths to lay bare the inadequacy of their arguments. The insouciant charm depicted by the contributors to this *festschrift* is only half the story. Wohlstetter tore to pieces the thesis of the arms control lobby, that the weapons policy of the Soviet Union was dictated simply by their perception of the US threat, rather than by their own very different agenda. His exposure of muddled, if not wishful, thinking on this issue did a great deal of good, but in his pursuit of adversaries Wohlstetter showed himself at his most Calvinistic: there was at times a distinct whiff of burning in the air.

For those who, like Wohlstetter and his colleagues, saw the build-up of Soviet capabilities as sufficient evidence of their intentions, the surge in Soviet weaponry at the end of the 1970s, combined with the incoherence of US policy under the presidency of Jimmy Carter, constituted a clear and present danger; one that was perhaps as effective in ensuring the election of Ronald Reagan in 1980 as 'the missile gap' had been for John F. Kennedy 20 years earlier. It would be premature to say that they were wrong. For a Soviet leadership that still thought in terms of 'the correlation of forces' and interpreted the uncertainties of the Carter period as a sign of weakness, nuclear dominance would have been an invaluable, perhaps a decisive element in their global policy, even if that policy fell far short of threatening, much less launching, a nuclear war.

Yet, paradoxically, it was at precisely this moment that the internal weaknesses of the Soviet Union were becoming terminal, and the gradual influence of the Helsinki process was opening up the Soviet empire to Western penetration. As the United States grew more alarmed about the military might of the Soviet Union, Europeans were becoming very much less. It was extraordinarily difficult for European visitors to Washington in the early 1980s (and, *a fortiori*, to California) to persuade US commentators and defence analysts that the progress of détente on their continent was the result of European confidence, not of European fears; and that if anyone was likely to be 'Finlandized', it was the lands of Eastern rather than those of Western Europe.

The third critique of the Wohlstetter school was of its alleged inhumanity, the cool way in which it assessed the cost-effectiveness of different targets, all involving perhaps millions of human lives. This was a cruelly unjust accusation and one that probably angered Wohlstetter more than any other. His analysis was precisely directed at trying to *limit* the inhumanity and destructiveness of war through careful selection of targets, the development of accurate weapons and guidance systems to hit them, and the creation of structures for command and communication that would ensure control even through the worst of nuclear wars. It could certainly be argued, as did Brodie, that such planning was so unrealistic as to be a waste of time and resources, but it was grotesque to term it inhumane. The inhumanity, as Wohlstetter quite properly replied, lay rather with those whose strategic vision did not extend beyond nuclear retaliation against cities: a group that embraced many arms controllers, old style SAC planners and, curiously enough, some church groups, in a far from holy alliance.[10]

The final accusation is that Wohlstetter's analysis was a recipe for an endless and debilitating arms race, exacerbating relations with the Soviet Union and sucking in resources desperately needed elsewhere. This was the charge made, with great prescience, by the British scientist and strategic analyst P.M.S. Blackett in a comment on Wohlstetter's 'Delicate Balance of Terror' article, in 1961. To accept the idea that stability could be obtained only by 'a great increase of expenditure on research and development of long-range missiles and a large increase in their invulnerability', wrote Blackett, was not only 'likely to lead to wrong allocation of priorities as well as a worsening of the international atmosphere'; it would destroy all hope of effective arms control and open the way to 'an endless and increasing arms race'.[11]

So it did, for a full quarter-century after Blackett wrote. For many people, this is the ultimate condemnation of Wohlstetter's work. But it is fair to ask again the irreverent question 'So what?'

Are 'arms races', so called, anything more than an assertion in peacetime of a determination to preserve or acquire power in the international system – a peaceful, if not a moral, substitute for war? Can they be abandoned or mitigated without abandoning the goals that they are intended to attain or the interests they seek to preserve? The archetypical arms race was the naval race between Britain and Germany before 1914. It arose because Germany was determined to challenge British maritime hegemony, and Britain was equally determined to maintain it. Britain 'won' that race, and Germany had to turn to submarine warfare in World War I to avoid defeat, ultimately with disastrous results. A comparable Anglo-American naval race was averted after 1918 because Britain was prepared to share maritime hegemony with a rival whom it did not perceive as a threat. Given an ideological confrontation that was still as bitter in 1980 as it had been in 1950, it is not likely that a comparable accommodation could have been reached between the United States and the Soviet Union, or have lasted long if it had; whatever marginal mitigation might have been achieved by arms control agreements.

Wohlstetter, with his steely logic, saw this clearly. An armaments competition lay in the nature of things, and it was important not to lose it. Further, in an era of rapidly evolving technology, the advantage lay increasingly with *quality*; something lost on those obsessed with 'bean counts'. What is not clear from this book is at what stage Wohlstetter began to realize, as became evident by the 1980s, that the arms race was effectively a war of attrition; bloodless, but no less remorseless than that waged between Germany and its adversaries in World War I; and, like that conflict, one in which the side with the biggest purse had the ultimate advantage. Some of the chapters here on net assessment hint that strategic planners in Washington had this objective clearly in mind. In such a contest, there was always the danger that the losing side, like Germany in 1918, would lash out in a last effort to avoid defeat, which made it all the more important to maintain effective deterrence at every level. Ultimately, the Soviet Union broke, as suddenly and unexpectedly as Germany had broken in 1918, leaving a comparable mess behind.

At the end of his life, Brodie despaired of strategy because nuclear war could never, in his view, be an instrument of policy. Wohlstetter would not have dissented from that conclusion, but he saw that nuclear *weapons* could be instruments of policy. Whether consciously or unconsciously, the United States used them as such. Historians will probably debate forever whether victory in the Cold War was due rather to Mikhail Gorbachev's perception that the Soviet Union could no longer sustain the military competition with the United States, or to the gradual but inexorable realization, on the part of all significant elements within the Soviet Union, that communism was not working but 'capitalism' was: a realization hastened by the communications revolution, which made possible increasing Western penetration in Soviet society. Both no doubt played their part; but if the Soviet Union had not been assured of Western benevolent intentions, as well as Western economic success and military power, it would not have given up so easily.

The victory has not come cost-free, any more than did the victory in 1918. The cost has yet to be counted of the long-term effects on the US economy and society; of the vast deficit piled up in order to maintain the level of military expenditure considered necessary to break the Soviet Union. It may well prove that in the long term the United States bought its victory, as did Britain in 1918, at the price of pre-eminence as a global power. We may certainly expect a generation of revisionists who will claim, as was claimed after 1918, that the whole conflict was unnecessary or that the risks run were excessive or that the price paid was too high. But not many of them are likely to come from the lands of the former Soviet empire.

Michael Howard, the President of the IISS, is the Robert A. Lovett Professor of Military and Naval History at Yale University.

Notes

1 See, for example, Ken Booth, 'Bernard Brodie' in J. Baylis and J. Garnett, eds., *Makers of Nuclear Strategy* (London: Pinter Press, 1991), p. 32.

2 Barry H. Steiner, *Bernard Brodie and the Foundations of American Nuclear Strategy* (Lawrence, KS: University of Kansas Press, 1991), pp. 10, 197.

3 *Ibid.*, p. 118.

4 *Ibid.*, p. 12.

5 *Ibid.*, p. 199.

6 *Ibid.*, p. 134.

7 Baylis and Garnett, *op. cit.* in note 1, p. 37.

8 Andrew W. Marshall, J.J. Martin and Henry S. Rowen, *On Not Confusing Ourselves: Essays on National Security Strategy in Honour of Albert and Roberta Wohlstetter*, (Boulder, CO: Westview Press, 1991), p. 284.

9 *Ibid.*, p. 174.

10 Wohlstetter's article on this subject in *Commentary*, June 1983, well deserves rereading. See Albert Wohlstetter, 'Bishops, statesmen and other strategists on the bombing of innocents', *Commentary*, vol. 75, no. 6, June 1983, pp. 15–35.

11 P.M.S. Blackett, *Studies in War, Nuclear and Conventional* (Edinburgh: Oliver and Boyd, 1962), p. 141.

CHAPTER TWENTY-FIVE

Old conflicts and new disorders

From Adelphi Paper 275, 1993

Western wars in the East

Although the Far East (to use an old-fashioned Eurocentric term) has never lacked for conflicts of its own, most of those that have been waged there over the past two centuries have resulted, directly or indirectly, from the impact of the West. For four hundred years the major powers of western Europe – Portugal, Spain, the Netherlands, France and Britain – exported their rivalries to the Far East in the form of competitive empires whose frontiers stopped only at the borders of a China that was too vast, a Thailand that was too wily and a Japan that was too tough to be conquered. The nineteenth century brought new actors on to the scene: the Russians, extending their reach as their railways spanned the continent of Asia; the Japanese themselves, imitating their European mentors in everything including their imperialism; and finally the United States, drawn by 'Manifest Destiny' into its own mission of enlightenment, civilization and, incidentally, the quest for a fast buck.

The colonial powers established their own balance in the region. It was disturbed primarily by the slow disintegration of

China; but while the Europeans divided the spoils peacefully if not equitably between them, Japan seized control of the Yellow Sea after the Sino-Japanese conflict in 1894, and went on ten years later to fight the first major war of the twentieth century with Russia over the control of Korea.

Thereafter the pattern of international politics in the Far East was to be wholly determined by events in the West. It was only European weakness and American isolationism that enabled Japan to extend its hegemony over Manchuria in 1931, and civil war in post-revolutionary China opened the way for further Japanese expansion on the mainland which the enfeebled European empires could do nothing to stop. Although the US had seen Japan as its major rival in the Pacific ever since the turn of the century and had built up its navy accordingly, it could do nothing to help its Chinese protégés without risking a war that the American people were morally and materially unprepared to fight.

Then, in 1940, the collapse of the old powers of western Europe before the Nazi onslaught and the resulting vulnerability of their empires in the Far East presented a temptation that the Japanese leadership found impossible to resist: to build a Greater East Asia Co-Prosperity Sphere that would be invulnerable to American economic pressure. Whether the United States would have allowed them to do so peacefully if the Japanese had not so disastrously attacked them at Pearl Harbour must remain one of the great 'might-have-beens' of history. As it was, the Japanese were the architects of their own downfall. The empire they established on the ruins of their European predecessors lasted barely four years. With the defeat of Japan in 1945 the US seemed set to establish a peaceful hegemony throughout the entire region not only of the Pacific, but of East Asia as well.

That hegemony, however, was not to extend beyond the shores of the mainland. A new Western conflict was already extending itself to Asia. The Marxist–Leninist revolutionary upheaval, which since 1917 had created virtual or actual civil war throughout Europe, had been given a new and powerful impetus by the victories of the Soviet Union in the Second World War. Lenin had already identified the anti-colonial movements in Asia as a fruitful area for the spread of communism, and between the wars ambitious young intellectuals from the East had been absorbing his doctrines in Paris and London as well as in Moscow. The combination of anti-Western nationalism and communist ideology would have been an immensely powerful agent for change in Asia even if it had not been encouraged by the Soviet Union. In China it proved irresistible. The victory of Mao Zedong in 1949 presaged the opening of a new era of conflict in Asia; one in which anti-colonial revolt, communist ideology and the emergence of new power rivalries were to be deeply intertwined.

In Washington the new developments were seen simply as an alarming extension of the confrontation with the Soviet Union which had already developed in Europe, and experts in the State Department who tried to indicate the complexity of the situation were given a very rough ride. The British were more phlegmatic. Experience in India had taught them that the best way to pre-empt communism was to come to terms with emerging nationalism, and they identified, far sooner than did the US, the emerging conflict between the Soviet Union and the People's Republic of China. The French, disastrously, tried to counter their humiliation in Europe by restoring their domin- ion in Indochina, and the United States, even more disastrously, supported them.

In Korea there was a clearer case. The invasion of the American protectorate of South Korea by Soviet-armed forces from the North could not but be seen, whether rightly or wrongly, as a deliberate challenge to the US and to the new world order it was aspiring to create through the newly founded United Nations. The United States felt bound to respond to that invasion by armed force, and its European allies felt equally bound to help, if only in return for American support on their own continent. With the outbreak of a shooting war in Korea the complex conflicts in Asia were suddenly simplified. Those who supported the US and its allies were friends, whatever their political complexion. Those who did not were seen as adversaries, actual or potential. Neutrals got short shrift. The resulting impact on American relations with India was little short of catastrophic; decades were to pass before they began to improve.

The starkness of this confrontation was mitigated when, at the beginning of the 1960s, the emerging hostility between the Soviet Union and the People's Republic of China became generally evident. Nonetheless, a continuing belief in the total nature of global confrontation between the forces of communism and those of the 'free world' led the United States into an involvement in Vietnam where none of its European allies were prepared to follow. It took the historical perspective of Henry Kissinger and the ruthlessness of Richard Nixon to accept the PRC as a partner in the power-game in Asia and to begin the long process – not yet completed – of normalizing relations with the largest nation in the world. But the virtual abandonment of the mainland of Asia outside South Korea did enable the US to consolidate its influence as the dominant maritime and nuclear power in the western Pacific, guaranteeing a peaceful order and a growing prosperity that transformed the economy of the region – and indeed of the world.

Justifying the American presence, and rendering it acceptable to the peoples of the region, was the continuing menace of a Soviet Union which possessed powerful satellites in North Korea and Vietnam, the second greatest navy in the world, and a continuing determination to exploit disorder to the disadvantage of the Western world wherever it was feasible to do so. But at the end of the 1980s that menace evaporated. There was no longer a hostile superpower for the United States to confront, whether in the Far East or anywhere else. The Soviet Fleet melted away from Cam Ranh Bay. That in Vladivostok rotted at anchor. At the UN the Soviet (later the Russian) delegate became a cooperative partner in the creation of a 'new' new world order. It seemed that the West no longer had any conflicts to export to the Far East. Would it – or rather, will it – now be peace?

Conflict areas today

The danger for a body like the IISS is that it should go round the world looking for conflicts to justify its continuing existence, like arms manufacturers seeking new markets to replace former valued clients who, infuriatingly, have decided to live together in peace. That is not the Institute's purpose. Nonetheless it is its job to identify seismic areas where conflicts might arise, and consider what is to be done about them.

Looking at the Far East today, the pessimist could find many such areas of conflict. The most serious lies a few miles north of where we are now meeting; that legacy from the darkest days of the Cold War, the border between North and South Korea. There are also legacies from earlier major wars, notably the two Russo-Japanese conflicts of 1904 and 1945 and the territorial disputes they have left behind them. Beyond that there are trouble-spots all round the vast perimeter of the People's Republic of China, not least that arising from the contested status of Tibet. There is fear that turbulence in Central Asia in the wake of the dissolution of the Soviet Union might spread over the borders into China. There is the continuing problem, in spite of the magnificent efforts of the UN, of Cambodia. There are contested islands in the South China Sea, notably the

Spratlys. There is the immensely delicate issue of Hong Kong. In South Asia, the dispute between India and Pakistan over Kashmir seems no nearer solution, and racial tensions still tear Sri Lanka apart. No doubt there are, and will be, many more.

The problem of Japan

On an entirely different level, not so much a trouble-spot as a vast problem in international and economic relations, there is the question of Japan which is almost a replica of the problem Europe has been facing with Germany. Both countries, since their defeat in the Second World War, have behaved faultlessly. They have introduced constitutions that are models for the rest of the world. They have demilitarized themselves, morally even more than materially, to such an extent that they are unwilling to use military force even for the most impeccable of international objectives. Their record of misbehaviour, abominable as it was, sinks ever deeper into a past in which no one has clean hands. Nevertheless those memories linger on for the generation that experienced them and, combined with envy and (in some cases) alarm at the economic achievements of those countries, infect the attitudes of their neighbours. And it must be said that the continuing reluctance of the Japanese to confront some dark passages in their past as frankly as have the Germans has made the task of reconciliation even more difficult.

Japan, however, or rather reactions to Japan, presents an even greater problem than does Germany. For one thing, the challenge posed by its economic achievement is greater. For another, it has been possible to absorb Germany into a European Community where its dominance is at least mitigated. For a third – and this must be quite frankly stated – there is, in the attitude of at least some Americans and even a few Australians to Japan, an element of sheer racism; one that long preceded the Second World War and which that war did nothing to mitigate.

The author's purely personal view, as someone who has had the privilege of living in the United States for three years, is that the problem is not so much the growth of Japanese economic power in itself as American reaction to that growth; and perhaps even more, Japanese perceptions of that reaction. A friend and colleague Paul Kennedy has pointed out the disquieting analogy between the US–Japanese relationship today and that between Britain and Germany almost exactly a century ago, when the success of German economic competition was a significant element in the growing hostility between the two countries that was to sharpen into the First World War. Fear that Britain might use its naval supremacy to stifle German commercial competition was used as a powerful argument by von Tirpitz and the builders of the German Navy which, in its turn, made the British fear for their very existence. No historical analogies are exact, and all are potentially misleading; but commercial rivalries have deepened into military confrontations in the past, and could do so again. So long as such possibilities exist, naval and military specialists are liable to make contingency plans that may, unless one is careful, turn into self-fulfilling prophecies.

But the Americans are not the only people who fear a possible renaissance of Japanese military power. The nations of South-east Asia, while enjoying the benefits of Japanese economic dominance, are happy to combine it with a simultaneous American naval hegemony, and are in no hurry to see the Americans go home. Neither are the two Koreas. Japan itself welcomes the continuation of American protection, both naval and nuclear, since it saves the nation from the tough decisions that would have to be taken if it found itself alone in a confrontation with a Russia which remains, whatever its good intentions, a formidable naval, nuclear and military power, and a China which, if not yet considerable in the first two of those categories, will become no less so with the passage of time. Soviet threat or no Soviet threat, the US presence in the Far East remains profoundly stabilizing, and one reason why the Pacific remains pacific. Such at least is the conventional wisdom, which in this instance the author shares.

The social roots of conflict

This survey so far has been a very old-fashioned one, as that of all strategists tends to be: looking at powers as powers and states as states whose actions are dictated by narrowly defined state interests, unaffected by domestic social changes within them. Few historians would today accept the adequacy, indeed the validity, of such an analysis. Leopold von Ranke's *Primat der Aussenpolitik*, the acceptance of the primacy of foreign policy in the conduct of human affairs, has long been discarded as an adequate explanation of international conflict. Changes within societies provide explanations for conflict at a very much deeper level. It is now known that the First World War cannot be understood unless the mentality of the peoples of western Europe is studied, particularly that of the newly united Germans, at a time of enormous social turbulence. The Second World War is even less understandable without examining the roots of National Socialism in Germany and its imitators elsewhere in Europe: the appeal of revolutionary nationalism to peoples uprooted from the past, bewildered by the speed of social change, nostalgic for old certainties while rejecting old structures, easily persuaded that their misfortunes are due to the machinations of external or internal enemies, pathetically anxious for leadership and prepared to pay almost any price to get it. This anomie underlay the appeal of communism as well as that of fascism, and both could be conveniently blended with old-style nationalism to mobilize entire populations. Both were fundamentally the result of the impact of modernism

on traditional societies: sweeping away old values and structures, questioning old certainties, destroying social hierarchies,
holding out infinite promise of material progress but leaving
individuals at the mercy of economic forces they could neither
control nor understand.

With the help of the Americans, this mess has been sorted
out in Europe; or rather, in western Europe; or rather, up to
a point in western Europe. Even so, nobody looking at these
western societies today can feel very happy about them. But in
eastern Europe and the former Soviet Union it is a very different story. The problems of that vast region are not the concern
of this conference, and perhaps that is just as well; but if 'new
disorders' are to be discussed, they can hardly be ignored.

What 'the new world disorder' does demonstrate is the
degree to which the West has been the victim of that old
Rousseauite fallacy that assumes that men are born not simply
free, but organized as discrete and coherent peoples who, if the
chains of despotism are removed from them, can automatically
create orderly and peaceful governments responsive to a clearly
identifiable popular will. Social organization is a more complex
matter than that, and the road to democratic self-government
is long and hard. The communist regimes in Europe and elsewhere were – and are – despotisms as repulsive as they were
inefficient, and their disappearance is no more to be regretted
than was that of the Nazis; but they did provide order of a kind,
certainties of a kind, even security of a kind. They protected
their peoples against the harsh winds of modernization which
are now blowing at full strength throughout the newly liberated region, presenting challenges and creating difficulties that
successor governments are finding almost insurmountable;
difficulties which are unlikely to be overcome by any amount
of foreign aid. And already the symptoms with which western
Europe became so familiar earlier in the century are reappear-

ing: authoritarianism, xenophobia, racism and ultimately, again, war.

The challenge of modernization

The way in which the West has exported its conflicts to the Far East has been mentioned above. But it has done a great deal more than that. It has exported the whole process of modernization, with all its gigantic problems and all its irresistible opportunities. This has had, on Eastern societies, the same disintegrating and transforming effect that it once had on the West; with the significant difference that, whereas in the West the transformation from traditional agrarian societies to modernized industrial states was spread over a couple of centuries (and even so caused enormous upheaval), in the Far East, as in the Third World in general, the process has been compressed into a single generation. Further, it comes as an alien import and so presents a double challenge to traditional values. Throughout the world and throughout this century, non-European peoples have been faced with the dilemma of whether to accept modernization at the cost of abandoning the traditional values that have bound their societies together for centuries, or to reject it at the cost of the kind of isolation and deprivation seen in the extreme case of Myanmar.

For a time, Marxist–Leninism and its Maoist variant seemed to offer an alternative path to modernization; an alternative as disruptive to traditional values as the Western model, admittedly, but one which created a new bond of social order and a new myth that protected the peoples who embraced it against the atomistic individualism and the ruthless challenges of the Western market economy. It has become painfully clear that such a model does not work. But it is equally clear that, for those who have embraced it, there can be no easy transition to Western-style democracy. In Beijing, the example of

Gorbachev can hardly appear a good one to follow: if the existing leadership does relax its grip, can it expect anything better in that vast and infinitely diverse country than the anarchy that has overtaken the former Soviet Union? How is uninhibited modernization, Western-style, to be made compatible with the preservation of any kind of social order? How is an orderly transition to be managed, and who is going to manage it?

The same problem has in one way or another confronted all the peoples of the Far East, as it has all the peoples of the Third World. Some have solved it more successfully than others. For many the transition to democracy has been painful: the political problems of South Korea itself are a case in point. It is not surprising that benevolent authoritarianism, supported if not imposed by the armed forces, has often been accepted as a necessary framework for the modernization process, whatever the cost to 'human rights' as understood and formulated in the West. Such infractions were winked at by the United States so long as the friendship of such governments was made necessary by the Cold War, but Western public opinion is likely now to become more critical. That in itself may provoke new tensions and inhibit cooperation within the region.

What are the implications of all this for the prospects of peace and stability in Asia?

It is generally assumed that democracies do not or are unlikely to fight one another. Yet it would be dangerous to place too much confidence in this: even if the American Civil War is excluded on the grounds that a slave-owning society cannot be a democracy, there was still a very nasty war between Britain and the entirely democratic Boer Republics in 1899–1902. Nor, having observed British public opinion at the time of the Falkland crisis and American public opinion during the Gulf War, can it be claimed that mature democratic societies are never belligerent. Conversely, autocracies and dictatorships are not necessarily belligerent either; they are usually too much concerned with preserving order within their own precarious societies, as was Franco in Spain and the bulk of Latin American military dictatorships, to risk external conflict. But there is a rough inverse correlation between the degree of successful modernization in a society and its propensity to go to war, however great its enthusiasm may be once the conflict is engaged. Democratic societies tend to place a high value on human lives – at least, on the lives of their own peoples – and a reluctance to see them put at risk.

In judging the likelihood of conflict, therefore, the nature of the societies involved as well as the sources of dispute between states must be examined. In the early part of this century both Germany and Japan presented the paradoxical spectacle of societies becoming rapidly industrialized within an archaic feudal framework, whose ruling elite watched with horror as the traditional martial values of their societies crumbled around them, and who embraced war, if indeed they did not actually provoke it, with a kind of cheerful desperation to show that heroic values had not perished from the earth. Such sentiments were still evident even in the Britain of Rupert Brooke and the America of Teddy Roosevelt, although they barely survived the experience of the First World War. In the aftermath of that war, when traditional values really had disintegrated, these feelings were reinforced by xenophobia and racial prejudice to become the basis for the populist phenomena of fascism and National Socialism; creeds that embraced war as a lifestyle to be welcomed, rather than a horror to be shunned.

Reaction against modernization can thus be a fruitful cause of wars. So can revolution. The three great revolutions of the modern era – the French, the Russian and the Chinese – have all followed the similar pattern of a revolutionary elite seizing power, regarding themselves, *ipso facto*, as being in a state of war with hostile neighbours anxious to destroy them, and provoking hostilities as much to guarantee their own internal security as to spread their ideological creed. In Western societies, therefore, fascism and communism have both presented threats to international order. Neither is now likely to recur in the guise familiar in the first half of this century. But if the circumstances that gave rise to them – the disintegration of stable social order, the collapse of functioning economic systems causing widespread hardship and despair – were to recur, they could re-emerge in new and even more terrible forms. No society is invulnerable. It would be reassuring to believe that Western societies are now sufficiently stable and successful to be immune from these diseases, but there are times when this seems doubtful. How immune are the emerging nations of the Far East?

Prospects for peace in Asia

The author is not an expert on Asian affairs. But in assessing the possibility of new conflicts and new disorders developing in this region, it is necessary to know about the problems caused by social and economic change as well as those of interstate tension; to look at the vertical conflicts as well as the horizontal ones. Will the People's Republic of China continue to be so deeply concerned with its internal problems that it will wish to remain on peaceful terms with it neighbours and attract as much external trade and investment as is compatible with the maintenance of its present political order; or will there be a new time of troubles in which it will go the way of the former Soviet Union, disintegrating into its constituent parts and provoking God knows what in the way of internal and external conflict? Will Japan remain sufficiently internally stable to maintain its deeply pacific stance and continue to extend its economic dominance in spite of the jealousy, hostility and mistrust that the nation provokes, in spite of itself, from its rivals and competitors? Will North Korea make a peaceful transition, if not to democracy, then at least to a regime open to the rest of the world; and if reunification does come about, will it be negotiated as amicably as was the case with the two Germanies? How peacefully will a reunited Korea settle into the power structure of the region? Will the eventual revival of Russian power bring a stable and friendly trading partner, settling in a business-like and harmonious fashion its differences with its Asian neighbours, or an angry nationalist regime anxious to avenge former humiliations? Can Vietnam and Cambodia develop, under UN auspices, into a friendly partnership? Can the nations of Southeast Asia maintain their present mixture of prosperity and benevolent authoritarianism? And in South Asia, will ethnic and other rivalries ultimately not simply disturb, but shatter the present stability and lead to major war in the subcontinent?

In the midst of all these uncertainties, one thing is clear. International politics in the Pacific and the Far East are no longer a subsystem of those in the West, and are unlikely ever to be so again. The United States will continue to participate in its own right as a Pacific power and to play a major role in the region; but its relations with other actors in the system, and their relations with each other, will be determined by indigenous factors and not by Western rivalries. But this region is now one of such importance that its continued stability is a vital factor.

CHAPTER TWENTY-SIX

Lessons of the Cold War

Survival 36-4, 1994–5

Sir Michael Howard, historian and President of the IISS, was the first recipient of the Paul H. Nitze Award of the Center for Naval Analyses, Washington DC, where he gave this presentation on 6 April 1994.

First, let us be clear: the West won the Cold War. I have little respect for those who maintain that nobody won. There are some – among them that great veteran of the Cold War, George Kennan – who maintain that we won it at an unnecessarily great cost and certainly the cost has still to be counted. But that can be, and has been, said of almost every war in the history of mankind. Historians will long debate this, as they still argue over whether it was necessary, during the First World War, to incur such terrible casualties on the Western Front and, in the Second, to flatten German and Japanese cities. What is beyond doubt, however, is that we effectively deterred the Soviet Union from using military force to achieve its political objectives, and thus provided the opportunity for the two political systems to compete peacefully. It was in this competition that the West ultimately prevailed.

Was the Soviet Union ever likely to use military force? Here again, historians will differ. We should probably admit that we were always more prone to overestimate that likelihood than to underestimate it – especially during those dark years at the beginning of the 1950s before the ground rules of the Cold War were generally understood. Most historians would now agree that in the immediate aftermath of the Second World War, Stalin, ruling an exhausted country that had narrowly escaped total destruction, was more concerned with security than with conquest. For all his ruthlessness, he was a cautious man who knew the limitations of his strength. But those who, like Winston Churchill, saw in his death an opportunity for resolving the Cold War were in my view too optimistic. Stalin's successors, Khrushchev pre-eminent among them, while sharing his ignorance of the outside world, lacked his political realism. They presided over an economy whose pace of recovery gave them good cause to believe that they might really 'bury' the West in peaceful competition, or by war if they had to. Even more important, the disintegration of Europe's overseas empires in the 1950s indicated to them that the foundations of capitalism were now really collapsing and that the West was becoming a beleaguered garrison surrounded by world armies of liberation that looked to Moscow for leadership. This euphoria was to lead to the Cuban missile crisis in 1962, which was a sobering experience for everyone concerned. It was probably this experience more than anything else that convinced at least the statesmen, if not all the military leaders and strategic analysts, on both sides that a nuclear war could never be won and must never be fought.

So a military stand-off was reached, and was over several decades preserved, that allowed the politico-economic systems of communism and pluralistic democracy to develop side by side; with results that we all know. The Cold War was not won by Western armed forces any more than it was lost by Soviet armed forces. Both performed their tedious and unrewarding tasks with great credit and can look back on their joint record with considerable satisfaction. The war was won by Western market economies, which by the 1980s embraced the entire non-communist world and were transforming global society in a manner that made Marxist–Leninist regimes look like dinosaurs surviving in a kind of Jurassic Park; dinosauric in their size, their ferocity, their inability to adapt themselves and, not least, their tiny brains.

It is hard to recall how improbable such an outcome seemed in Europe during the immediate post-war years. It was then barely a decade since the apparent collapse of capitalism in the early 1930s had devastated the economies of the West and made possible the rise of fascism. It was not just a handful of cranks and fanatics who saw in communism the last best hope of mankind. Marxism was a creed that captured the imagination of many of our brightest and our best. There was huge sympathy for the Soviet Union in post-war Europe and goodwill for the communist system; sympathy deepened by doubts as to whether capitalist economies would ever get on their feet again.

Had it not been for the intervention of the United States and the generosity of the Marshall Plan, perhaps they would not have recovered. But once those economies did expand again, and the presence of US forces provided reassurance that they would not be overthrown from outside, the enormous strength of an increasingly global market system, now made politically stable by social democracy, quickly became clear. Within a few years the Soviet system found itself on the defensive, literally having to build walls to keep foreign ideas out and its own citizens in. The newly liberated countries of the Third World, except for a handful most deeply scarred by colonial wars, embraced the economic, if not always the political, systems of their former masters. The Soviet Union's most powerful associate, communist China, in the eyes of many Americans its most formidable conquest, became its most dedicated adversary. It was not the West that became an island of obsolescence surrounded by an ideologically hostile world; it was the Soviet Union. After 40 years of confrontation the Soviet leaders themselves came to realise it.

Let me reiterate: it was not the military strength of the West that won the Cold War; military strength did no more than make victory possible. If the Soviet economic and political system *had* worked, and if it had delivered the prosperity and social justice that its founders had promised and for which generations of Russians had suffered and died, then the Soviets would have won and would have deserved to win. No amount of Western military power could have prevented it. Western Europe would have shifted from social democracy into socialism, from neutrality into clientism. The Third World would have welcomed the tools to build the socialist paradise of which so many of the first generation of their leaders had dreamt. The US would have relapsed into bitter isolation. But it did not work. Marxism–Leninism was given its chance but failed; as George Kennan had prophesied at the very outset of the Cold War, if properly contained, it was eventually bound to fail.

It was President Mikhail Gorbachev's great achievement to realise that Soviet military strength was both irrelevant to the success of Marxism–Leninism and harmful in the distortions it imposed on the Soviet economy. Soviet military power could conquer nothing that the Soviet Union needed; the territories in Eastern Europe that it garrisoned were economic liabilities and political embarrassments; and it deterred an adversary who did not have to be deterred. Further, in the event of general war it could offer no prospect except the virtual destruction of the Soviet Union itself. Only by ending the confrontation that made that military strength necessary, Gorbachev realised, could the resources be made available to give the ailing Soviet economic system the slightest prospect of success.

What Gorbachev failed to understand, however, was the extent to which the Soviet Union had become a garrison state. If the garrison was unnecessary, the whole legitimacy of the state disappeared. Georgei Arbatov, you will remember, teased us with the warning that Gorbachev was going to inflict on us the severest blow conceivable – he was going to deprive us of an enemy. We survived that. Free societies do not need enemies. But for totalitarian societies they are essential. The Soviet Union had had its 'necessary enemies' ever since 1917. Only their existence – real or alleged – justified all the sufferings and injustices that the regime had imposed on its unhappy peoples. When the enemies vanished the regime itself disappeared; it had lost its *raison d'être*. The Soviet Union was like a rotten tree, supported only by the ivy that was killing it. It is for these things that President Ronald Reagan will be remembered, long after 'Irangate' and the Strategic Defense Initiative are forgotten: his magnanimity, his courage and, above all, his skill in persuading the Soviet peoples that they really did have no enemies and that it was safe for them to come in from the cold.

So we won without a military victory, and without even having to fight. To fight at all would have been a confession of failure and victory a catastrophe indistinguishable from defeat – even though we had to make it clear that we would fight if it was absolutely necessary and that in any conflict our adversaries would suffer a great deal more than ourselves.

Now a historical epoch is over and we are entering a different and perhaps no less dangerous world; certainly a more disorderly one, both domestically and internationally. While no one would deny the possibility of an eventual resurgence of Russian power, and the continual likelihood of its causing problems to its immediate neighbours, a renewed global ideological confrontation providing a unifying force for the confusion of world politics is barely even a possibility. So, are the forces that we raised and the skills that we developed during the Cold War as obsolete as the situation that called them into being? Are there any lessons to be learned, especially by the military, from that historically almost unique situation: 40 years of non-shooting conflict?

Hopefully, I think there are. Although such a global confrontation is unlikely to recur for a generation or two, there will be, and already have been, comparable problems, if on a very different scale.

Today we are confronted by a confused and deeply disturbed world, the causes of whose confusion we only dimly understand. No part of it is totally at peace and much is in a condition of endemic war, often brought to our attention only in a random and unsystematic way by the good offices of CNN. Thanks to global communications there is today no part of the world that can be completely ignored, but equally no part that can be entirely and permanently pacified. The US is no longer likely to swing wildly between its two traditional poles of isolationism and globalism, based on those opposite but interconnected illusions that, on the one hand, the outside world can be ignored and, on the other, that it can be coordinated in a world order impregnated by American ideals and controlled by American power. Even those regions that we thought were settled and pacified for good, notably Europe, are revealing themselves to be surprisingly unstable. I would like to believe those of my academic colleagues who declare that mature democracies never go to war with one another, but I would not lay any money on it. Democracy is a very elastic term. Democratic institutions are liable to decay and abuse, and electorates can show themselves to be remarkably immature in their political judgement. Even in democracies, economic failure is liable to trigger social disorder, social disorder to trigger internecine violence, and internecine violence to trigger regional if not global instability. There is nothing necessarily permanent about democracies – even for them, even for the US itself, history may have some nasty tricks up its sleeve.

So our first priority must be to set our own houses in order and ensure that we are not ourselves part of the problem rather than part of the solution; that we are in a position to export stability rather than risk importing instability. The fact that communism failed does not mean that market economies will necessarily succeed. If they also fail, the whole dreary cycle will probably begin again, in Europe as elsewhere, with the forces of the moderate centre being squeezed out between the competing nostrums of Left and Right, and fanatical totalitarianism once more threatening international peace.

Beyond that, what can we do to bring stability to the world and, in particular, what use can be made of our military power? Is American military strength still relevant to the maintenance of world peace? My belief is that it is as relevant today, and will continue to be in the future, as it has ever been. Military power has three functions – deterrence, compellance and reassurance. We have become rather expert at deterrence: in the hands of such masters as Paul Nitze it made it possible for us to win the Cold War. Military power will still be needed in the future to deter other states, if ones less formidable than the Soviet Union, from using force as an instrument of policy. Deterrence has spawned an entire academic profession of strategic analysts, who are not going to be put out of business in a hurry.

The military themselves, however, are more at home with compellance, a term coined long ago by Tom Schelling of Harvard University, which is the actual use of armed force to make people do things. Compellance was used to get Saddam Hussein out of Kuwait. There are those who, rightly or wrongly, urge compellance in Bosnia to make the Serbs cease and desist from their hostilities against the Muslims. We are having at least to contemplate compellance to make North Korea abandon its nuclear programme, and the same need may arise again to prevent the proliferation of further nuclear states. Compellance usually signals a failure of deterrence, but deterrence is not likely to be credible unless the possibility of compellance is evident.

Perhaps reassurance (a term for which I can myself claim paternity) is more important than either deterrence or compellance for the preservation of world stability, for it determines the entire environment within which international relations are conducted. Reassurance provides a general sense of security that is not specific to any particular threat or scenario. The best analogy I can provide is the role played by the British Royal Navy in the nineteenth century. For nearly 100 years, British naval power exercised a global and usually benign hegemony that was taken for granted by other powers because it conflicted with the interests of very few of them. While Britain itself profited most from that hegemony, nobody else suffered. Under its auspices the world enjoyed an era of peace that made possible an unequalled growth of prosperity. Towards the end of the century other powers, not least the US and, more disastrously, Germany, began to resent having their security depend on the goodwill of an unpredictable foreign power. The system disintegrated, but the Pax Britannica was a good epoch in the history of mankind.

After the Second World War, the US had aspirations towards a comparable Pax Americana which were dampened, if not extinguished, by the onset of the Cold War. The end of that conflict has not seen their revival. It is generally admitted that the US remains the only superpower, but it has no appetite to act like one. The American electorate is deeply reluctant to accept imperial responsibilities, while American policy-makers have learned the hard way that the world is too complex and diverse to be controlled by US power. Nonetheless, disorderly and uncontrollable as the world may be, it would be a great deal more disorderly if American military power did not exist, as we can see if we examine three major regions of the world.

Even with the disappearance of the Soviet threat, the American presence remains an intrinsic part of the European security system. The Soviet Union may have dissolved and its successor states be too impoverished and divided to pose any serious immediate dangers, but Russia remains a power, and a nuclear power, on a scale that still requires American strength to balance it if Europe is not to militarise itself to a degree inconceivable even at the height of the Cold War. Further, the reunification of Germany, however benign the policy of its leaders, has created a new, or rather recreated an old, power centre on the continent that makes the states of Eastern as well as Western Europe (and not excluding those of the former Soviet Union) anxious to retain the US as part of the regional balance. The disappearence of American power would leave Europe from the Atlantic to the Urals prey to terrifying uncertainties. There are indeed those in Europe, notably the French, who seek to reinsure themselves against a possible withdrawal by the development of a new 'common military identity' for the European Union, but I suspect that even they would see the disappearance of the American presence as a disaster. For Central and Eastern Europe it would be a real catastrophe.

Much the same can be said of the Pacific. There we see the development of a peaceful multipolar system of wealthy independent states, all of whom, unfortunately, regard it as the privilege of their wealth, independence and statehood to arm themselves to the teeth. But they would all agree (even perhaps the Republic of China) that their peace and prosperity depends not on any regional balance, but on the presence of a benign and dispassionate US whose military capacity would outclass any of them. Like the British in the nineteenth century, the US may lament that its military power provides the opportunity for its economic rivals to develop, but as with Britain the answer must be to compete more successfully and not eliminate the condition that makes possible the stability and prosperity of all.

In the Middle East the elimination of the American presence would open a Pandora's box of regional wars which would be unlikely to remain regional. The US has in the past tried to provide surrogate policemen for the region – Iran and Saudi Arabia – with highly unsatisfactory results. A misleading appearance of disinterest led to Saddam Hussein's invasion of Kuwait – a classic example of the failure of deterrence making necessary the exercise of compellance. There can be no substitute in the region for American power as the ultimate arbiter of disputes and American power means an evident capacity, and readiness, to intervene with armed force if all else fails.

The dismantling of armed forces in the past few years has been termed 'the peace dividend', but unless we are very careful it could be precisely the opposite. The Cold War was won by the triumph of the global market economy over the Marxist–Leninist command economies – or, if you prefer it, pluralist democracy over totalitarianism. But this triumph was made possible only by the stable framework provided by military deterrence. Peace and stability can now be preserved only if that economy continues to operate successfully, but it can only do so within a framework of world order underwritten by the military power and presence of the US. Nobody else wants the job. Nobody else could do it effectively. So please, soldier on.

CHAPTER TWENTY-SEVEN

When are wars decisive?

Survival 41-1, 1999

This essay is based on a paper presented to the 40th Annual Conference of the IISS at Oxford in September 1998, and has been modified in light of the subsequent discussion. The author acknowledges with much gratitude his debt to the work of Professor Brian Bond, *The Pursuit of Victory: From Napoleon to Saddam Hussein* (Oxford and New York: Oxford University Press, 1996) and Elliott Abrams (ed.) *Honor among Nations: Intangible Interests and Foreign Policy* (Washington DC: Ethics and Public Policy Center, 1998).

Wars are fought, or should be fought, to attain certain political objectives and decide specific issues. 'No one starts a war', wrote Clausewitz, 'or rather, no one in his senses ought to do so, without first being clear in his mind what he intends to achieve by that war and how he intends to conduct it'. He did accept that irrational elements, what he called 'the passions of the peoples', were likely to play at least as important a role in the conduct of war as the rationality of governments and the strategic calculations of the military. Even so, people seldom if ever take up arms (and this applies as much to civil as to international conflicts) without intending some preferred outcome, even if it is no more than the survival of their own group. So, what are the factors that will enable them to achieve their objective? When, if ever, are wars 'decisive'?

In Clausewitz's time, there was little problem about the definition of 'war': it was armed conflict between discrete and recognised states. Today the situation is more complex. Military activity is now as likely as not to be conducted, not against organised states, but against small, organised political units – 'sub-state actors' – attempting to take or retain control of territory or to overthrow the incumbent authority. The definition of war must therefore be extended to embrace all armed conflict between political entities, whether or not these are or claim to be recognised as sovereign states. Journalists and politicians often confuse the issue by suggesting that war can be waged against such abstractions as 'drugs', 'crime' or, particularly, 'terrorism'. 'The Cold War' notwithstanding, none of these usages makes sense unless they involve the use of armed force against specific political adversaries; in the case of terrorism, those who use terror as their primary political instrument, usually because they have none other available.

Whoever the adversary may be, what are wars intended to 'decide'? Again, let us take Clausewitz as our starting point. He divided wars rather arbitrarily into 'limited' and 'absolute': those intended to achieve a precise objective, usually territorial (as, in our own day, the possession of the Falkland Islands/ Malvinas or the liberation of Kuwait), or those intended to overthrow the adversary and destroy his political independence; as Humpty Dumpty succinctly put it, 'who's to be master – that's all'. But the distinction is not so easily drawn. The 'limited' objective may be sheer survival, as was the case with the Soviet Union during the Second World War, or with Israel in 1948 (if not indeed in her subsequent wars). In such cases the limited object may demand total commitment. Japan was fighting a 'limited' war between 1942 and 1945 in so far as, like Frederick the Great in the Silesian Wars 200 years earlier, she was concerned only to hold on to her initial conquests; but both found themselves fighting total wars against adversaries determined to crush them. In such civil wars as those in North America in 1776–83 and 1861–65, or Ireland in 1920–21, or Kosovo in our own day, the object of those who initiate the conflict is normally limited to gaining independence, but the incumbent authority may have to fight a total war to prevent it. It was the unwillingness, or inability, of England to fight such a total war that enabled both the United States and Ireland to achieve independence; whereas it was the readiness and ability of the United States to make total war that prevented the Confederacy from doing the same.

Furthermore, the struggle for an apparently 'limited' aim may be only symptomatic of a 'total' objective. Hitler initiated the Second World War with the apparently limited intention of 'liberating' the German city of Danzig and revising Germany's eastern borders. But his evident intention to go on to destroy Poland and assert the mastery of Europe compelled the British and French to plan a total war for his overthrow from the very outset, one in which the original objective was quickly forgotten. So the categories of 'limited' and 'total' objectives overlap. The objective of one side may be limited while that of the other is total; the objective itself may be limited but the means used to achieve it total. Finally, the limited objective may only be the symbol of a total struggle, rather as the independence of Belgium in the First World War and Poland in the Second World War became for the British.

There is a further complicating factor which is all too often ignored. Thucydides listed three causes of war – interest, fear, and honour. 'Interest' corresponds fairly closely to the idea of

'limited' objectives. 'Fear' of political if not physical annihilation certainly motivates at least one side in total wars. But
'honour' – whatever part this may have played in antiquity, in
medieval or even early modern warfare – has not this archaic
concept not totally disappeared in the modern world?

Far from it. Its name may have been changed to 'prestige', or
sometimes 'credibility', but the concept of 'honour' has played
a part in twentieth-century warfare quite as great as it did in
earlier ages. 'Interests' may determine the issue in limited wars,
and 'fear' may tend to make them total, but 'honour', however
defined, is what inflames 'the passions of the people'. Like 'fear'
it removes decisions from the controlling hands of the diplomats. Britain's decision in 1914 to fulfil her written guarantee
to Belgium and her unwritten obligation to France may have
been determined by a combination of fear (of German hegemony) and interest (in preserving the independence of the Low
Countries). But it was the concept of 'honour' that mobilised
public opinion, and kept it mobilised on both sides. Once blood
had been shed, and in terrible quantities, any settlement short
of final victory was depicted as a betrayal of those who had
already 'laid down their lives'. 'Honour' demanded that the
enemy should be forced to surrender, admit his guilt, and pay
full recompense. Much the same applied in the Second World
War. Whatever President Roosevelt's calculations may have
been about the *interests* of the United States, it was the insult
to their *honour* at Pearl Harbor in December 1941 that brought
the American people so whole-heartedly into the war; while it
was the same concept of honour that impelled the Japanese to
go on fighting virtually to extinction even though defeat stared
them in the face.

Thirty years later, although it may have been a combination
of fear (of global communism) and interest (in preserving her
control of the Pacific rim) that got the United States involved

in Vietnam in the first place, it was the desire to preserve her 'credibility' both with her allies and her adversaries that made it so difficult for her to get out again. In the Middle East, it was largely the desire to restore the prestige and dignity of his country that led then Egyptian President Anwar Sadat of Egypt to launch the Yom Kippur war in 1973; and it was certainly honour, rather than any conceivable calculation of narrow interest, that made the British people support so wholeheartedly the expedition to recover the Falkland Islands in 1982. Today the concept of honour, and its evil twin 'vengeance', still plays a large part in the conflicts in the Balkans and in tribal warfare everywhere, whether in Africa or Northern Ireland. It was certainly a sense of offended 'honour', and probably a desire for vengeance as well, that led the US to retaliate so precipitately against Afghanistan and Sudan when their embassies in Nairobi and Dar-es-Salaam were bombed in August 1998. We would be unwise to assume that 'honour' is any less significant in causing and prolonging conflict today than it was in the days of Thucydides.

So it will be these Thucydidean coordinates – interest, fear and honour – that determine the object for which war is fought. But whatever that objective may be, the means of attaining it in war are primarily military. Such ancillary methods as economic or psychological pressure may be used to make military victory easier, but if they are used on their own the conflict cannot properly be designated as 'war'. The military means used to obtain the purposes of the war were divided by Clausewitz and his successors into two: *Vernichtungsstrategie*, 'strategy of annihilation' – the destruction of the enemy's capacity to defend himself by destroying his armed forces on the battlefield; and *Ermattungsstrategie*, the use of attrition to wear down his will to resist. The first disarms the adversary, leaving him literally at the mercy of the victor. The second persuades him that victory is, if not impossible, only obtainable at an unacceptable price.

The first outcome is the ideal at which the professional military will, understandably, always aim – the truly 'decisive' victory on the battlefield. Napoleon remains the hero of all military buffs. The secret of this 'decisive victory' is the philosopher's stone for which the military are continually seeking. There are those who believe that it was found with the 1991 Gulf War, and that the so-called 'Revolution in Military Affairs' will ensure that it is here to stay. But victories on the battlefield, however overwhelming, do not necessarily lead to a lasting peace, as the aftermath of the Gulf War has made very clear. Even Napoleon's spectacular victories at Austerlitz, Jena and Wagram produced political settlements that were no more than truces. Even in their time such victories were exceptional, and there have been few examples since. The outcome of the American Civil War, to say nothing of the First and Second World Wars, was not decided on any particular battlefield, but by a whole succession of battles in which the defeated side was slowly, and almost literally, bled to death. In all these cases those who initiated the war, whether Confederates, Germans or Japanese, hoped to achieve a rapid decision on the battlefield that would make it clear to their adversaries that victory was either impossible or obtainable at too high a cost. All became wars of attrition and, with some rare exceptions, that became the pattern for war in the first half of the twentieth century.

We must not exaggerate the extent to which battles were decisive even before the nineteenth century. Edmund Gibbon famously congratulated his own age on its 'temperate and indecisive' wars. Such 'famous victories' as Blenheim in themselves decided nothing, as old Kaspar had ruefully to inform his grandchildren in Southey's well-known poem on that battle. The long duel fought by France and Britain between 1689 and

1815 for control of the oceans and the colonial wealth to which they gave access – a duel that was truly decisive for the future of both nations – was a long drawn-out war of attrition, which France abandoned only when victory became clearly unattainable. In the perspective of history, indeed, the Napoleonic era of 'decisive battles' was atypical. Its disappearance has often been attributed to the development of weapon technology, but it was not the introduction of rifled firearms that prolonged the American Civil War, or machine-guns and recoilless artillery the First World War. It was the development of communications and, with it, the mobilisation of nations. Lost battles, operational setbacks that might once have been 'decisive', became mere episodes in campaigns that could be indefinitely prolonged so long as fresh forces could be brought into the field, recruited from and supported by large and enthusiastic populations; populations that may have had little sophisticated understanding of national interests, but were easily moved by propaganda that played on emotions of fear and, even more, of honour.

It was thus the advent of 'people's wars' that made war total, shifting the centre of gravity away from armies on the battlefield to the people on whose endurance and support the continuance of the war depended, making it ever harder to reach a 'decision'. Not simply the armies but the will of the enemy people had to be crushed. When, in the autumn of 1870, the Prussian High Command, in spite of having totally defeated the French armies in less than a month, found themselves still confronting a French population that showed no signs of accepting defeat, the American General Philip Sheridan drew on his own experience in the Civil War (and perhaps Indian warfare) and advised Bismarck to leave the French people 'nothing but their eyes to weep with'. It was advice to be followed, so far as it lay within their power, by all the belligerents in the twentieth century's two world wars.

Whether wars are limited or total is thus likely to depend not so much on the original object for which they are fought, but on the nature of the society fighting them, and in particular on the degree of popular involvement in the conduct of the war. The greater that involvement, the greater is the part likely to be played by such non-rational factors as 'honour'. It has been suggested that democracies do not start wars, a generalisation that needs to be at best heavily qualified. What is beyond contradiction, however, is that in the era of democracy, wars may have been harder to begin but have also been very much harder to bring to an end. Nor is democracy (however that may be defined) necessary for popular participation and support. The Russian people fought for three years between 1914 and 1917 to support a dynastic autocracy, and a further four years in the Second World War to defend a totalitarian regime. In both world wars German armies, with the wholehearted support of their people, fought effectively and courageously for years at the behest of undemocratic governments. It would be a grave mistake today to believe that because a hostile state does not have a Western-style democratic constitution and is stigmatised by the West as a 'rogue state', its people would not support their leaders, with a minimal degree of coercion, in defending their country against its enemies, and remain bitterly resentful in defeat. Iraq today is no exception.

Few wars, in fact, are any longer decided on the battlefield (if indeed they ever were). They are decided at the peace table. Military victories do not themselves determine the outcome of wars; they only provide political opportunities for the victors – and even those opportunities are likely to be limited by circumstances beyond their control. In his excellent study *The Pursuit of Victory* Professor Brian Bond reminded us that 'at least two other considerations have to be added to success on the battlefield: namely, firm, realistic statecraft with specific aims, and the willingness of the vanquished to accept the verdict of battle' (p. 61). To study a war without taking into account the circumstances in which it is fought and the peace to which it led is a kind of historical pornography; like the study of sexual intercourse in isolation from the relationship within which it takes place and the consequences that flow from it. It is certainly an inadequate approach to thinking about war in the future.

A case in point is the First World War and the peace settlement that followed. The military victory of the Allies in that war had been as total as any in recorded history. Their enemies had either disintegrated altogether or surrendered at mercy. But because the war had to be fought again 20 years later, the memory of the war itself is, quite unfairly, one of military incompetence and bloody deadlock. The charge of incompetence is better laid at the door, not of the generals who had fought the war, but of the political leaders who made the peace. If the settlement after the Second World War had been equally indecisive, we might be rather less certain that it had been 'a good war' and remember more keenly its frustrations and failures. But this time there was 'firm, realistic statecraft with specific aims' – the destruction of the power of Nazi Germany and Imperial Japan. The vanquished *were* made willing, as they had not been in 1918, if only through physical conquest and occupation, to accept the verdict of battle. It was as much the work of the statesmen and diplomats as the achievements of the soldiers that military victory led to a peace that has lasted for more than half a century, provided the framework for the unexampled prosperity of both vanquished and victors, and shows no signs of collapsing.

It is worth comparing the settlement after the Second World War with that, equally successful, after the Napoleonic Wars. The object in both cases had been the destruction of the power of a formidable state which had attempted to assert an imperial hegemony. It had been achieved, not by any specific battles (although Waterloo certainly provided a satisfactory denouement) but by the exhaustion of the defeated peoples after many years of warfare, and the discrediting of their bellicose leaders. In 1815 France was left intact, but the map of Europe was redrawn to ensure a balance of power to check any revival of Napoleonic ambitions. More important, France was rapidly readmitted into the Congress of Powers as a partner in preserving the settlement. Alarm bells were to ring at intervals when internal upheavals seemed to bring revisionist groups into power in Paris, but France remained a cooperative partner in the Concert of Europe for half a century – which is about as far as any prudent statesman can hope to foresee. After 1945, German power was contained by the division of the country; an unintended result, certainly, but one that was accepted by the victorious powers as preferable to any likely alternative, even if their leaders did not find it prudent to say so in public. But even that might not have worked if the allied occupying powers had not made the division of the country, and its continuing military occupation, acceptable within Germany by finding leaders who commanded the support of their own people and were prepared to cooperate with their conquerors with varying degrees of effectiveness and enthusiasm. Certainly one can hardly equate the Federal Republic of Germany's willing acceptance of partnership with its former adversaries to the philosophic acceptance of Soviet hegemony by the population of the DDR. Nonetheless, both accepted the decision of the Second World War as irreversible, including the massive transfer of some 12 million Germans from East to West that accompanied it – surely the greatest example of 'ethnic cleansing' Europe has ever seen. No serious *revanchiste* threat ever developed within Germany, such as had emerged after the First World War for far more trivial reasons.

So what went wrong after the First World War? Why was the Allied victory in 1918 not 'decisive'? Were the Germans not sufficiently defeated, or not sufficiently conciliated? Perhaps both. Certainly they had not experienced the horrors of war at first hand, as they did a quarter of a century later: indeed their armies had been everywhere triumphant until the very last three months of the war. The trouble was that the German people did not 'internalise' their defeat. The leaders thrown up by their revolution in 1918 lacked domestic credibility and did not, when they reluctantly signed the Treaty of Versailles (and with it, in some cases, their own death warrants) carry with them the support of the people they claimed to represent. The German people felt *dishonoured* by the Treaty, with its imputation of a 'war guilt' that none of them accepted. To compel them to accept it, it would have been necessary to build against them a military balance so strong that for at least a generation they could do nothing to reverse the verdict – much as Bismarck forced the French, by depriving them of allies, to accept the humiliation of 1871. As it was, any government, whatever its political complexion, that pledged itself to avenge that humiliation and to restore German military power in order to do so, was assured, as were the National Socialists, of massive popular support.

So there are at least two requirements if the use of military force is to be decisive. First, the defeated people must accept the fact of defeat and realise that there is no chance of reversing the verdict in the foreseeable future, whether by military revival, skilful diplomacy or international propaganda. Second, they must become reconciled to their defeat by being treated, sooner or later, as partners in operating the new international order. Honour must be satisfied, unless the defeated peoples are to be massacred or reduced to perpetual slavery. This means either that the incumbent government of the defeated power must itself accept the defeat, persuade its people to do the same, and continue to be treated with respect by the victors; or that it is replaced by a new leadership that is both cooperative with the victors and has an independent credibility with its own peoples. New leaders must not be seen, in short, as 'quislings' who themselves become the targets of new resistance movements as were Michael Collins in Ireland and Matthias Erzberger in Germany. It was one of the many shortcomings of British planning for the Suez operation in 1956 that, although the ultimate objective of the British government was to 'topple Nasser', they had no idea who would take his place. On the other hand, although it was not the British intention to 'topple Galtieri' when they reconquered the Falklands, the loss of the war in itself was enough to discredit his regime and bring to power a more amenable leadership with which peace could be made, and has been kept.

In summary, the problem may best be considered across a spectrum of possibilities, which is a more realistic way of analysing the subject than any arbitrary distinction between 'total' and 'limited' wars. At one extreme are ritual confrontations where neither fear nor interest plays a major part, and honour can be satisfied with a minimum of bloodshed. Anthropologists believe that these were by no means rare in so-called 'primitive' societies, although today their equivalents are probably football matches, a healthy and necessary catharsis of largely adolescent aggression. At the other extreme are wars of true annihilation in which the defeated are destroyed in mass acts of genocide, and their lands either devastated or taken over by the conquerors: conflicts common enough in antiquity, but not unknown in more recent times. The mutual massacres of the Hutus and Tutsis come very near it, as have episodes in wars of European colonial settlement, not least in the New World; while this, as we now know, was the kind of war that Hitler intended on the Eastern Front. But even if we exclude those extreme examples, we have a wide range of possibilities, examples from which can be found almost in living memory.

Consider just the Second World War in Europe. Here, Hitler was fighting a comparatively limited war in the west between 1939 and 1941, and a total war of conquest and colonial settlement on the Eastern Front. His victory in the west in 1940 made him master of Europe, and only the intervention of the United States would have been able to reverse that decision. That, exceptionally, was the result of a single decisive battle, one that deserved to rank with Austerlitz, Wagram or Sadowa in that it led to the immediate capitulation of Germany's continental adversaries and the conclusion of peace on the victor's terms. Ultimately it was not 'decisive' because Britain remained undefeated, and (as after Austerlitz and Wagram) a wider war went on. Nevertheless, like Austerlitz and Wagram, the operational victory of his armies gave Hitler an opportunity to make a political settlement that might in itself have made further war unnecessary. The peoples of Europe in 1940 had no appetite for further war. In every country, élites emerged who were prepared to accept and enforce German hegemony if it guaranteed peace and prosperity for their own peoples, as it very well might have done. Britain had few friends on the continent after her armies had been beaten off every battlefield on which they had appeared. Neither interest nor honour demanded that the states of mainland Europe should continue the war, and if Hitler had been prepared to make a peace that took full account of both those factors, there would have been very little that the British could or the Americans would have done about it. The issue – who was to be master in Europe – would have been decided at least for a generation. But instead Hitler, like Napoleon before him, used his victory not to reconcile but to pillage his victims, using their resources to carry on further wars which he ultimately lost.

With regard to Hitler's 'other war', he never intended any settlement with the Soviet Union. This was a war of colonial conquest, in which the government of the vanquished would be destroyed and its peoples either massacred or enslaved. But here again, even the most complete military victory could have done no more than provide opportunities for a political solution. Had Hitler studied the European wars of imperial conquest that he so much admired, he would have realised the immensity of the problem with which his military victories presented him. However complete the conquest, some measure of cooperation from the defeated people is necessary if the victory is to be exploited. The more advanced the society, the greater is the cooperation needed. Local leaders and specialists have to be found if empires are to be made to work. Hitler admired the success with which the British ruled India using a handful of administrators, but failed to realise that this was possible only because, subject to a minimum of direction and advice, the British left the Indians to run themselves. Conquest could be made fruitful only through conciliation. Hitler, on the contrary, systematically destroyed the indigenous élites who might have cooperated with him in ruling Russia, and had no plans for long-term pacification except settlement maintained by terror.

There was a further factor that had made European colonial warfare 'decisive'. The victims were isolated, and could look to no outside sources of help to delay or reverse defeat. The indigenous inhabitants of North America and South Asia could for a time retain their independence by playing their European conquerors against one another. But once the French had been beaten out of both continents, the inhabitants were at the mercy of their Anglo-Saxon conquerors, and the world left them to their fate. But by the mid-twentieth century there were few parts of the world where such 'decisions' could be insulated from world politics. The unsuccessful attempts of the European powers to maintain or re-assert their colonial dominance after the Second World War showed the impossibility of insulating colonial repression from world politics in the latter half of the twentieth century. Even decisions imposed on the aboriginal peoples by yet more remote conflicts in Australia, New Zealand and the American West are now being reconsidered by the world court of appeal. Few if any victims are now friendless. The effect of defeat in the field, as the Palestinians have successfully shown, can be delayed or mitigated, if not reversed, by skilful propaganda and diplomacy at the United Nations. Given the globalisation of politics, the use of military force to impose 'total' solutions is nowadays very unlikely to be decisive.

So when are wars today likely to be decisive? The Clausewitzian formula still applies. First, operational victories must be gained, so convincing that the adversary is either disarmed altogether or made to realise that the cost of continuing the conflict will be prohibitively high. In the case of such limited objectives as the possession of the Falklands or frontier adjustments in the Himalayas (the Sino-Indian War of 1962) this is still entirely feasible. Such a decision is all the easier if one side is overwhelmingly strong and is seen to be so, although physical strength can be matched if not overmatched by moral determination, as the United States found in Vietnam. Second, the defeated power must be deprived of all sources of outside support in reversing the military verdict – something that the British successfully accomplished at the United Nations during the Falklands War, and Bismarck achieved against France after 1870. Even if the defeated adversary remains unreconciled to its losses, it must, however reluctantly, be prepared to live with them. But third, and most important of all, in a conflict between states, a government must be found in the defeated country that is able and willing to take responsibility for enforcing the peace-terms on its compatriots. The difficulty of doing this will be in direct ratio to the harshness of the terms that the defeated power is being required to accept. If no such government can be found, the victorious power will have to assume the responsibility itself: that is normally the way in which empires grow. The decision after the Gulf War to leave Saddam Hussein in place rather than to install US General Norman Schwarzkopf as an imperial pro-consul showed a fine judgement as to the lesser of two evils.

That is why in general wars today – wars, that is, between states – tend to be decisive mainly in maintaining the status quo. The Falkland Islands remain British, Kuwait remains independent. Even the Second World War was successfully fought to reverse two bids for imperial expansion, though the world had to be drastically reconstructed after it. But a war, fought for whatever reason, that does not aim at a solution which takes into account the fears, the interests and, not least, the honour of the defeated peoples is unlikely to decide anything for very long.

CHAPTER TWENTY-EIGHT

Are we at war?

Survival 50-4, 2008

I

This year we are celebrating the 50th anniversary of the foundation of the IISS. I shall not bore you with a blast on our own trumpet, except to remark how astonishing and gratifying it is to see how the acorn that Alastair Buchan then planted should have grown into such a flourishing tree and continued to bear such nourishing fruit. But I would stress the point that the founders of the Institute never had the audacity to claim to tell people *what* to think about strategic affairs, much less what to *do* about them. Our hope was simply to persuade people at least to *think* about them – not only the military and political experts whose job it was, but everyone with a vote – and to provide them with accurate information so that they could think intelligently; possibly also to provide some guide to priorities, as to what was important and what less so.

At that time there could be no doubt as to what was most important: it was the acquisition by the major powers of the world, at a time when they were bitterly divided by incompatible ideologies, of nuclear weapons capable of destroying mankind several times over. The destruction of Hiroshima and

Nagasaki seemed to open a new and grimmer era in the history of mankind, and we were only beginning to learn how to come to terms with it. So, unsurprisingly, the work of the Institute focused for several years on questions of nuclear deterrence, disarmament and arms control before broadening out to consider less existential, if more immediate, questions. Now I would just say that those questions of nuclear war have not gone away: the proliferation and control of nuclear weapons remains one of the ineluctable problems of our time. The nuclear dragon may be sleeping, but it is certainly not dead, and the IISS continues to keep a wary eye on it.

Then seven years ago another event occurred that was in some ways even more epoch-making than the development of nuclear weapons: '9-11', the destruction of the World Trade Center in New York by a dozen or so terrorists, with the massacre of some 3,000 people who were peacefully working there. The perpetrators had themselves been virtually unarmed, with none of the resources of a major state behind them. The implications were terrifying. How many more of them were out there? What if they had access to nuclear weapons? We had to come to terms with the fact the most powerful state in the world could now be seriously harmed, not by another state equally powerful, but by small private groups owing allegiance to no state at all. For the past 300 years wars had been waged, but also peace had been kept, by States, one of whose defining characteristics was that they enjoyed a monopoly of violence. That monopoly had now been seriously breached by elements apparently beyond state control. Fifty years ago the challenge to world order had come from the transformation of weapons systems. Now it appears threatened by the transformation, if not disintegration, of the entire states-system that has provided the framework for international relations for 300-odd years.

The American government reacted to 9-11, understandably enough, as if the attack had come from an enemy state. It declared war, and from that day to this many, if not most, Americans still believe that they are 'at war', although the precise definition of the adversary has varied over the years. But many, if not most, of America's friends and allies believed this reaction to be mistaken. For what it is worth, I was one of them. We have now had seven years to think about it and I still believe that America was wrong, and dangerously wrong. The United States and her allies are certainly engaged in armed conflicts in many parts of the world, but that is a different matter from being 'at war'; and the difference matters. I hope that you will forgive me if I take this opportunity to share with you some further thoughts on the question. I need hardly add that they are my own thoughts, and they certainly don't carry any imprimatur from the IISS as such.

II

When I use the term 'epoch-making' to describe 9-11, I choose the words carefully. What we are witnessing is the close of an epoch that opened some 350 years ago; an epoch generally known as 'Westphalian' after the Peace of Westphalia, concluded in 1648, that remoulded the decaying feudal order of Europe into discrete sovereign states with distinct frontiers, whose rulers went to war to protect or extend their national interests very much as they thought fit. National loyalties might be complicated by transnational affiliations: in the seventeenth century by loyalty to the Catholic Church; a century later by the appeal of revolutionary France; in our own day by that of international communism. But on the whole the state could rely on the overwhelming support of its citizens – never more so than during the First World War, when the loyalties of armies fighting for their countries was unadulterated by considerations of transnational ideologies. The object of war was simple – victory; and victory was attained by the overthrow of the enemy, the destruction of his will and capacity to resist. Once victory was achieved a peace was made that enhanced the power and interests of the victors, but the framework of the system, not least the sovereignty of its members, normally remained unaffected.

But there was one belligerent to whom this simple Westphalian pattern did not apply – the United States; or rather, the president of the United States, Woodrow Wilson. When Wilson brought his country into the European war in April 1917 it was not as an ally of either side, nor did he endorse the war aims of his co-belligerents. For him the war was a crusade, one, as he himself put it, 'for a universal domination of right by such a concert of free peoples as shall bring peace and safety to all nations and make the world itself free'. It was a war, in fact, to change the world.

This was not a path down which Wilson's own people were yet prepared to follow him, let alone those of his European allies. The Europeans were still thorough Westphalians. They had made war to protect their national interests and those interests determined the peace that they eventually made. Nevertheless, Wilson's vision, of Westphalian wars being replaced by what we might term 'Enlightenment Wars', crusades for the establishment of 'a Universal Domination of Right', was to remain the declared objective of the United States throughout the twentieth century. Her wars were fought not simply to defeat her adversaries but to convert them so as to make further war inconceivable.

So unlike Westphalian wars, Enlightenment wars were fought not for purely national interests but on behalf of mankind. The object was to create a *community* of nations which, if they went to war at all, would do so not to prosecute quarrels with one another, but to enforce a commonly accepted law against a transgressor. To bring such a community into existence it might certainly be necessary to use force against a member who did not share its values. This was the case both with Imperial Germany and its Nazi successor, both of which had to be converted to democracy before they could be admitted to the comity of nations. But after the defeat of the Axis powers in 1945 the United States was able to put its principles into practice, with 'democratic values' and the principle of 'collective security' being accepted, if only notionally, by all members of the United Nations.

As we know, this happy state did not last for long. The Cold War quickly brought it to an end as the leading powers divided into two blocs, each identifying itself with a different concept of 'democracy' and a different vision of 'world order'. But stability of a curious kind did result, if only from the fact that, in the nuclear age, neither side dared go to war. New states were thus able to emerge peacefully onto the world stage, largely because, with a few exceptions, their former imperial masters had neither the will nor the capacity to prevent it. Some of them flirted with the Soviet Union so long as its ideology and power gave them some leverage on the world scene, but most joined the world of the market economy, even though this made them dependent on the West. Ultimately, the failure of the communist dream forced both the Soviet Union and People's Republic of China to do the same. It was the stability provided by the Cold War that by the end of the twentieth century enabled a new global order to come into being that was gradually to render the Westphalian system of states obsolescent, if not yet obsolete.

This order was of a different kind from that visualised by Wilson and implemented in some measure by Franklin Roosevelt. It was not international, but transnational. It did not result from agreement between governments; indeed it had often come into being in spite of them. It had been created by the silent operation of a market economy that had originated in Europe and the Atlantic region in the early nineteenth century and developed ever faster as sail gave way to steam, steam gave way to oil, electricity gave birth to electronics, telegraph was replaced by radio and television, which in turn led to the Internet that has now made instant communication possible not only between every nation, but every man, woman, and, not least, child, on the planet. It is a process that has swept away social structures, political hierarchies and religious beliefs, opening up unimaginable opportunities for mankind but leaving in its wake a trail of confusion, bitterness and anomie. No state, even the most powerful, can remain immune from its effects: the communist world struggled in vain to insulate itself, and eventually gave up in despair.

In this post-Westphalian world the function of the state is no longer simply to create and preserve an acceptable order for its citizens and defend them against their rivals. It is also to enable its citizens to participate fully in this new transnational global order while protecting them so far as possible from its ravages; to cooperate with other like-minded states in so doing; and to assist in the evolution of such states where they do not yet exist and to restore them when they are threatened.

The Westphalian system is far from extinct and traces of it will be with us for many years yet. States may no longer enjoy a monopoly of violence but wars between them are still possible, especially between small new states with ill-defined frontiers. It is also still conceivable between great powers – China, the United States, Russia, India, and as some would have it, the European Union – and all arm to face that possibility. But today the major threats to world order do not come from rivalry between great powers, but from the inability of weak states to exert control either over their own citizens or over highly volatile regions where no effective writ runs; and this weakness creates threats of disorder with which traditional military power has shown itself ill-adapted to deal. The world is in fact increasingly divided, not between freedom and tyranny, nor between democracy and dictatorship, but between states that are successfully adjusting themselves to membership of global civil society and those that are not.

This 'new world order' has three primary characteristics. It is *global*, embracing the entire planet. Disorder anywhere in the world may have universal implications. It is *dynamic*: today there is no region that is not experiencing increasingly rapid and socially disruptive change. The effectiveness – indeed the *legitimacy* – of governments depends on their capacity to manage that change, a capacity itself dependent on social consensus, uncorrupt administration and the rule of law.

Above all, this global society is highly *vulnerable*. I shall say nothing here about climate change, which is perhaps the greatest threat of all, but in addition to that, increasing urbanisation is making an ever larger proportion of the world's populations dependent on exogenous supplies of vital fuel, and creating huge conglomerations – hardly deserving the name of 'cities' – whose critical infrastructure can easily be disrupted by a few malevolent individuals who can cause at best widespread inconvenience, at worst destruction on a scale far transcending that of 9-11.

There is no lack of people ready to so disrupt it. Although the transformation of our societies increases the wealth, the health, the life expectancy and the opportunities open to mankind to a degree inconceivable even a century ago, it also creates losers: uprooted peoples whose livelihood and lifestyles have been destroyed, whose traditional political structures have been demolished, and whose core beliefs –

beliefs that held their societies together for centuries – have been dissolved. Their grievances may be regionally and politically specific as were those of the Irish or the Jews a generation ago, or those of the Palestinians today. They may be based on a more general resentment at the injustice and oppressions inherent in a global economy that may put the prosperity of entire societies at the mercy of decisions taken in boardrooms at the other end of the world. They may be provoked simply by visceral reaction against the hedonistic secular materialism that has destroyed faiths that sustained their ancestors for millennia. Whatever the cause, there will be no lack of angry young men and women in a generation whose numbers are swollen by increased life expectancy beyond their capacity to find employment, and who will not hesitate to use violence to redress or revenge their grievances. They may revert to atavistic tribalism. They may be recruited to messianic creeds, religious or secular, that promise a new and glorious future. Sometimes their protests may be channelled into political parties that gain control of a state, as happened so disastrously in the case of Germany after 1918. But initially they are all likely to turn to 'terror': first *demonstrative*, 'the propaganda of the deed', to give expression to their resentment, advertise their existence and recruit supporters; then *intimidatory*, to cow their opponents into submission; finally *provocative*, to tempt the government into overreaction and so delegitimise its authority.

There is nothing new about these techniques: in Europe they have a pedigree dating back nearly two centuries. But in our own day they have been rendered far more lethal: first by the vulnerability of urban societies to which I referred; and secondly by a readiness for self-sacrifice that was perhaps more common in our own societies a couple of generations ago – when young men were positively encouraged 'to lay down their lives for their country' – than it is today. For whatever our political leaders may say about the atrocities perpetrated by suicide bombers, these are not 'mindless'. They are often carefully calculated and regrettably effective. And they are certainly not 'cowardly': people who are prepared to die for a cause in which they believe may be misled, but they are not cowards. If we do not accept that we are often dealing with people who are both intelligent and courageous we would be very stupid indeed.

III

The threat of terrorist protest thus accompanies the development of our global society like an inescapable shadow, and is likely to remain a major social problem as far forward as we can foresee. In our own day it has been made especially lethal by the coincidence of the problem of Palestine, affecting as it does the entire Muslim world, with a profound crisis of modernisation within Islam that has produced a school of extremists whose influence extends beyond the Middle East into the Muslim diaspora in Western cities – a diaspora that has its own problems of cultural assimilation. It is a combination that presents a formidable challenge to the stability of the entire world order. But there is no point in 'declaring war' on it, let alone adopting the apocalyptic language of religious extremists who stigmatise their opponents as the embodiment of evil.

This is not a mere matter of semantics. There is no harm in speaking of wars against poverty, or crime, or disease. These are mere metaphors: they do not give a license to kill. But in the world of international politics 'war' has a specific meaning. It means quite specifically the abandonment of civil restraints and the legitimisation of the use of whatever force is necessary to achieve one's objectives. Restraints inherent in the culture of the belligerent societies may be observed in the conduct of war – restraints recently described by one American attorney general as 'quaint' – but they will be very quickly abandoned under duress. The leaders of nations at war have always considered themselves entitled, if all else fails, to use any means to defeat their adversary and avoid defeat themselves, whether it be the torture of individuals or the destruction of entire cities, and they will usually enjoy massive popular support when they do so. Let us be clear about it. To 'declare war' is formally to espouse a set of values and to legitimise activities normally outlawed in civil society.

But in dealing with terrorists our object should be not to abandon those values. It is to enforce them. '9-11' and similar atrocities should be seen not as acts of war, but as 'breaches of the peace' – not just the peace created by international treaties, but the peaceful order that makes possible the functioning of a global civil society on which the well-being of the entire planet depends. Our approach in dealing with them should not be that of 'warriors' but of *police*, whose function is the preservation of civil order, and for whom the use of force is the last and least desirable resort. The object of terrorism is to destroy the legitimacy of the incumbent authority. The object of government must be to preserve and exert it, and to avoid being dragged into a conflict on the same level as its adversary. That is possible only so long as it retains the confidence of the community on whose behalf it claims to act.

This should not be too difficult in dealing with domestic terrorism, unless the extremists have a cause – as they did in Northern Ireland – that can command substantial public support. But intervention to deal with terrorist activity in foreign countries is a very different matter. It is true that the global civil society whose peace we are trying to keep has yet to develop its own transnational structure of government, so its agents have often to be the armed forces of old-fashioned

Westphalian states whose very presence, however well-intentioned, is likely to arouse a very natural xenophobia; especially if they carry a great deal of their own tribal culture with them. However well they may behave, however many sweets they give children, foreign soldiers can never be very popular, certainly not for very long, and certainly not if they believe that they are 'at war' and are therefore immune from normal civil restraints. It then becomes all too easy for their opponents to depict them as the agents not of a global civil society, but of an alien hegemony, and condemn those who support them as traitors.

For all these reasons we should not become involved in the affairs even of the most incompetent and failing states unless our intervention is a matter of vital importance to global stability and has clear international legitimacy. I would argue that our intervention in Afghanistan meets these criteria, while that in Iraq did not. And if we do become involved, our object must be neither to subdue nor to convert – not even convert to Western-style democracy. It is to assist where necessary in destroying hard cores of nihilistic extremists and to aid the construction, or reconstruction, of a civil society whose government can fulfil its basic obligations: to maintain a socially acceptable order; to connect its citizens with the benefits of transnational civil society while protecting them from its hazards; and to act as a dependable member of the community of states. If there is no immediate prospect of doing any of this, we would be ill advised to try.

I am afraid that all this is now pretty platitudinous, but it would not have been seen as such in Washington – or even, I am afraid, Downing Street – five years ago. Experience in Iraq and Afghanistan has now made us sadder and I hope wiser people. After a similar if rather less traumatic experience suffered by the British in South Africa at the beginning of the last century, the poet Rudyard Kipling – whose observations on war in Afghanistan still have a poignant relevance – remarked:

> Let us admit it fairly, as a business people should
> We have had no end of a lesson; it will do us no end
> of good.

At least, I hope it will.

CHAPTER TWENTY-NINE

Review Essay: History, tragedy and farce

Survival 51-1, 2009

The white war: life and death on the Italian front, 1915–1919, by Mark Thompson (London: Faber and Faber, 2008)

In the spring of 1945 the Allied Armies in Italy at last levered the Wehrmacht out of the mountain south of Bologna which they had held all winter, swept across the Po valley and headed past Venice into the Julian Alps en route for Vienna. My own unit had a more limited role: to get to Trieste and the valley of the Isonzo before Tito's partisans did. We spent the next year sitting in the bleak hinterland of Trieste to prevent the Yugoslavs from 'liberating' the territories that the Italians had 'liberated' from the Austrians 30 years earlier. We had not yet heard of the term 'ethnic cleansing' but we saw what it meant, close up. The Italians had done their best to 'cleanse' the Slavic population from the land they regarded as *Italia irredenda*: now the Yugoslavs were repaying in kind, and we could do little to stop them.

This was my own introduction to the Brave New World we had been fighting to create. But we also found a different kind of testimony to the region's tormented past. On our way through Friuli we briefly halted in the village of Redipuglia outside the largest war memorial I have ever seen, equal to if not dwarfing those on the Western Front: a vast staircase of terraces, each a hundred yards wide, containing the bones of over a hundred thousand Italian soldiers who had died on those huge, and to us unknown, battlefields in the First World War.

All that I, like most of my countrymen, then knew about the Italian performance in that war was that their army had shamefully disintegrated at the battle of Caporetto in 1917 and had to be rescued by British and French troops; a performance they had repeated more recently when they had tamely surrendered to the forces of General Wavell in the Western Desert. We had no idea that between 1915 and 1917 the Italian army had launched 11 successive offensives across the stony plateau of the Carso that now confronted us; attacks on the same scale, and with much the same results, as our own Battle of the Somme. When finally in November 1917 an Austro-German army launched their counter-offensive the Italian army had already been eviscerated. By the end of the war it had lost nearly half a million dead, most of them on the Carso. In 1918 Italy was able with Allied help to defeat an Austrian army as exhausted as her own and earn her place at the top table at the peace conference. But although the Italian prime minister declared that Italy's victory was 'one of the greatest that history has ever recorded', nobody, least of all his allies, believed him, or treated the country as if it were. In fact Italy had been as broken by her 'victory' as Germany by her defeat.

Perhaps it has been a combination of native shame and foreign contempt for the disastrous performance of the Italian armies that accounts for the remarkable absence of any serious study in English of the Italian front in the historiography of the First World War; but now the gap has been filled by Mark Thompson with this brilliant and definitive book. It is a work not simply of military but of political and, even more importantly, cultural history as well. All these dimensions are needed if we are to understand why the diverse, heterogeneous and often barely literate peoples of the Italian peninsula came to be pitch-forked, by a deeply divided political class dominated by a small group of ultra-nationalist fanatics, into a war of choice against her former allies of the Triple Alliance; and even more remarkably, how the very disaster of the war would strengthen that group so effectively that they were able to seize power and hold it until they were overthrown in a yet more disastrous war 30 years later.

The political reasons for Italy's entry into the war are clear enough. In 1914 her political leaders still had unfinished business. Her wars of unification in 1859 and 1866 had still left extensive Italophone territory south of her 'natural frontier' the Alps under control of the Austrian Empire. The Western Allies were thus able to bribe her out of neutrality by offering her, at the expense of the Austrians, not only these *irredenta*, but non-Italian territory beyond the Adriatic that would make her a major Balkan power; together with a hefty slice of Anatolia at the expense of her old enemy Turkey. The mouth-watering prospect of such Great-Power status was too great for the Italian cabinet to resist, and the nationalist enthusiasm stoked up by a hysterical press too great for its opponents to overcome. The cry that had once inspired the followers of Garibaldi, *fuori i stranieri!*, drive out the foreigners!, carried all before it. Good liberals, not only in Italy but throughout the Western world, believed that Italian honour demanded no less.

The trouble was that such 'good liberals' were rather thicker on the ground abroad than they were in Italy itself. In fact the Italian people had never been very enthusiastic about unification. Nationalism was largely a middle-class phenomenon and in Italy the middle class was slow to develop. The bulk of the population were still very largely peasants – overwhelming so in the south – who took their cue from a Catholic Church who saw a unified secular Italian state as a challenge to the political and spiritual authority of the Pope. The conservative ruling classes in the north were quite content with the enlarged Kingdom of Savoy bequeathed to them by Cavour, and regarded everything south of Rome – as many of them understandably still do – as a liability rather than an asset. Mazzini, the great father of Italian nationalism who spent most of his life in exile, constantly lamented the lack of enthusiasm among the actual inhabitants of the Italian peninsula for his great ideal of 'Italy'; and his followers were only too conscious of the fact that when 'Italy' was in fact made and the foreigners driven out, it was as a result not of any great popular uprising, but of deals between her more powerful neighbours after wars in which the Italians themselves had played a minor and largely inglorious part. The great cry of Italian patriots was *Italia fara da se* – Italy will do it on her own. But she never yet had.

In consequence Italian nationalists believed that the Italy in which they lived was not the true Italy to which they aspired. That had still to be made, and could only be made by war – not a war won by proxy, but one in which Italians would fight and die, preferably in large numbers; showing by their sacrifice the greatness of the nation that had borne such heroes. Of course the Italians were not the only people who felt like this in 1914. The same ideals drove thousands of young British, German and French patriots to the recruiting offices and ultimately to their deaths, and the numbers in which they died were seen as evidence not of the incompetence of their generals, but of the virility of their nations. Nor were Italian intellectuals alone in their espousal of the creed of 'vitalism', that denial of all the values of the Enlightenment, which taught that action was its own justification and that both intellectual reflection and traditional morality were matters only for wimps; a twisted kind of social Darwinism that saw nature as a struggle for survival in which thousands had to die in order that the species best adapted for conflict could prevail. But nowhere else were such ideas driven to the verge of lunacy as they were in Italy by the Futurists under Filippo Marinetti; or well beyond it, as they were by that ludicrous but sinister figure Gabriele d'Annunzio, in whom romantic excess reached its furthermost bounds and who in any other country would probably have been quietly locked up, instead of becoming a national icon.

This lethal combination of frenetic nationalism and anti-rational vitalism, burning away at the core of an otherwise somnolent and inward-looking people, helps to explain not only why Italy joined in the war in 1915, but why she fought it in the way that she did. Her overt objectives were the Friuli plain northeast of Venice, the mountainous region of South Tyrol (including Alto Adige, most of which was German in language and culture) and the port of Trieste; Italian-speaking, but entirely surrounded by Slovenes. The first objective was overrun almost bloodlessly, but its inhabitants greeted their liberators with a marked lack of enthusiasm. The second involved fighting in the high Alps that showed the Italians at their heroic and ingenious best; a campaign fought largely in bitter cold and perpetual snow that provides the title for Mark Thompson's book. But that was as untypical an experience for the bulk of the Italian army as was the Palestine campaign for the British. In the same way as the typical experience of the war for the British was the Western Front, the campaign in which the Italians died in their scores of thousands was that fought on the stony plateau of the Carso that barred the way to Trieste.

The Carso is a horrible place; a bare, gnarled, stony plateau bereft of cover, baking in summer, freezing in winter, and tilted at an angle ideal for providing defensive positions with excellent fields of fire. The Italian mode of attack was, to put it mildly, unsubtle: repeated frontal attacks by infantry en masse. The Italian High Command shared the belief, common throughout the European military in 1914, that the advantage provided to the defensive by modern firepower could always be overcome by the high morale of the attacking infantry. But by 1915, when Italy entered the war, both their allies and their enemies were already learning the bleak lesson laconically expressed by General Philippe Pétain – *fire kills*; and were beginning to explore less lethal ways of conducting war. Their learning process was painfully slow, but in the Italian army there was no learning process at all, and their High Command saw no reason to acquire any. Thompson's account of these attacks is quite heart-rending. The officer corps consisted largely of Savoyard monarchists who had little interest in the welfare of the largely illiterate peasants from the south from which the army was recruited. (It is significant that when Italian infantry attacked, their battle cry was not *Italia!* but *Savoia!*) At their head was General Cadorna, who blamed the failures of his offensives on a lack of *slancio* ('dash') on the part of his troops, and sacked any of his subordinates who suggested otherwise. Again, the Italians were not unique in this. Left to themselves, both Joffre and Haig took the same line. But they were not left to themselves: political pressure ultimately forced Joffre to retire and Haig to accept more realistic advisers on to his staff. But the Italian government stood firmly behind Cadorna, his parliamentary critics were howled down by nationalist fanatics, and the press meekly submitted to being muzzled by the High Command. The war in fact saw the destruction of Italian parliamentary democracy: Mussolini would simply administer the *coup de grâce*.

If the war was a tragedy for Italy, the peace was an ugly farce. Her allies had now been joined by the United States, who did not recognise the validity of the promises made to her by France and Britain; certainly not of those involving non-Italian territory now claimed by Yugoslavia. The Italian government had kept quiet about these in its wartime propaganda. Now they declared that if they were not granted regions of Dalmatia and Slovenia in which the Italians were a tiny minority, the heroes whose bodies lay on the blood-soaked slopes of the Carso would have died in vain. Italy's allies treated these claims with contempt. The seizure of the port of Fiume, which did not even figure in Italian war claims, by a private army under Gabriele d'Annunzio was a farcical piece of operatic bravura that even the Italian government had to disown. But the government found itself increasingly helpless in face of the *fasci* (bands) of hardline demobilised troops, termed by their leader Mussolini a 'trenchocracy' who claimed to represent the true Italy, with a mission to cleanse the political Augean stables at home and assert Italian greatness abroad.

For the British the lesson taught by the Somme and Passchendaele was 'never again'. For the mass of Italians the comparable holocaust on the Carso was a meaningless disaster better forgotten, but the Fascists claimed that it proved Italy to be truly a warrior nation, one that would now in future *fara da se*. But for one man at least, lessons had been learned. General Giulio Douhet had been one of the few open critics of Cadorna's conduct of the war and was determined that nothing of the kind should occur again. In 1921 he published a seminal book *The Command of the Air* which was to transform strategic thought. In future the target for military offensives should be not the armies of the enemy, but his civil population. There would be no more Carsos: war would in future be a matter for heroic elites, warriors destroying the soft centres of enemy power from afar. It was a doctrine eagerly embraced by Mussolini. Others were not slow to follow. We were billeted in a smelly little village on the edge of the Carso when we learned over the radio of the bombing of Hiroshima. Then I saw no connection. I do now.

INDEX

Adelphi books are published six times a year by Routledge Journals, an imprint of Taylor & Francis, 4 Park Square, Milton Park, Abingdon, Oxfordshire OX14 4RN, UK.

A subscription to the institution print edition, ISSN 1944-5571, includes free access for any number of concurrent users across a local area network to the online edition, ISSN 1944-558X. Taylor & Francis has a flexible approach to subscriptions enabling us to match individual libraries' requirements. This journal is available via a traditional institutional subscription (either print with free online access, or online-only at a discount) or as part of our libraries, subject collections or archives. For more information on our sales packages please visit www.tandfonline.com/page/librarians.

2020 Annual Adelphi Subscription Rates			
Institution	£832	US$1,459	€1,230
Individual	£285	US$488	€390
Online only	£707	US$1,240	€1,045

Dollar rates apply to subscribers outside Europe. Euro rates apply to all subscribers in Europe except the UK and the Republic of Ireland where the pound sterling price applies. All subscriptions are payable in advance and all rates include postage. Journals are sent by air to the USA, Canada, Mexico, India, Japan and Australasia. Subscriptions are entered on an annual basis, i.e. January to December. Payment may be made by sterling cheque, dollar cheque, international money order, National Giro, or credit card (Amex, Visa, Mastercard).

For a complete and up-to-date guide to Taylor & Francis journals and books publishing programmes, and details of advertising in our journals, visit our website: http://www.tandfonline.com.

Ordering information:
USA/Canada: Taylor & Francis Inc., Journals Department, 530 Walnut Street, Suite 850, Philadelphia, PA 19106, USA. **UK/Europe/Rest of World:** Routledge Journals, T&F Customer Services, T&F Informa UK Ltd., Sheepen Place, Colchester, Essex, CO3 3LP, UK.

Advertising enquiries to:
USA/Canada: The Advertising Manager, Taylor & Francis Inc., 530 Walnut Street, Suite 850, Philadelphia, PA 19106, USA. Tel: +1 (800) 354 1420. Fax: +1 (215) 207 0050. **UK/Europe/Rest of World**: The Advertising Manager, Routledge Journals, Taylor & Francis, 4 Park Square, Milton Park, Abingdon, Oxfordshire OX14 4RN, UK. Tel: +44 (0) 20 7017 6000. Fax: +44 (0) 20 7017 6336.